THE THINGS OUR FATHERS SAW

THE UNTOLD STORIES OF THE
WORLD WAR II GENERATION
FROM HOMETOWN, USA

VOLUME VI:
THE BULGE AND BEYOND

Matthew A. Rozell

WOODCHUCK HOLLOW PRESS
Hartford · New York

Copyright © 2020, 2023 by Matthew A. Rozell. Version 3.28.24 LARGE PRINT. All rights reserved. No part of this publication may be reproduced, distributed, or transmitted in any form or by any means without the prior written permission of the publisher. Grateful acknowledgement is made for the credited use of various short quotations also appearing in other previously published sources. Please see author notes.

Information at matthewrozellbooks.com.

Maps by Susan Winchell.

Front Cover: "American soldiers of the 289th Infantry Regiment march along the snow-covered road on their way to cut off the Saint Vith-Houffalize road in Belgium on 24 January 1945." Public Domain Photographs, National Archives Number 531244, Unrestricted.

Back Cover: "Chow is served to American infantrymen of the 347th Infantry Regiment on their way to La Roche, Belgium, 13 January 1945." United States Army. National Archives, public domain.

Any additional photographs and descriptions sourced at Wikimedia Commons within terms of use, unless otherwise noted.

Publisher's Cataloging-in-Publication Data
Names: Rozell, Matthew A., 1961- author.
Title: The Bulge and beyond : the things our fathers saw : the untold stories of the World War II generation, volume VI / Matthew Rozell.
Description: Granville, NY : Matthew A. Rozell, 2020. | Series: The things our fathers saw, vol. 6. | Also available in audiobook format.
Identifiers: LCCN 2020918993 (print) | ISBN 978-1-948155-48-9 large print pbk. | ISBN 978-0-9964800-9-3 (paperback) | ISBN 978-1-948155-19-9 (hardcover) | ISBN 978-1-948155-17-5 (ebook)
Subjects: LCSH: Ardennes, Battle of the, 1944-1945--Personal narratives, American. | World War, 1939-1945--Personal narratives, American. | World War, 1939-1945--Campaigns--Belgium. | World War, 1939-1945--Campaigns--Luxembourg. | Veterans--United States--Biography. | Military history, Modern--20th century. | BISAC: HISTORY / Military / World War II. | HISTORY / Military / Veterans. | BIOGRAPHY & AUTOBIOGRAPHY / Military.
Classification: LCC D756.5.A7 R69 2020 (print) | LCC D756.5.A7 (ebook) | DDC 940.54/219348--dc23. Library of Congress Control Number: 2020918993
www.matthewrozellbooks.com

Created in the United States of America

*~To the Memory
of
Francis S. Currey MOH
and
The World War II Generation~*

"There's one thing about these medals that bothers me. I'm proud that I did some good and was recognized. The thing that bothers me is, I hate the idea of glorifying war, and I can't help thinking that when you show your medals, you're glorifying war. The last thing I want to do is glorify war. I hate war. Old men make war, and young men die."
— Battle of the Bulge Survivor

THE THINGS OUR FATHERS SAW VI:

THE BULGE AND BEYOND

THE STORYTELLERS

(IN ORDER OF APPEARANCE):

Francis S. Currey

Alfred H. Meyer

Angelo B. DeMicco

Robert F. Kirk

Harold L. Bloom, Jr.

Carrol S. Walsh

George C. Gross

Frank W. Towers

William E. Bramswig

Sydney Cole

Rosario Catalano

Frederick S. Dennin

MARTIN SYLVESTER

GERALD M. DAUB

JACK BLANCHFIELD

THE THINGS OUR FATHERS SAW VI:

THE BULGE AND BEYOND

TABLE OF CONTENTS

AUTHOR'S NOTE 13
THE BATTLE OF THE BULGE 23
PART ONE 28
THE FOREST 28
THE REPLACEMENT 31
    The Hürtgen Forest 31
    Replacement, 4th Infantry Division 36
    'This Is It' 40
    'Made It Through Four Campaigns' 47
THE RIFLEMAN 51
    Inland 54
    Mortain 55
    The Cold 60
THE REPLACEMENT RUNNER 65
    Great Britain 70
    Medals 73

    Experience 75
    The 28th Infantry Division 77
    Paris 79
    'We'll be Home for Christmas' 80
    The Forest 81
    'Say Hello to Hitler!' 83
    Private Eddie Slovik 86
    The Replacement System 90
    'They Made Them Go Back' 92

THE SCOUT 105
    College Man to Rifleman 109
    The Repo Depot 112
    'Combat Team' 121
    The Minefield 123
    'Don't Leave Us Here' 127
    Evacuation 131
    Rocket Science 137
    Payback 138

PART TWO 141

MALMÉDY 141

MEN OF OLD HICKORY 143
    The Battle of the Ardennes: Malmédy,
    Belgium 153
    The Attack 156

   Axis Sally Reports *158*
   Malmédy *159*
   Pfc. Francis S. Currey, MOH *164*
   'The 9th U.S. Luftwaffe' *165*
   T/Sgt. Paul Bolden, MOH *171*

THE SERGEANT **175**
   Overseas *180*
   Digging In *188*
   Replacements *189*
   The Accident *197*
   Weapons *199*
   The Prisoners *202*
   Across the Rhine *205*

PART THREE **211**

GUESTS OF THE REICH **211**

THE ARTILLERY SPOTTER **213**
   Canada *216*
   Field Artillery Spotting *219*
   The Last Mission *221*
   The Stalag *230*
   Liberated by the Russians *233*
   'I Just Couldn't Believe What I Saw' *235*
   Home *241*
   'I Had to Get On' *245*

THE GLIDER PARATROOPER 249

The Glider Crash 255
The Battle of the Bulge 259
The Country Sharpshooter 263
Surrender 265
Alone 270
Slave Labor 271
'Smart for Self-Preservation' 272
Collapse 273
Liberation at Bad Orb 275
The Spoon 276

THE SURVIVOR 281

Shipping Out 286
The Suicide 289
'An Awful Racket' 292
Tiger Tanks 293
Wounded and Captured 295
Strafed 298
The Estate 301
The Gauleiter 304
On The Move 305
Going Home 311
A Survivor 315

THE ESCAPEE 317

- The Hürtgen Forest 321
- The Battle of the Bulge 322
- 'We Just Cheered' 326
- Captured 327
- Wounded 329
- Interrogation 333
- The First Escape 335
- The Second Escape 341
- 'We Are Going to Execute Them' 343
- Strafed 345
- Slave Labor 346
- The Last Escape 347
- Home 352
- Antisemitism 354
- The Saddest Thing 356

BERGA 361
- The Whiz Kids 366
- 'The First Scout is a Target' 370
- 'Not me, Howard. I'm Jewish!' 373
- Interrogation 378
- Bad Orb 381
- 'Step Forward' 384
- Berga 386
- The Germans' 'Final Solution' 389
- Slave Labor 392

The Death March 395
'My Bittersweet Day' 405
'Justice' 410
'They Thought We Were All Dead' 412

THE INTERPRETER 417

Growing Up 419
'All Safe 'Til Peace' 422
'We've Got Company' 427
Captured 429
The Work Detail 437
The Prisoner Who Lost His Mind 438
Interpreting for the Germans 440
The Work Strike 444
The Captives Become the Lords 447
Free 451
Home 452
My Enemy is My Friend 455

"YOUTH" 459

ABOUT THIS BOOK/ 489

ACKNOWLEDGEMENTS 489

NOTES 493

"Chow is served to American infantrymen of the 347th Infantry Regiment on their way to La Roche, Belgium, 13 January 1945." United States Army. National Archives, public domain.

Author's Note

"I had no idea where I was, or why I was fighting, or where I was fighting—I had no idea. All I knew was that they'd tell me to go here, and I'd go there. And they'd say shoot, do this, do that. I knew my lieutenant, and I knew my sergeant. I didn't know who the commanders were. You don't know one day to the next. We had the saying that if a bullet's got your name on it, it's going to get you. And you just never knew; it was just luck and chance."

— Infantryman, 4th Infantry Division

As is my nature, and as I suppose is the nature of all writers of history, I started this book with a lot of questions.

How does one write a new book around the Battle of the Bulge, when there are so many good books on the subject out there? How does one even begin to make sense of a battle where over a million soldiers were committed to fight—a battle, like many, where incompetence and 'uncommon valor' existed side-by side? How does the author do justice to the memory of the nineteen thousand American GIs who never saw their mothers again? How does one attempt to tell the story of the tens of thousands more who staggered or were carried out of the aftermath with the physical and mental wounds that would afflict them for the rest of their days? Of those men forced into captivity and slave labor?

It's a daunting task. But like all of my books, I have chosen to thread a narrative by letting the soldiers speak for themselves. If you are looking for an hour-by-hour account on the strategic, operational, tactical, and technical aspects of the Battle of the Bulge, I did not write that book, and you can do better elsewhere.[1] I hope the narrative flow serves up enough of the above to keep the reader engaged in a chronological and contextual 'big

---

[1] There are so many good books. One of the best, by a historian who was there, is *A Time For Trumpets: The Untold Story of the Battle of the Bulge* by Charles B. MacDonald. I also highly recommend Rick Atkinson's Liberation Trilogy, Volume 3: *The Guns at Last Light: The War in Western Europe, 1944-1945*. For an excellent account of the pivotal fight for Bastogne, see Peter Schrijvers' *Those Who Hold Bastogne: The True Story of the Soldiers and Civilians Who Fought in the Biggest Battle of the Bulge*, and so many others.

picture' fashion, keeping in mind that in most cases the common soldier had no idea what was happening around him. I just wanted to talk to the men who were there, and that is what I share with you—their words.

In sorting through the stories as another worldwide crisis unfolds, I am confident that we need them now more than ever before. For as long as I can remember, I wanted to know: how did these young people, thrust into a world of unknown and uncertainty, handle the most cataclysmic event in the history of the world? How did the American soldier—like my late friend, scrawny orphan and replacement GI Francis Currey, MOH—average age just nineteen, cope with being thousands of miles away from family, freezing in the most brutal temperatures in modern European memory, pushing back against a quarter-million-man counterattack through the Ardennes Forest in the bloodiest single battle fought by the United States in World War II? How did the kids like Frank, who admittedly went into the Army "to get the hell out of Hurleyville, New York"—only to be deemed 'too immature' to be an officer—stand up against an onslaught of German tanks and infantry in endless days where fighting began long before daylight?

"We were not prepared for it because we were told it wouldn't happen," he remarked to an interviewer in later years. "We didn't even know where we were." But as the first German tank crossed his path at 4:00 AM on December 21, 1944, his instincts and training kicked in. Seven months later, on July 27, 1945, the Medal of Honor was presented to Currey by the 30th Infantry Division commander, Major General Leland Hobbs, in front of the assembled division. The official citation reads:

> "He was an automatic rifleman with the 3rd Platoon defending a strong point near Malmédy, Belgium, on 21 December 1944, when the enemy launched a powerful attack. Overrunning tank destroyers and antitank guns located near the strong point, German tanks advanced to the 3rd Platoon's position, and, after prolonged fighting, forced the withdrawal of this group to a nearby factory. Sgt. Currey found a bazooka in the building and crossed the street to secure rockets,

meanwhile enduring intense fire from enemy tanks and hostile infantrymen who had taken up a position at a house a short distance away. In the face of small-arms, machinegun, and artillery fire, he, with a companion, knocked out a tank with 1 shot. Moving to another position, he observed 3 Germans in the doorway of an enemy-held house. He killed or wounded all 3 with his automatic rifle. He emerged from cover and advanced alone to within 50 yards of the house, intent on wrecking it with rockets. Covered by friendly fire, he stood erect, and fired a shot which knocked down half of 1 wall.

While in this forward position, he observed 5 Americans who had been pinned down for hours by fire from the house and 3 tanks. Realizing that they could not escape until the enemy tank and infantry guns had been silenced, Sgt. Currey crossed the street to a vehicle, where he procured an armful of antitank grenades. These he launched while under heavy enemy fire, driving the tankmen from the vehicles into the house.

He then climbed onto a half-track in full view of the Germans and fired a machinegun at the house. Once again changing his position, he manned another machine gun whose crew had been killed; under his covering fire the 5 soldiers were able to retire to safety. Deprived of tanks and with heavy infantry casualties, the enemy was forced to withdraw.

Through his extensive knowledge of weapons and by his heroic and repeated braving of murderous enemy fire, Sgt. Currey was greatly responsible for inflicting heavy losses in men and material on the enemy, for rescuing 5 comrades, 2 of whom were wounded, and for stemming an attack which threatened to flank his battalion's position."

Frank's matter-of-fact comment, years later: "It was just one day in nine months of steady combat."

*

Some time has passed since I sat with the veterans I interviewed, but my memory of the smiles, the laughs, the emotion, and the tears have not faded, though the day is approaching when no one with firsthand memory of World War II (and then, even people like you and me who may have heard these stories directly) will be alive. According to the U.S. Department of Veterans Affairs, 'between Sept. 30, 2019, and Sept. 30, 2020, 245 WWII veterans are expected to be lost each day. These projections were calculated before the COVID-19 pandemic and do not take any deaths related to that disease into account. The last living American veteran from the war is projected to die in 2044.'[1] Most veterans have gone the way of the World War I and Civil War generation without ever having told the tale outside of their own brothers and sisters who experienced it with them. So, thank you for your interest in this book series; it's the culmination of a mission that for me, as a history teacher and oral historian, turns out to have been lifelong. In reading it, you will have done something important—you will have remembered a person who may be now long dead, a veteran who may have lived out his or her final days wondering if it was all worth it. You will witness with me the extraordinary achievements of the participants and survivors of the most catastrophic period in the annals of history, which brought out the best—and the worst—of mankind. And these people were our everyday neighbors, our teachers and coaches, shopkeepers and carpenters, millworkers and mechanics, nurses and stenographers, lawyers and loggers, draftsmen and doctors, people from every walk of life, high school dropouts and college graduates. They were the World War II generation, and there was a time after the war when we just simply took them for granted.

When I began *The Things Our Fathers Saw* series, I began in the Pacific Theater and worked my way through the stories of that arena of the war, from Pearl Harbor to Tokyo Bay. Most of the veterans hailed from an area where I grew up and taught surrounding Glens Falls, New York, a small city that *Look Magazine* renamed 'Hometown, USA' in 1944 and devoted six wartime issues to, illustrating patriotic life on the home front.[2] That book was

---

[2] *Most of the veterans hailed from an area surrounding Glens Falls, New York, that Look Magazine renamed 'Hometown, USA'*-In keeping with the hometown theme, the series title remains the same for this book. Some of the veterans have a direct connection to 'Hometown, USA,' and others a more circuitous one, but most hailed from New York hometowns bound together by the simple hope that the boys would return. Many did, and many did not.

well received, and a nationwide readership clamored for more veterans' stories in the vein I wrote in. The second and third volumes highlighted the men who fought in the skies over Europe, and the fourth tackled the war in North Africa and Italy, a campaign so brutal that news of it was downplayed at home. In the fifth book, I set out to have our veterans guide you through their experiences on *D-Day and Beyond*. And now, in *The Bulge And Beyond*, we will walk with them as they sense the fear of the unknown, the crush of impending doom, the scale of being amongst the columns of young, tired men slogging into a forest, medieval and dark, with the complete inability to ever get warm again.

Matthew Rozell
Washington County, New York
-October 8, 2020-
The first anniversary of Frank Currey's passing

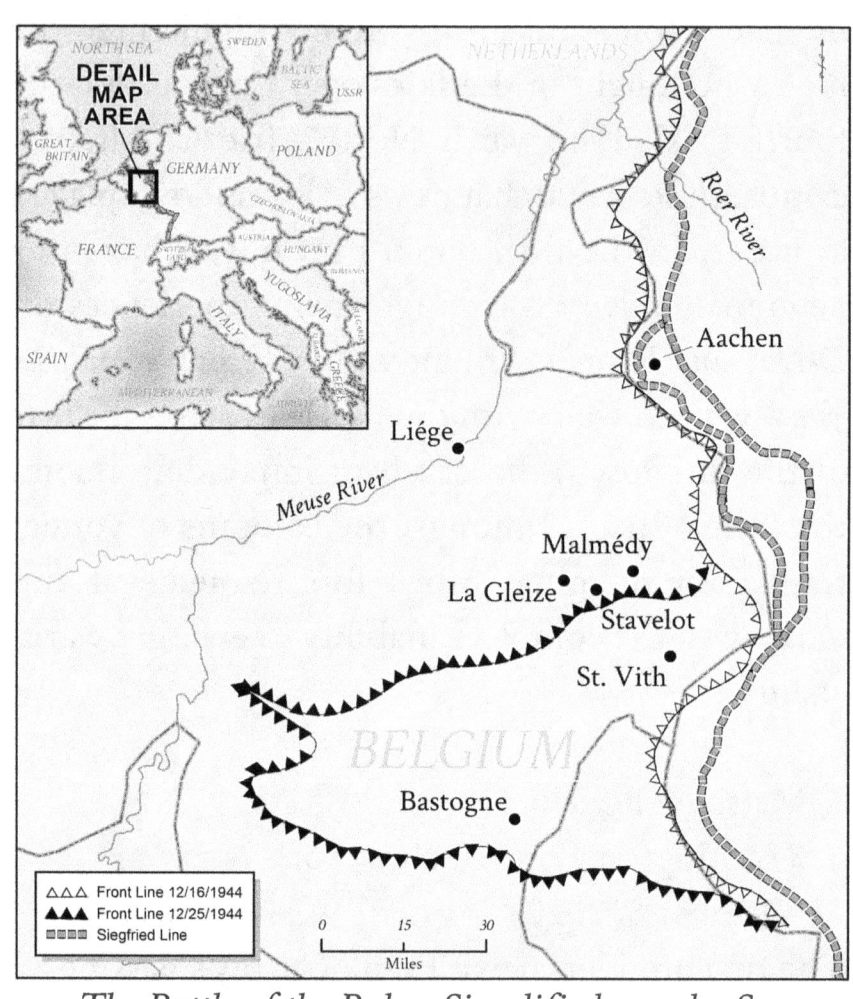

The Battle of the Bulge. Simplified map by Susan Winchell.

OVERVIEW

The Battle of the Bulge

"About midnight I was sleeping—my buddy was on duty—and somehow or other, the Germans got within 20 yards of our position. Gordon got ripped by a machine gun from roughly the left thigh through the right waist. Well, when you're that far from your home base and it's snowing and the temperature's zero, you don't have a chance. We were cut off. The Germans had overrun our position and we were in the foxhole by ourselves, so basically, we both knew he was going to die.

He slowly froze to death, bled to death. The next morning, as we looked at our gear, it looked as if I'd have spent a day in a butcher shop. My clothes were all covered with blood; his clothes were all covered with blood, and the territory we were in was all covered... he just... it was a butcher shop."

—*Bob Conroy, Private, 75th Infantry: 1944*[2]

Five months after the landings at Normandy, the Germans launched an all-out surprise counterattack against scantily defended American lines in the Ardennes Forest. Hitler's last gamble to counterattack between the advancing American and British forces in Northern France and the Low Countries had been in the planning stages since around the time the U.S. 28th Infantry Division paraded down the Champs-Élysées in Paris, which, in late August, foreshadowed the German Army's final collapse in France. The incredible magnitude of American industrial capacity dictated to Hitler that somehow the supply lines had to be cut, and he chose the Ardennes Forest for the avenue of attack in the hopes of reaching the port of Antwerp. By combining the elements of surprise, hostile terrain, and bad weather with a massive quarter-million-man offensive, the ultimate goal was to have the Germans encircle and split Allied forces and thereby push the Western Allies to the conference table to accept a favorable peace agreement with Germany to end the war in the west.

In the early morning frozen hours of December 16, 1944, six hundred German tanks broke through the thinly manned American lines after a tremendous artillery barrage, creating a 'bulge' or pocket they hoped to exploit to the sea, sowing desperation, panic, and confusion in the blitzkrieg's wake. Allied soldiers, including those of the hapless 28th Infantry Division, recently pulled from the Hürtgen Forest, found themselves in a desperate struggle for survival as temperatures plunged to the coldest in European memory during the winter of 1944–45. Many had little experience, having replaced those killed and wounded in the Normandy campaign thus far. The average American replacement was 19 years old, and in this battle, the second bloodiest in United States military history, just over 19,000 were killed.[3]

---

[3] *the second bloodiest in United States military history-* 19,276 Americans were killed between December 16, 1944 and January 25, 1945.The bloodiest campaign/battle was World War I's Meuse-Argonne Offensive from September 26 to November 11, 1918, with 26,277 Americans killed. Source: List of battles with most United States military fatalities, en.wikipedia.org/wiki/List_of_battles_with_most_United_States_military_fatalities#Campaigns

More than 700,000 Americans would eventually be engaged in yet another death match that would herald the outcome of World War II in Europe, many just a year or two beyond lazily daydreaming in a high school or college classroom. This is a story, told in the veterans' own words, of how their worlds were upended.

PART ONE

THE FOREST

"FROM THE FRYING PAN INTO THE FIRE"

"After you were in combat a while, you see the guy next to you, like Corporal Robinson, be killed. Then you realize it could very well be you, you know? Or you're in the Hürtgen Forest at night, you might be saying prayers, you kind of believe in God then, 'What did I ever do to deserve a fate like this?' The shrapnel, or the Germans are firing up into the trees, it's coming down, hitting all around you. You're cold. You're frozen. You have no warm meal. You open up a wax-covered carton with a couple little crackers in it and maybe a little thing of cheese, and that's about it. That's all you get."

– 28TH INFANTRY DIVISION SOLDIER

CHAPTER ONE

The Replacement

The Hürtgen Forest

'Our gains in the forest proper came inch by inch and foot by foot, delivered by men with rifles—bayonets on one end and grim, resolute courage on the other. There was no battle on the continent of Europe that was more devastating, frustrating, or gory.'

—Major General William G. Weaver, 8th Infantry Division

A few weeks after the liberation of Paris, the longest single battle the U.S. Army has ever fought began just three miles into Germany on September 19, 1944. It was a stop-and-start horror show in the worst conditions in Europe—ice, mud, fog, rain, sleet; damp, cold, and wet—and it did not let up until February 1945. Pushed off the front pages by the opening salvos of the Battle of the Bulge that unfolded back across the border that December, it remains relatively unknown today, despite—or maybe because of? —the high costs. Thirty-three thousand Americans were killed or wounded for very little gain. Foxholes filled with water, shells bursting in treetops terrorized and maimed countless GIs. Many rifle companies turned over 100 percent—out of one company of 160 men of the 28th Division, one recalled, 'By the time I left the forest, I had the instincts of an animal,' being only one of the twenty lucky enough to walk out.

Alfred H. Meyer and others were also lucky enough to walk out. He sat for this interview in October 2001.

Alfred H. Meyer

I was born in Brooklyn, New York, I grew up in the Red Hook section on Brooklyn. I went to elementary school and Brooklyn Technical High School. In December '41, when World War II started, I was 16 years old. At that time they had a draft on but they were drafting men from 21 years of age and up.

So, since I was 16 years old, I figured the world wouldn't last that long and I wouldn't be in it. It wasn't long before they dropped the draft age down to age 18. When I was finished with high school I didn't want to go in the Army, so I volunteered for the Navy. The Navy wouldn't accept me because of my eyesight, I wear eyeglasses. So, I was 18 in January of '43. I figured, 'Well, I'm not rushing. I'll just wait until they call me.' In April '43, I was drafted. The reason I wanted to get into the Navy to begin with was I figured maybe I could learn something while I was in the Navy that would be useful in civilian life, but it didn't work out that way.

I was inducted in the Army. I went to Camp Upton, New York, and that was just the place where they process people, where you get your clothes, and your shots, and things like that. We got on a Pullman train and we went down to Camp Blanding, Florida. I was homesick. I lived, sort of, a shelter to life until I was taken away, but that was good that I got away from my mother's apron strings. I didn't like close order drill. I figure I'm not doing anything that's useful, marching up and down, and left and right. If they put me on garbage detail, or something like that, I feel I was doing something worthwhile.

Things were going bad in Africa and they wanted volunteers to go to Africa. If you're a volunteer they give you a furlough immediately; when they come back, they would ship you out. I wanted to get home for a visit, so I volunteered, and I always wanted to see Africa. So I went home on a furlough. When I come back and I reported they say, 'You're not going.' And I said, 'Why not?' They said, 'Well, we lost your shot records, so we can't send you. You have to take your shots all over again.' So I took my shots all over.

*

I was assigned to the 66th Infantry Division. I was in company D, which is a heavy weapons company. It consists of machine guns and 81 mm mortars, and I was trained as a mortar man.

After we left Camp Blanding, Florida, then we went to Camp Joseph T. Robinson in Arkansas. That's near Little Rock and it was nice there. I liked the Arkansas, Little Rock; I was in with a bunch of hillbillies. And I was telling stories, you know, about things that happened in New York. So, I was there about eight months, then we went to Camp Rucker, Alabama. I was there for a little while, and meanwhile they had the Normandy Invasion and they were having a lot of casualties over there, and they needed replacements. So, then they shipped me out as a replacement to go overseas. I sailed on the *Queen Elizabeth* as she went up to New York. I had posh accommodations—I was in a state room on the top deck, so that was a good spot on the ship. The voyage was pleasant, but because of the submarines they changed course every 20 minutes. So it took about eight days and we landed in Glasgow, Scotland. From there we got on a train and we went to England. I stayed in England for about a week. I moved down to Southampton and went across the channel in a ship, and I landed in France. A couple of days later, I was assigned to my outfit in the 4th Infantry Division, the 12th Infantry Regiment, Company D.

Replacement, 4th Infantry Division

[As a replacement], I was nervous and scared. The first day I landed in France, they dropped two bombs and 20 men got killed. So, I was nervous and uneasy, and I'm standing there with a long face on and a couple young men come up to me and said, 'Relax, take it easy.' Said, 'Won't be long, a couple of days, you'll get used to what's going on.' So then I felt much better.

Now, at that time the Normandy Campaign was over, and we moved through Northern France and we got to Paris. We were digging our foxholes to sleep for the night, and we could see Paris over the horizon. The one fellow said, 'Hey, that must be Paris.' The other one said, 'Hey, we'll probably go in there tomorrow.' And the other guy said, 'No, I think we'll probably go around it.'

So, we got up the next morning and we were waiting and waiting. Meanwhile, there was a lot of things going on; Eisenhower and de Gaulle were having an argument. Eisenhower wanted to go around Paris and de Gaulle wanted the glory of re-taking Paris, so politics won out. The best thing would be to go around, but we went through Paris, so I took part in the Liberation of Paris. Everybody was going crazy there. The French people had all the British flags hanging out, they must have thought the British were coming. I don't know where they got all the flags. All of a sudden, they changed the flags and they put American flags out. They were passing out drinks and eats, and everybody was so happy. I looked all over the sea of happy faces and I said, 'Oh boy, it must have been terrible living under the German occupation.' I said, 'This is worthwhile, what we're doing.' I think it was on a Saturday, August 25, '44. We went to a park, we dug foxholes there, and stayed there for the night. In the morning, whoever wanted to go to church could go to the Notre Dame Cathedral for the church service there.

We stayed there for about a week and then we moved on, going north into Germany. When we got to the German border, we were at the Siegfried Line. We walked right through it; we didn't have any resistance there. [There were] a lot of pillboxes and, you know, the 'dragon's teeth' [concrete obstacles] for the tanks and such. We captured a couple of Germans there. Nobody knew who they were there, I think, so we kept on going, now we're getting into September. We went on and on, and the next big thing was the Hürtgen Forest.

*

The mortars are usually about 300 yards behind the actual front, you see. I was what they call a second gunner. I was the guy that drops the shell down a tube. After a while they made me a radioman. I carried a radio on my back, weighed about 35 pounds, and you go up the front where the lieutenant directs the mortar fire. When I went in to be a radioman, I figured, oh, that was it. That was a more dangerous job, but I pulled through.

[The Hürtgen Forest] was terrible. We were in a forest and the Germans put up a stiff resistance there and both sides had heavy losses. One division after another went in there and got cleaned out. The weather was bad, and it was during the month of November and it rained every day for a whole month. It was cold. One or two days when it stopped raining, the wind blew the rain out of the trees. I put my overcoat out to dry and it froze. Everybody was getting either sick, wounded, or killed. Casualties were terrible. They had men out there on the battlefield, they were lying out there for three days and nobody could get to them. They asked for volunteers to go out and pick them up and bring them to the aid station. So, in my company, we had eight men volunteer, I was one of the volunteers. We managed to go in and get them out without getting hurt. After the war was over, I received the Bronze Star for that.

When we left the Hürtgen Forest, the 4th Division had been in combat for about six months at that time without any relief. We were supposed to go to Luxembourg for rest, that was sort of a dead front. So they moved us to Luxembourg, and that's when the Battle of the Bulge started. [*Chuckles*] We went from the frying pan into the fire. During the Battle of the Bulge, we were in Patton's Army at that time. Patton's Army was on a flank and flanks held out, so we didn't have too much trouble in that battle.

*

Time went on. A lot of snow, a lot of cold. If I had a cup of coffee, before I could finish the coffee, it would freeze in the cup. It was so cold, bitter cold. We bundled up. I had two pair of pants, overcoat, gloves, boots, and when you got cold during the night, you would wake up and dig a little more in your foxhole. Warm yourself up and go on back to sleep. Some people froze to death in their foxholes, it was so cold. We weren't prepared for this [winter] war, so we didn't have the right equipment, good equipment for the cold weather. It was the first time the Americans fought a winter campaign since the Revolutionary War. The other wars, they used to cease for the wintertime, and start a spring offensive.

'This Is It'

A little while later, we were walking through the woods; we were supposed to settle down for a night, we're in a patch of woods and there was a clearing and another patch of woods. We were going to move from one patch of woods to the other and settle down for a night. Well, they sent one man across and he was shot by a sniper. They sent another man across, he was shot.

I was the next man to go, so I figured this was it. This was the end, and I said a prayer. Two artillery shells come in and you could hear them coming, but I couldn't duck—I didn't know whether to stand up or lay down. Sometimes if you stand up in the woods the tree will shelter you, though I got shrapnel in my kneecap and I went back to the aid station. So little by little I was taken back to France, and they operated on me in Paris, and they moved me to a tent hospital in the Normandy area. I recuperated from my wound and I was ready to go back and be reassigned. I spoke to a sergeant, he was doing the paperwork, and he said, 'I'm going to put you in the rear echelon.'

I said, 'I want to go back to my outfit.'

He says, 'You do?'

I said, 'Yeah!'

He said, 'Are you sure?'

I said, 'Yeah, I want to.' I said, 'Can you do it?'

He says, 'Yeah, we can arrange that.'

So, I figured this war ain't going to last too long, the Germans are just about beat. When it's over they'll have no use for the infantry and they'll send us home. See? So, I rejoined my outfit and hostilities ceased. We did various things for a while. One time we're in charge of a prison camp there, and then we were... we were shipped back to the States.

The prison camp was bad. They had war criminals there, real bad people, not ordinary soldiers, you know? So you had to be careful. Mainly I was guard duty, you know?

So, I come back. I went on what they call a Victory ship. This time I didn't have posh accommodations. We were stacked in there like sardines, but it was a pleasant trip. We sailed into New York Harbor. I had a bunch of the fellows from down south around me. I was pointing out the various buildings, like the Empire State Building, and the Woolworth Building, and this and that, you know? They were looking, you know, like this [*drops jaw, opens mouth wide in mock wonderment*].

They never saw those tall skyscrapers. We passed by the Statue of Liberty, and Governors Island. Right across from Governors Island is where I used to live. You could almost see my house. When I had left New York on the *Queen Elizabeth*, I looked over where I lived and I said, 'Oh boy, I wonder if I'm coming back?' [Now there was a] big reception.

*

We went up to Camp Shanks, New York. We got off the ship and had all female reporters there, and oh, they looked beautiful because we never saw any women dressed up, or with makeup. All we saw were peasants most of the time, in farm clothes. They weren't bad women, but they weren't that attractive, you know? We went up to Camp Shanks and they had a telephone exchange. You could go in a telephone booth and call home, you go up to a desk and you pay them whatever it cost. So, I went to the booth and I called home, told them I was back in the States, and of course everybody was excited. From there I went down to Camp Butner in North Carolina, near Raleigh. This was in July '45. Little did I know we were scheduled for the invasion of Japan.

They gave us a 45-day furlough. In August I was home on furlough, and they dropped the atomic bombs, and then in a couple of days, it was over. I was home and it didn't take too long to be discharged, in November '45. When I was being discharged they had us all lined up and everybody was anxious to get home, naturally. A sergeant was coming down the line and he'd say, 'You all right?

You all right?' This was at the Hospital Separation Center, and they were using their facilities to discharge people. It had nothing to do with medicine.

Sergeant comes to me and says, 'You all right?'

I said, 'No.'

He said, 'What? You ain't all right? What's the matter?'

I said, 'Well, I got shrapnel on my knee and that bothers me every day.'

I wanted it down on the record that I wasn't satisfied, and I was hurt. So he pulled me out of line. The other guys are thinking, they're all afraid to say something. They were thinking, 'Oh boy, this guy will never get home now.'

They sent me to see two doctors, I saw one doctor and another one. When they were finished examining me, they said, 'We're going to put you in for a disability. After you get home, you'll hear what the disposition was.' So, I was awarded the 10% disability for my wound.

*

After the war, I drifted around. First thing I do is I had to get a job immediately, any job, as long as

I got back to work—I didn't like my mother going out to work every day, and me sitting at home.

When I left, I had one suit that was nice. I told my mother don't throw that suit out, save it. I got home, but it didn't fit anymore. She had saved the suit for me. The war, it was very hard on the mothers. I was sitting in a cafe in Paris, outside sipping a glass of wine, watching the women go by. I said, 'Oh boy, here I am. I'm sitting here.' I think this was in April, and spring in Paris. 'I'm sitting here relaxing and my mother's home worrying about me.'

When I was wounded, I wrote a letter home immediately, saying I was wounded. 'Don't worry, I'm okay.' When I got to Paris, I wrote another letter saying, 'Well, the nurse just gave me a bath.' And it didn't say much, that I was all right, or what. My mother got a telegram from the War Department saying that I was seriously wounded in action. She got the second letter first, so that was a shock to her. When she went to work the next morning, it was published in a local newspaper, at that time they had the paper called *The Brooklyn Eagle*. She walked down the block to get to the bus.

Everybody comes out of their house. Said they were sorry, that they read in the paper that your son was hurt. Neighbors were friendly at that time. They used to sit out at night on the porch. They didn't stay in the house with the air conditioner on and the TV going. When it got hot, they used to sit down outside together.

I had to buy clothes to wear and I got a job as a messenger in Manhattan. I drifted around from one job to another, each one would be a little better. Then I had a chance to get into the Post Office, a temporary appointment, so I went to work in the Post Office. Then I got an attack of appendicitis, I had to have my appendix out. I went to the hospital, and had the operation, and I'm lying in the hospital and I was making good money in the Post Office. I said to myself, 'I don't need all this money.' I said, 'I ought to go to school.'

So I went to the Veterans Administration and told them I want to go to school. I had found out some public law that they have for disabled veterans, so I went to school to study cabinetmaking. I took a course for a year and when you get done, they find employment for you. While I was taking a course, I visited a furniture factory and I saw the working conditions there, and I figured it was no job for me. I figured I'd be better off in a Post Office. I worked there 15 years and I wasn't satisfied at it, there wasn't much chance of advancement. So I quit the job, and I'm still living in Brooklyn there, and I went to work for the New York State Thruway Authority. I worked up in Albany, New York, and we moved up in that area, East Schenectady. I managed to advance a couple of times. I worked there 26 years, then I retired, and that's the end of the story.

'Made It Through Four Campaigns'

I don't care for the Army too much. I'd go willingly if they need me, you know, but I'd rather be in the Navy. They were taking a beating, they needed men in the infantry, it didn't matter. We had guys that were civil engineers, lawyers in the infantry. [I was in a good squad], only you couldn't make many friends because people went missing all the time. I know one time, I almost got captured. We had outpost with a section of machine guns. You know a section of machine guns is two machine guns and a couple of squads of men. An outpost is something that's set up in front of the front lines. They want to string telephone wire from where we were to the outpost. So me and another guy, we strung the wire and we hooked up the telephones. We went back, and when we got back, the telephone didn't work. So, we had to go back, and check to see what the matter was, and everybody at the outpost was missing, Oh God, they must have been captured. So, I missed [being captured] like that. You have a lot of close calls. I was lucky, and I had to be careful too. You know, don't do anything foolish. Don't make a lot of noise.

I [made it through] four campaigns, with the mortar and the radio, but I didn't shoot any rifles; see, that wasn't my job. In fact, I never shot a gun over there. It wasn't my job to shoot people or shoot at people. Instead I had to duck the bullets, and shells. [But], you know, I was young at the time. I was 19 when I was overseas. I was [more worried] about what I was going to do when I got home. I had faith that I would get through it. I had a good mental attitude. I used to get up in the morning, [and of course], there was no future there. I said to myself, 'Well, who knows what new and exciting adventures I'm going to have today!' You know, I psyched myself up a little. A mental attitude, it helps a lot to pull you through any situation. So, it was an interesting experience. That was worthwhile for me. I grew up while I was there. Now I'm happy, relaxed, and retired. Oh, I am a little disappointed that we're in another terrible war. Everybody's sad about that.[4]

---

[4] *another terrible war-* Mr. Meyer sat for this interview in October 2001. Operation Enduring Freedom (2001-2014) in the Global War on Terror had just commenced.

CHAPTER TWO

The Rifleman

Angelo B. DeMicco was a kid who had not even finished high school when he felt the pull of getting on with his life and joining the service. He became a rifleman with the 4th Infantry Division, a replacement soldier who soon found himself, at age 19, in the thick of the fighting, nearly killed, and like many, with a disability for life.

Angelo B. DeMicco

I was born on January 29, 1925. I went three years of high school. Then I came here to Mechanicville; I had one year at Mechanicville and then I had to get out of there, start going to work. I quit three years of high school. Of course, when

I heard Pearl Harbor, I probably was out of a job, looking for a job or something like that. Right away I asked a buddy of mine, I says, 'If they're going to start drafting and stuff like that, [we might as well] volunteer.' So me and my buddy Johnny, who's dead today, we went down and volunteered when we heard about that. We were 17 years old, but they wouldn't take me on account of my age. They took Johnny, but they didn't take me because I was only 17. I turned 18 in January and then I volunteered—just wanted the Army, that's all. My brother, Tony, he tried the Navy or first the Marines. They wouldn't take him because he had his slant eyes like this and they wouldn't take him because they thought he was Japanese. [*Gestures with fingers at corners of his eyes*] Honest to God, this is the truth. After that, he went to the Navy or the Army, then they wouldn't take him in the Army. They finally took him in the Navy and he spent forty years [in the service]. He became Master at Arms and everything in there. Then he went in the Army for 26 years—that's when he was a professional fighter. He spent three or four years professional fighting.

I went for the induction in Camp Shanks in New York. And then from my basic training, I went down to Camp Butner, North Carolina, just infantry training mostly, learned how to shoot the guns. Then we had what they call 'dig your foxhole and we'll have a TD, a tank destroyer, going over your foxhole while you're in there,' to see how strong it was. Well at that time, I had mine on the end and everybody else [who dug theirs] ran in the woods. I didn't know that. I'm down there like this hanging underneath there [*makes crouching motion, covers head with arms*]. So the tank destroyer came around, it spun around, and everything came down on top of me—I was buried alive! Geez. So some way or another, I got my head up and I'm yelling, 'Help! Help!' And everybody in the woods came. I says, 'Did you guys get in the foxhole?' 'Oh no. We ran in the woods.' So I got two days off anyhow for possible sickness…

We transferred out in the 78th Division and I was transferred into the 4th Infantry Division; I became a rifleman in S Company, 2nd Squad. We went up to Camp Shanks right away and we were shipped overseas.

We were way up in Scotland area, then [moved to Southampton for the Normandy invasion]. We went in on the first wave on Utah Beach; I don't think we lost [more than] one, two guys. That's about it. But we went in with probably no resistance at all because we landed, I think it was five miles down too far. And then when we got there, our division commander, Teddy Roosevelt Jr., he says, 'Well, we'll start from here.' He died within two or three weeks after the invasion, I'm pretty sure it was Normandy because he had a bad heart, but he went against all the deferments. They wanted him to stay home, but he wouldn't stay home. He went in anyhow. He was a good man though. And I don't know what general took over after that. I was too busy. You were too busy fighting up along the coast.

Inland

And then we started going inland from that beach to all of the cities along the coast, and we relieved the 82nd Airborne at Sainte-Mère-Église. We relieved that outfit and we got them together, and then they came along with us fighting up towards Cherbourg; that was our biggest place we hit. When we hit Cherbourg, we had house-to-house fighting with stiff resistance. Then we captured the island of Saint-Malo. I don't know if you ever heard of it, it was an island right off of Cherbourg, and it was loaded with thousands of Germans, but they gave up all of a sudden after some bombardment. When we went in there, we found a cave full of all kinds of whiskey and cognac and wine, everything. I don't know. Everybody in the whole division could have 20 cases if they wanted it. We had a few bottles of it, celebrating the capture of Cherbourg.

*

Mortain

On August 7, a sleepy little French town called Mortain was the very place that the Germans would launch a major counterattack with four panzer divisions, conceived by the Führer himself.

The summertime breakthrough in Normandy had telegraphed to the German High Command the unwelcome possibility that the Germans might have to withdraw from France or risk being encircled and trapped. Neither option was acceptable, so Hitler himself drew up the plans with the expectation of punching through the American lines and driving to the coast at Avranches, forcing a wedge into the advancing armies and stopping the hemorrhaging, perhaps even pushing the invader back all the way to the sea. Having survived the July 20 assassination attempt, he was in no mood to listen to objections; and so it was that the 30th Infantry Division, 743rd Tank Battalion, and the 823rd Tank Destroyer Battalion came to one of the crossroads of the entire Normandy campaign. DeMicco's regiment of the 4th Infantry Division would be sent in to plug the gaps.

Twenty-six thousand Germans and the first of 400 tanks, including the lead elements of the black-uniformed crews of the 1st SS Panzer Division *Leibstandarte SS Adolf Hitler*, began to attack. With a barrage of rockets, artillery fire, and mortar rounds, they enveloped most of the American positions on the roads surrounding the town in short order. The afternoon would bring counterattacks by the rockets of RAF Typhoon fighter bombers targeting the panzers, but also taking out some of the 743rd's Sherman tanks. As dark fell on the evening of the 7th, the men on Hill 314 were surrounded by the 2nd SS Panzer Division.[5]

As the Germans repeatedly tried to scale the hill, an artillery spotter called down round after round through his fading radio set, delivering death on his doorstep from five miles distant.[3] The hill held. Watching the battle closely, Hitler called for a renewed effort to take Mortain and this troublesome obstacle. Under a white flag of truce, the SS officer expressed his admiration for the stand and demanded surrender. The senior officer refused, releasing a pent-up, colorful reply and calling in an artillery barrage on his own position as the Germans attacked it.[4] The hill held, and on August 11 the Germans began their withdrawal amid constant shelling and harassment from the air. While the 30th had lost over 2,000 men, the Germans had

---

[5] *2nd SS Panzer Division* – The 'Das Reich' SS Division had already distinguished itself in keeping with the standards of barbarity the SS has been noted for. In a reprisal raid on June 10 in the quaint Norman town of Oradour-sur-Glane, members systematically murdered 642 French civilians and razed the town. Men were herded into garages and barns and shot; women and children were forced into a stone church and burned to death. The town was never rebuilt and stands today as a silent memorial to wartime atrocity. See Atkinson, Rick. *The Guns at Last Light: The War in Western Europe, 1944-1945.* New York: Henry Holt & Co., 2013. 94.

had their attack blunted and nearly 100 tanks knocked out or abandoned.⁵ It was the start of the German movement to the Siegfried Line and their westward defenses on the border of the Reich itself; by the end of August, some 10,000 Germans had been killed in the pocket and 50,000 captured.

Angelo B. DeMicco

So I went into Cherbourg, then we went down towards Mortain. Now in Mortain, we had to go in and take a little area. We had captured Crossroad 148, just before Mortain; the Germans were dug in, so we surrounded them, and we killed a sniper that was in a tree to protect the area. And then all of a sudden, we heard [voices] from the Germans; after they knew they were already beaten, they gave up. And we didn't lose any of our men, because we grabbed that sniper before he could kill any one of us.

During the overnight, the Germans pulled a big counterattack. That's when I got machine gunned in my right leg. And [some of the Germans] were dressed up in American uniforms, the ones that got me. They came in and infiltrated because we thought they were Americans, and then they started opening fire around us. And when they did, they hit me in the back of the leg and ripped almost the whole thing off, but I survived it. In fact, I think this bone right here, right there is a bullet wound, I shoved the bone right back through. But it hurts all the time now, after over 50 years that it happened; I've been going down to the VA [hospital].

The counterattack was still going on. They got me on a rack on a jeep, and the Germans are shooting at this jeep with burp guns and all kinds of machine guns. And I can feel the [rounds] going right by me; you hear a bullet that sounds like a crack of a whip—crack! —you hear it going by you. We finally made it to an aid station, then I went into the evacuation area towards Cherbourg. And that's when a doctor, a colonel, operated on my leg.

*

I went back to England and then I finally came back to my outfit, and that's when Patton made the breakthrough. The 4th Division made for the Ardennes and then I was pulled out of that, on the outskirts of the Ardennes, the forest. In fact, I was in the Battle of Bastogne. And when they were surrounded, we went up there with Patton on his tanks and relieved the troops at Bastogne. He didn't believe in sitting down and digging a hole. He believed in keeping going. In fact, we had him in the Falaise Gap, when I first came back from the hospital; that's when I teamed up with him, and my division again. We teamed up with him. He went on a rampage. He was good. No question about it. Smart.

The Cold

I had regular combat boots and then they wanted to give out the galoshes. I didn't want them because a lot of guys were freezing their feet with the galoshes because when they would walk with them, they'd sweat. And then when they stopped, they would get frozen toes; a lot of them went back with frozen toes. They couldn't stand.

My buddy and I, we had two blankets. He had one, I had one. One guy stood guard and the other guy slept. And the body contact between both of us was warm enough to keep us alive, to keep us warm. We did have covers over the foxholes; we'd built it with branches, with snow on top of them, camouflaging ourselves. But it went like that. This other guy, he got the frozen feet, like I said, because he had the galoshes. So I took his shoes off and everything, I rubbed his feet. We built a little fire, he had frostbite, but not as bad as the other guys had it. That was after they pushed through to Bastogne, when it was 20 degrees below zero, in that area at that time. That's why a lot of things didn't move. It was so cold and so foggy, you couldn't move.

*

I went as far as the Siegfried Line; I wound up in what they call the Prüm area. We were now starting to fight near towards the Siegfried Line and that's when I got blown out of my little foxhole; what they call a Screaming Mimi came over my head and blew up, concussion bomb. It lifted me right out of the hole I was in and blew me up right against the tree. And I was bleeding all over, out of the nose. So actually, I had two wounds, and then I went back to the front lines again. Finally, they sent me back after about another month in combat and they were heading towards Germany. They said I needed more rehabilitation. [We had had no rest at all]; I was starting to hear things in my head, starting to get wobbly, I wasn't up to par. So, they finally said, 'Well, send him back to a Camp Philip Morris.'

At that time, they were giving out points so much in combat and so much for being wounded. I think we got 15 points extra for being wounded. So I picked up 30 points more and I was almost one of the first to go back to the States, I think on the *Queen Mary*, shooting craps on this boat, picked up a few bucks, a few souvenirs, pistols, German SS knives, a Luger and a Mauser, which I gave to a couple of captains there who wanted them—I didn't want them anymore. I caught pneumonia or bronchitis before I got discharged and I was supposed to get discharged on December the 14th, but they kept me another month, Camp Shanks because I had to take penicillin [intravenously]. Then I met my oldest brother, we were getting discharged together. He had been in the [Army] Air Force up in Alaska. Tony was in the Navy in England, and our other brother Armand was with the

104th Timberwolf Division. He got captured. He was a prisoner of war for nine months. He landed in Le Havre, and that division was in [the Battle of the Bulge] on the first day. About a week in there, the way I got it from Armand, he went on a seven-man patrol. The Germans shelled that seven-man patrol; the shell hit right in the middle of them and killed four of them, and he, the sergeant, and another guy were captured, and he was in the prison [camp] for nine months.

*

I think the war changed my life when it comes to working on the railroad, because they wouldn't take a service man with disabilities. I would have had 45 years [on the job] there because I worked in the roundhouse when I worked for the railroad. [Somebody] turned me in about my disability and then I lost my job. I used the GI Bill to go to the Veterans Vocational School in Troy. I became a body and fender man. So I worked odds and ends, body and fender work, until I had to give it up [for health reasons].

I'm a life member of the DAV, Disabled American Veterans. And I pay dues every year to the

VFW, [but I did not stay in contact with anyone that I served with]; I never got their names, half the time, they come in and go out. You don't even [really know them, just] 'Hi, Bill' or 'Hi, Joe' or something like that. That's it. All those guys, and most of my friends, are dead and gone now.

Angelo DeMicco passed away in 2016 at the age of 91.

CHAPTER THREE

The Replacement Runner

Robert Kirk knew he was blessed. The happiest day of his life was when he got out of the Army. He speaks quickly; he has a twinkle in his eye, but it does not hide the emotions that have long since been buried. He gave this interview in 2001.

"*I think [at some point], you're worried about being killed because there's so many being killed around you. At first, you're going, and someone would brag, 'They haven't made the bullet yet that's going to get me.' At the Hürtgen Forest, we fought bitterly and lost most of the outfit, but we didn't gain anything because it was near the Siegfried Line, the top of a big hill in the forest. The Germans were dug into cement pillboxes and they'd shoot down at us; it was a mistake to try to take it, we should've bypassed it. It was a thing when they were throwing 88 shells up into the trees. You're down below. The shrapnel comes straight down. And the Germans would come out at night. If you were in your trench they could jump in and knife you and kill you. We'd come the next day and you'd find the guys dead or they disappeared entirely."*

Robert F. Kirk

I was born in Corning, New York, on March 10, 1920. My father was a farmer and a supervisor in the railroad yards down in Corning. They folded up [in the Great Depression] and he lost his job, so we went to Rochester where he got a job at Eastman Kodak. I was raised mostly in Rochester from 1927 on. I went to Holy Rosary Parochial School and Sacred Heart, which is the cathedral today in Rochester, and I attended Aquinas Institute, which is a well-known Catholic college there. I was brought up strict religious. Like I said, my family didn't allow any guns. I never fired a gun or a thing. They were very, very strict in parochial schools, as you know, and like that, and there was no swearing, or cussing, and everything. The worst offense in school at that time would be chewing gum or whispering.

I went to business college after I finished and got a two-year associates degree, and I had heart problems. I've got a heart murmur, and when they had a draft, they classified me as 4-F. I got a job with the defense plant, and I was working there in the cost accounting department at the time. [Later], the war wasn't going too good, and they rechecked everybody, and they said, 'Oh, you're fit to go in,' so they took me in the service.

I went into it the day before Thanksgiving in 1942. It was entirely different than any life [I had experienced to that point]. In fact, I went from Fort Niagara, and at the time my brother went in they were taking all Army Air [Corps]. He went in as a bombardier. But when I went in later that year in '42, it swung over to ground warfare, and I didn't have much chance, they put me in the infantry, shipped me by train all the way down to Camp Livingston, Louisiana. They put me in basic training. It started as thirteen weeks, but they kept dropping it so that when I got in, it was only five weeks. We started out seven days a week about 6:00 AM, and after supper, we were made to go and march. You could never please the sergeant, you know? He had you salute and you'd bring your hand up. What would happen, he'd come and grab it at the right angle, and they'd yell at you, and they really put you through [hell]. In basic training, as you probably know, we weren't allowed to do anything, to even think for ourselves.

Well, after basic training, then they assigned us, and I was assigned to Company H. Right from day one, I was in the 28th [Infantry Division] and I was assigned to the 109th Regiment, Company H, which was heavy weapons. It's not as bad as a rifle company, and that's where I was.

We had amphibious training in Florida in February, I remember, 1943. It was extremely cold down there, we're in the Panhandle, and we'd get out about 7:00 or 8:00 in the morning and we'd have to go out in an amphibious boat. Then we'd step off into the water and you have to go out diagonally and you had to walk in the water. But once you hit the beach, you run, and you throw yourself on the ground. I must've done it a couple dozen times in a day. You'd be shaking and everything, and then we'd go out on the firing range. I had to qualify with the M1, the .03, the carbine. I had to qualify with the mortar, the .45, and the heavy machine gun. And they said anyone that could do it gets a leave of absence, and I was one of two, and so in March 1943, I was given a week's leave.

I went back home, of course. It was good to get home, get away from the service, which I really didn't like. I didn't like the change in the life. It's not a democracy. You have nothing to say at that time, and taking someone like myself with an entirely different background, I didn't like [some of the people I met]. They're always thinking of going out and getting the girls, and swearing, and cussing, and everything else. It just was so different than what I was brought up to know. My parents didn't even allow us to have a BB gun. My oldest brother, three years older than me, he had a BB gun and he used to hide it in the attic, and they found it. Oh, and he got hell for that. And [the Army] was an entirely different experience, a wake-up call for a young person like me. You know?

We left there and we went to Camp Pickett in Virginia and went on maneuvers in West Virginia. Those were always a little rough, and then from there we went to Camp Myles Standish outside of Boston, and we went overseas in I would say October 1943. We were stationed in Wales.

Great Britain

When we were in the States, we had a lot of marching. We had to do a five-mile march with full equipment, about 70 pounds. When we were in Florida, we had to do that in one hour or less. We always had a contest with the other companies, and I think we did it in 51 minutes. You walk some. Then you run and walk. I think the next group was nine miles in two hours. Then you had to do 25 miles in eight hours. If you fell out, you were in trouble.

But when we were in Wales, we had to go across the moors. We had one week to do one hundred miles. We went nights and everything. We thought that was tough, but it didn't compare with combat. When we were in England we were training like mad. I don't know if you ever heard of that infiltration course. They had this barbed wire and you had to go on your stomach and under it like that, and they got guys on towers. They hit the bombs that go off right next to you. Some of the men got real scared and jumped up. They got machine guns about 20 inches above you there, and they were killed. It was always gloomy and dark because we were there in the wintertime. There wasn't much... They're further north than us and like that. I ended up in the hospital when I was there because you got no sunshine. They used to give us a special drink for vitamin C or something and like that, and it was cold and dreary.

The people were very friendly, very nice. We were very well accepted. I even got a furlough into London. That had to be '43. I remember the Rainbow Club down there, and the bombs would be dropping, and we'd be dancing. You could hear them, and a lot of the women would run for the shelters, but we were 'too brave' to do that. We'd look like a coward if we ran, so we had to stay there. I stayed in an apartment house I think, and when they were bombing at night I climbed up to the flat roof and I could look off and see the bombs dropping. I got a small room. One little dresser, and I said, 'Gee, I'd do anything to have this permanently,' because when you're living, say, in barracks with bunk beds up and down, there's no privacy. You really have nothing, everyone is together, but I think we got along pretty good. We had one fellow... Maybe I shouldn't bring this up. We had one fellow who was probably... There was segregation at the time. Would you like me to talk about that? In the States, he came to us and he was mostly white, but you could tell by his features that he had Afro-American blood in him. When we marched, or had anything to do with any other company, [we'd hear], 'Here comes the nigger company.' They'd say things like that! Everybody wouldn't have anything to do with him, but I did, you know? He was a corporal and I was only a private, probably, or PFC. He was a pretty nice fellow and I went out with him over to the PX, had a few beers, and like that. I'd always get ribbed along.

'How is your nigger friend?'

There were expressions like that, but I remember the last time I saw him I think was in Northern France. He got shot in the leg. He was lying there bleeding, and I went over and talked to him, and he said, 'Boy, am I ever lucky. I'm going home now.' It was a flesh wound.

Medals

I never got a Purple Heart for anything because [sometimes fraud was suspected]. You'd be battered and bleeding and everything, but if you went in and complained or asked for it, they'd say, 'It's a C-ration thing.' You know what C-ration is? It's a can of food. It's a can. You open the can and they have different things in there, hash or bean soup or something like that. The edge of the can is sharp. You could cut yourself, take yourself like that over to the medics and say you were wounded in battle, and some guys, I believe, did that. They wanted to get a Purple Heart. 'Here I am, a wounded veteran,' you see? Also, I'll bring up [my feelings on] the prisoner of war issue. I think most of them, if they're in the Air Force and shot down, there's nothing they can do but surrender. Maybe they can try, but they're not used to fighting on the ground. But I would say any infantryman that would quit when he had his gun and his ammunition is not following the rules they should. This one guy I heard about was a general, West Point general. Kept radioing for help during the Battle of the Bulge. They couldn't give him any. He says, 'We're practically out of ammunition. We have to surrender.' And they told him he could not surrender, but he did surrender, and they said, 'Well, he's ruined for life in the service after that.' But he was pretty lucky though—he died in a prisoner of war camp, so he never had to face that. But when I was caught at the Battle of the Bulge, the last thing in the world I wanted to do was surrender. I'd rather be shot and killed than surrender because we heard all kinds of stories. In fact, when the Germans captured some of them, they took them out in a field and mowed them down, as you know from studying that, and we heard stories like that. I had more combat experience than a lot of others who were there, scouting missions, so at that point, I figured, 'Maybe I won't make it.' You know what I mean?

I would say we were well trained because if they had any doubt, they send you out to the range. You're out there all day, shooting, every day. We never wore any plugs, and years later I went to a hearing aid doctor, and he says after he tested me, 'I'll tell you one thing. You were in the service, weren't you?'

I said, 'Yes. How'd you know?'

He said, 'All you fellows have trouble with hearing!'

And where I fired the gun up here [*puts imaginary gun butt on right shoulde*r], this ear here is almost dead completely, and the other ear is not too good. With the hearing aids, I get by all right, but if I'm in church or something I can't hear the voices, there's noise around me. I can hear some sound, but I can't distinguish it. But I went to apply for [financial help with the] hearing aids, they said, 'No, it's not on your service record. You're out of luck.'

Experience

[Our training was good], but I don't really know if it ever would completely [prepare you for combat] because you've got to get the experience. You knew how to, say, throw a grenade. You knew how to fire your gun. I was an ammunition carrier for a machine gun. I carried two big boxes with the ammunition in it. It was water-cooled. One guy put the tripod around his neck. The other guy had the barrel on his shoulder, and we had a lot of ammunition guys. My immediate commander at that time was Corporal Robinson, and we moved into our first battle, and right away, the Germans were dropping their mortars in, and he got killed. I turned him over and there was [a hole] right in his neck. He didn't move, and there was only maybe half a dozen of us at the most still left at the end. [So I got my experience], and it's an experience I'm glad I was part of, but I never want to go through it again. I would say it was a pretty rough, tough life, and after I got home, I put it completely out of my mind as well as I could. But as my wife said, 'You never joined an organization. You never talked about it or anything, but now you do.' I think a lot of the wounds might be healed with time. It's 56 years now since the end of the war. I didn't join anything; when I got back, I had one thing on my mind. I had a girlfriend, but I didn't want to get married until I got established. So, I went back to college, graduated in '48, and got married the following year.

The 28th Infantry Division

The 28th got a nickname, probably way back in France, because we had the red patch [a red keystone, a symbol of Pennsylvania], and the Germans would say it's a bloody bucket. You know? Probably our blood. [*Laughs*] It was no fun at all. When I first got home, I used to wake up in the night and sweat, you know? You go back. And even today occasionally I have a nightmare; I come back to those days, but it's less and less.

[Being in the 28th], I would say, like Omar Bradley found, there were a lot of incompetents. There were a lot of lawyers. I'm not picking on lawyers or anything, or other professional people who for years had the rank. They were National Guard, but they didn't know what they were doing. If you ever read his life story, the hardest job he had was trying to get ready to go into service. Another thing was there was little chance for any [non-combat] promotion like you might get in other branches. During combat, I was offered promotions, but I didn't want any. They used to call me 'Staff' because I always ended up where the staff sergeant was when he was wounded or killed. They'd want to give it to me, and I would say, 'No, no, no. I don't want it,' because the German snipers [would target you]. We had a general in Northern France it was, and he... We had an awful lot of casualties, about 115-120%. This general came up to the front lines because they fired Colonel Blanchard, he was the colonel from the 109th. The general, I can't think of his name, came up there to find out why we had so many casualties. The first day he was up, he went right to the front to find out; a sniper got him and killed him.

There were a lot of snipers [looking for you] if you were there. The officers didn't wear [insignias], as you can understand. If you saluted them or even looked to them, they would get mad at you.

Soldiers of the 28th Infantry Division march down the Champs Élysées. Paris, August 29, 1944.

Paris

I spent the entire war practically never being in a bed. I don't think I was from the time we entered at Saint-Lô all the way through into Germany. I fought in all the battles. Normandy, Northern France. I fought in the Ardennes. I fought in Germany and the Rhineland.

I was in Paris there before it was [technically] free because I took off with another fellow; it was rather loose at that time. We were getting ready to march over the Champs-Élysées, and we commandeered a car. We had cigarettes. I didn't smoke, but we had them, and the Free French had taken over. It was awful rough there, but we moved in and there were bars open and everything. One place, they had thrown a German officer out, they shot and killed him, and I had a few drinks. I'm laughing as I step over his body right there, the blood all over and everything. You go up into the bar, you know, and they had really, really treated us royally. But we didn't have any time.

'We'll be Home for Christmas'

After we got through Normandy and Northern France, they said, 'We'll be home for Christmas,' which we weren't. I think the good part about going through those villages, we were accepted not as conquerors but liberators, and the people came out with flags. They cheered us. In fact, at one point my mother got *Life Magazine*. There was a picture of the 109th, and it was a picture of me holding an M1—I got it yet, you know? She cut it out and saved it for me after the war. But that was the good part. We had them on the run. But once they stopped us at the Hürtgen Forest and the

Battle of the Bulge, it was an awful experience, but we finally got through.

*

After we marched through Paris, like a day later, we continued right on. Then we had an awful letdown. We moved right into Germany in September, but then what happened was we ran out of fuel to keep moving out. We had gone over the Siegfried Line. They told us to pull back, there were no Germans there. We had it. And we had to sit and wait several weeks because of the other battle in Holland, you know, where all the supplies were going. And then by the time the Germans had come back and dug in and everything, they moved us into the Hürtgen Forest.

The Forest

The worst battle I was in was the Hürtgen Forest. By far the worst, because you'd dig a trench, you'd be there at night, and they'd throw shells up in the trees, and they'd be hitting around you, and we had always dug in close to trees when we were there because it was a little safer. They didn't come right down on you. At the Hürtgen Forest, we fought bitterly and lost most of the outfit, but we didn't gain anything because it was near the Siegfried Line, the top of a big hill in the forest. They were dug into cement pillboxes and they'd shoot down at us; it was a mistake to try to take it, we should've bypassed it. The Germans had these bunkers up there, cement bunkers, and they were right there, and they had all the men, it's almost like D-Day. We had to attack into that [scenario], and we only had one division fighting them. There was a time where both sides had so many dead and wounded out there—I don't know if you read this or not, but we had a truce for 24 hours where we allowed no firing so that they could come in and get their wounded and dead out.

It was a thing when they were throwing 88 shells up into the trees. You're down below. The shrapnel comes straight down. And the Germans would come out at night. If you were in your trench they could jump in and knife you and kill you. We'd come the next day and you'd find the guys dead or they disappeared entirely. There was one fellow I knew rather well, and I thought he was killed, but we had a reunion in Scranton,

Pennsylvania, I think, in the early '80s. He came in, and he said, 'Staff, is that you?' I said, 'Jerry, I thought you were killed!' He wasn't. He was a prisoner of war and he got out. There was another outfit in ahead of us and another came after, but the Hürtgen Forest was really [a disaster].

'Say Hello to Hitler!'

In December '44, they sent us back to rest at Wiltz, Luxembourg, and we were just sort of resting there on December 16. The Army took over a theater and they were going to show us the movie *Watch on the Rhine* with Paul Lucas. We never did get to see it, because the Germans came at us, and I was cut off at that point from the rest of them. I was the last one out of Wiltz, Luxembourg.

Well, what happened was they sent me back to command headquarters to get directions on what to do. While I was there, I laid down [for a minute] and fell asleep. They were going to send me as a runner back, but when I woke up, they were breaking all the radio equipment and I said, 'What's happening?'

They said, 'The Germans are on the outskirts. They're coming in.'

I said, 'I can't leave. My orders are I have to stay here until we're relieved!'

The two radiomen ran out of there and they said, 'Okay. Say hello to Hitler when he comes through!' [*Laughs, waves hand in air*]

So, I ran out of there and down a hill, and there was a big convoy headed towards Bastogne. All I have is my M1 rifle and some ammunition, a few grenades, and there was a jeep there with nobody in the back. I said, 'Can I jump in?'

They said, 'Okay,' and we started down the road. This is at night, now, I'd say 7:00, 8:00 at night, and we came around [a curve] towards Bastogne, and there was a Tiger tank sitting right in the middle of the road! It opened up and hit the vehicle ahead of me, blew it right up. Threw me up in the air; I landed in the road and crawled over to the ditch, and [some of us] got together there. The Germans threw flares. I forget the German word; do you know the German word for surrender? I can't come up with it, but they were yelling that, for us to surrender. They asked us to surrender and they'd give us a little time before they opened up. There was one fellow from division headquarters, and he was an administrator, a major, and he was the top man [in the convoy]. He said, 'We got to surrender,' so I fell to the outskirts [with another] fellow and I said, 'I don't want to surrender. We'll never make it if we do.' I said, 'Let's take off. They're going to surrender.' So, we took off and I was about one week behind the lines and finally worked my way back on Christmas Day.

During that time, we had practically nothing to eat. You had one box of K-rations with the chocolate in it, and we came to a road, and we looked down, and a whole bunch of German tanks and everything else are moving along. Of course, we kept down, and at one point, we wanted to go into the village. We looked in, the Germans were already there.

Finally, we got back to [our lines]. [We were sent to] a big barn, and the officer in charge said, 'You're through.' They had a doctor there, and the doctor said, 'Are you hit? Are you hurt?'

I said, 'No. No.' They gave us a meal and said, 'We're going to send you right back to Bastogne. How many grenades you want?'

I asked for four, but they gave me double that. They put us into trucks to bring us back up then, and the Luxembourg people on the side of the road, women and older men, said, 'Boy, those guys are brave going up there again.'

I thought to myself, 'We're not brave. We just have to go.'

When we got up there, we couldn't get into Bastogne, but we had artillery on the outskirts, so they sent us to dig in there, to make sure the Germans didn't come in. There were a few Germans that came up and we fired at them. It kept them away, but they were concentrating on Bastogne.

Private Eddie Slovik

After that, I went back to my old outfit and we went to the Colmar Pocket to fight. That was the time I was there on January 31, 1945, when they brought Private Slovik back and they executed him. [6] You're probably familiar with that.

At that time, we were moving in on the Germans. I remember moving up and there was one German guy who was hit or something in the middle road, and the tanks rode right over him. He was flat, you know? Those are the types of things you'd see. After a while, you get used to it. You go into [combat] with the idea that you're going to make it, but after your buddies all get their heads blown off or get shot and killed... If a person's wounded,

---

[6] *Private Slovik-* Eddie Slovik (1920-1945) was the first American soldier tried and shot for desertion since the Civil War. Out of 21,000 American deserters and 49 death sentences in World War II, his was the only one carried out. Eisenhower upheld the execution. Joseph Lentz of Cambridge, NY, was an official witness:

Joseph F. Lentz: "I joined 28th Infantry Division, 109th Infantry Regiment, Second Battalion, H Company, heavy weapons. I became number three man in the squad of seven or eight. All had been killed or wounded in Bulge fighting. From Charleville, we went to holding positions in Vosges mountains. While there one day in daylight, two men down in the Valley walked up through. Our sergeant was called, and we were told not to fire on them and give away our position. After a few days, we left this area and went to a village. January 31, I was picked to be a witness to an execution. There was 17 of us. It was Private Slovik and two others. At the time, I didn't know who he was. Later at home, I saw the movie and bought the book. The army took all kinds of protection of guarding our identity, phony [names] and serial numbers. He refused to fight. To this day, there is controversy why he had to be killed. The only man executed since the Civil War. The other two, I think were German soldiers wearing GI clothes." Interview, April 16, 2004. Cambridge, New York. Wayne Clarke/Mike Russert, NYSVOHP.

you can give them temporary help and call for the medics. If they're killed, you have to leave them there, move on. You can't stop or anything, so sometimes you get so worked up, you laugh, when you shouldn't be laughing at all, you know? It wasn't good at all. It was an awful experience. [*Shakes head*]

You never got to, say, a bathroom or anything. You had to use your helmet, to get water, to wash. A couple times they'd move the big tents in, and they'd give you a delousing. You throw all your clothes in a big pile. Pants here, shirts there, and you go through the tent... Then when you came out, they had laundered all of them. You pick out some that fit you, you know? I got trench foot. I got about everything. But one thing I discovered during the Battle of the Bulge, any of these battles, was that you could lay down and go to sleep and you didn't die, even though the temperature's way down. I had a heavy coat, two pairs of pants, long johns, and two pairs of socks. But you had a continual cold and coughing. You didn't eat. You didn't get enough sleep—at night, you couldn't sleep. It was impossible to do that. You just get by and you say, 'Gee, when will this ever be over?' And you often say to yourself, 'What did I ever do to deserve a fate like this?' Say someone commits a crime, today they go to jail. They don't treat [inmates] like we were treated during the war, especially in the infantry, you know? I caught a break because with so many of our people killed, they were looking for someone with battle experience to bring up replacements. That took me out of the front lines temporarily, you see; I might've brought Slovik up. I don't remember, I went back [at that time]; Captain McCloud and I rotated. When they needed [replacement troops], they sent me back and they gave me a jeep and a driver and the trucks I needed to bring them up. I knew where the companies were in the 109th; I'd have to bring them up and turn them over to the first sergeant. Many times, going up, we'd be fired on. I remember guns were firing around and Captain McCloud said he didn't want to do it, and I can't blame him, so he assigned me to do it. I had to be able to type, too. They had a portable typewriter. I had to be able to type up the names and some things that he wanted done, so he used me. But I took people [up to the front] ...

One fellow, he was in supply or something, and he wanted to come up to the front to get a little experience. He showed me a picture of his wife and his kid. I brought him up. Before I got back, we heard news that he had been killed; there were all kinds [of incidents] like that. Eventually, later in the war, I got transferred from H Company to Service Company. I think it was after the Battle of the Bulge because they had to rebuild, and they needed me to bring more troops up and get them to the right companies. Even though you were right near, you weren't up that close. That's probably the only reason I went all the way through because I had been to business college and we had to be able to type 50 words a minute for 15 minutes with three or less errors in order to finish. That's how I made corporal, company clerk, for Service Company.

The Replacement System

I formed strong opinions about the system of replacement of soldiers. It was very poor. They bring these young kids up [to the front], and they're just out of high school. They have very low training. They don't know what it's all about. They don't know anyone. Even the other ones they met coming over, they don't stay with them. I might take them up, one or two, to each company, you see, and I'd drop them off there. That's what happened to Private Slovik when he came in. Eddie Slovik, when he came in, we were under fire... A fellow wrote a book saying, 'Who wouldn't act the way he did under circumstances like that?'

We didn't even know [the replacements'] names. They had dog tags. No one knew them or said anything. When I was back in Service Company, the Red Cross guy had some other guy write the letters home. [The letter writer] didn't know [the soldier who was killed]. Just, 'He was a fine young man and soldier, and he died heroically.' [The writer] wouldn't even know how he died, just that he died, but he would write that. When a soldier died, anything he had on him, pictures of women, or girls, or anything like that, they would never send back, because maybe he had a girlfriend, it would upset her. They didn't know who it was [in the photograph], so they would just set that aside.

*

Well, it's hard to say [what I think of my experience in my outfit]. I'm not a military man. I was a young draftee, didn't know what's happening. Even when I was fighting there, I did not know where I was or anything. The only thing I wanted to do was get enough food and live, you know? To keep going. We just did what we were told and that was it. Most of the [leaders] I knew, Sergeant Petrie and others, they were all killed. Within Company H, they'd bring up replacements. At the end, it's not the same ones. I was about the only [original man] who was in Company H who came out at the end. The only reason [I think that happened was] because as I explained to you, I brought up the recruits and they moved me over eventually to Service Company. I wouldn't be here.

'They Made Them Go Back'

And being with a heavy weapons company, you're not on the direct front like a rifle company. We're behind them firing the machine guns over their heads at the enemy ahead. There were two fellows that I knew, one was Sergeant Davis, and Evans, I think was his friend's name, his best buddy in school. And we're into Northern France where they had the hedgerows, and it's hard to get through. The men were pinned down, and Sergeant Davis was the staff sergeant. 'Goddamn, men, let's go.' I remember he was ahead of me, and he got up and started running across the field. They mowed him down. They killed him. His buddy, his lifelong buddy, went berserk after that. He went out of his mind. They had to take him back.

To briefly tell you about that, if an officer couldn't make it—and a lot of them couldn't—it was awful. They brought them back and they re-classified them. But he was an enlisted man. They brought the enlisted men back to a psychiatrist... 'Come on, you have to revenge your buddies!' 'Go back. Just kill a few more Germans and go back.' So, they really... I saw some of them, you couldn't even talk to the ones who I knew. Those guys were just out of it, but they still made them go back. They'd either go out of their mind or get killed. They used to call it 'shell-shocked' in World War I. They said, 'There's no shell-shock. There's nothing like that. There's no mental problem. It's all you, and you're not going to get out of it by pretending this is it.' They wouldn't let them out.

Once you were out there, you just stayed. When you're with an infantry company like me, you might be called in the middle of the night. They need a prisoner. They need to check the territory. Many a times I had gone out middle of the night, dark, to find a German to take prisoner or to check out [the situation]. I don't care how courageous you might be, how you feel, but when you get out there and people are firing at you and everything...I'd try to get big guys, taller than me, to go with me. You know why that was? Because if it was a German there, sharpshooter, who would he pick off first? The leader or the big guy, you know? I remember going down and some guy said to me, Harman, I think was his name. We're going down the road to find the location. He said, 'I know why you go with me. I know I'm taller than you.'

He said, 'They'll pick me off first.' If they picked him off, I'll jump in the [ditch]. Never really happened like that with me, but it happened with others, and I was always conscious of that.

It wasn't who deserved awards that got them, it was how they wrote them up. In the very beginning in Normandy, there was a Captain Brooks. He was handicapped, his leg or something, and he wanted to go ahead, and he was with Company G, I believe. He had a whole bunch of other officers, including a major, I think it was, they all met together to talk over things, and Germans came in and killed every one of them. But the chauffeur to the top officer jumped in the jeep and got back, and they gave him a Bronze Star for bravery, you know? If you happened to be an officer or something, they could write it up and they would give them that. This one fellow, I told you, Sergeant Davis, he got the Silver Star. He probably deserved it.

Well, I think you just had to accept [the things about being in the Army that you did not expect], to the running after the women, to the profanity, everything, you know? When you're in Rome you got to do like Romans. You got to do it. I know their thing is to train you to where they tell you to go up right into the machine gun [fire]. You got to do it, because you can't think about it; they don't want anybody to think about it! They go, 'Let's go!', you got to get up. The biggest problem they had with a lot of men, they're being fired at. Initially, you want to get down. You don't want to fight back, but you got to fire your gun. Your M1, you got to fire it. You've got to move up; you've got to fight. You just can't stay there, you know? You'd like to, but they'll jump on you. You're considered a coward if you did anything like that, you've got to go with the group. You've got a company or a squad. You have to have every man doing his part. A machine gun squad's a closely-knit group. We've got the machine gunner, but everyone's got to be able to do their part. I fire the gun, and I have to have the ammunition, and you have to continually work together. You can't fall back. You wouldn't be accepted. You've got to do what they want. When the head guy is shot, or wounded, or killed, you've got to step forward. That's why they called me 'Staff' and they even offered me a first sergeant, but I said, 'No. No, I want to live through this. I'm not an Army man. I'm willing to follow orders, but I'm not willing to [constantly] lead.'

*

I think [at some point], you're worried about being killed because there's so many being killed around you. At first, you're going, and someone would brag, 'They haven't made the bullet yet that's going to get me.' After you were in combat a while, you see the guy next to you, like Corporal Robinson, be killed. Then you realize it could very well be you, you know? Or you're in the Hürtgen Forest at night, you might be saying prayers, you kind of believe in God then, 'What did I ever do to deserve a fate like this?' The shrapnel, or the Germans are firing up into the trees, [tree bursts]; it's coming down, hitting all around you. You're cold. You're frozen. You have no warm meal. You open up a wax-covered carton with a couple little crackers in it and maybe a little thing of cheese, and that's about it. That's all you get. There's no bathroom or any way you can shave or do anything like that. You know you had to go and you hope and pray that the war will end. Do you know what I mean? We got back to Fort Dix and they said, 'I got to talk to you about re-signing up. We're going to Camp Shelby.' Later, he said, 'I see this is hopeless. We'll skip that part of it,' because he couldn't get anyone who was in combat to go back. I think one of the happiest days of my life was September 20, 1945, when I was discharged.

[When the war ended], I was in Germany at the time, but after the Colmar Pocket, we sort of fell back. We had lost so many, and I think we stopped fighting. I remember [April], I believe, President Roosevelt died. I was sleeping on the floor of a house in Germany, and my staff sergeant came in and he woke me up. He says, 'I got bad news for you.'

I said, 'Oh, we have to go up again,' and I remember I was relieved when he told me it was the president had died, rather than me having to go up there to the front again.

*

We weren't doing much. We'd have movies to keep us busy and outdoors, but they always sent in movies of the Japs. What it was like, fighting the Japanese over there, but the same thing had happened to us. You'd shudder. We weren't ready for that.

After it ended, because I had some photographic experience—I had a camera with me all the way through, it was a Kodak, and I had taken a lot of pictures. At that point, we had taken over a town in Germany and they put me in charge of a photo lab. There were women working there, and they used glass plates. I had to make sure there was no espionage or anything like that, but I couldn't talk to them because I can't speak German. But I made arrangements for [the soldiers] to come over and get their picture taken. You know? But that didn't last too long because then they broke our group down. Those that had a lot of points—and actually had a guy who had 120 to 150 points—they were told to wait. [The rest of us] went back to Le Havre, France, and we're going to go to Shelby, Mississippi, to train to fight the Japanese. We all went home, and I was there when they dropped the bomb. I was home to celebrate when the war ended; the others were still over there, and I got out September 20, 1945. They were still there, even with all these points and everything, so I got a break there.

*

I'm telling you, the government did a lot for us. The GI Bill was very, very good to me. They paid for your books. They paid for the tuition. My family was not rich or anything. I had a sister, a brother, myself. There's five of us. We always rented in two-family houses, I think my father only made, at that time, about $25 a week, but you didn't pay a lot in rent. He didn't even have a car because he couldn't afford it. We didn't have a telephone back in those days. It just was a situation that when I got out, I said, 'I've got to get a degree. I'm 25 years old. I've got no time to waste. I'm going to do it right away,' and I spent full time and effort in getting that degree.

I got a 4% government loan at the time in Rochester, and I bought a place. Then I started with the New York State Tax Department in Rochester, but I got a promotion and I moved to Syracuse in 1952, where I stayed until I retired 30 years later. I got the job in the '40s; I retired in '82, and at that time, I was in charge in Central New York here of the income tax section, you see, so I was 62 years old. I figured I couldn't live forever, so I better get out and enjoy it. [In retirement], you don't want to do nothing. I've been doing a lot of volunteer work. I take photos of different groups. I belong to these organizations. When I retired, I joined AEF. It's the 28th, AEF, it stands for Allied Expeditionary Force. The 109th Infantry also has a group; I'm a member there too, and I'm a member of the Battle of the Bulge group. We have had reunions, too. In fact, I went to St. Louis to celebrate the 50th [anniversary] year, 1994, and they had opened up the whole city for us, they gave us a key to it. The Secretary of Defense was there, I forget who it was. Budweiser furnished all the beer for us, and it was a tremendous affair, a whole week, you know. I got to meet different people from around the country. Now, we have a local branch of the Battle of the Bulge too, which I'm part of. Every December 16 or the Sunday nearest there, we have a dinner. They come from all other parts of the state, even Buffalo and Utica.

My neighbor was a German fellow, and he was after me all the time to join the German club because I was half-German, you know? So, I did, [and met some German veterans]. I knew a lot of them. I wanted to arrange to allow them to march in the veterans parade; some of them had marched in Utica at the veterans parade, but when I presented to the VFW, [they said], 'No, that's for Americans. We can't do that at all. They're the enemy.' They wouldn't tolerate it, but they were nice guys. One guy said, 'I was in the Battle of the Bulge,' and another said, 'So was I. I had a Tiger tank I was in.' A lot of them came over here after.

*

My respect for the German soldiers and civilians is very high at the end because when it was all over, they picked up for the women and the kids. All the stones, rubble, they'd grab them. They cleaned up after them. I think nothing was as neat and clean as the Germans were. But at the end of the war, for the Germans, we were not allowed to fraternize at all. If you were caught fraternizing, you got 'six and six.' Six months in the stockade and six months, two-thirds a year, pay taken. After the war, I remember one time having a few drinks. We were in a house, but you had some other fellows upstairs. A lot of the German women were fraternizing, and the MPs come up. I'm in the second floor, and we dropped out the window, ran into the field, and they're looking for us with flashlights. Of course, we knew how to do combat, we got down low. [*Laughs*]

But I didn't quite agree with that [non-fraternization policy]. There were a lot of German kids who were hungry. When we ate, we'd throw the stuff in the garbage cans, and there'd be little kids who'd grab any food you have, like ham, or bacon, or something. This was in, I would say, probably May or June 1945.

*

I think I'm proud of being part of helping them, to get them back on their feet with the Marshall Plan and things like that. I think without the US getting involved, the world would be entirely changed today because I think Germany and Japan would've easily won the war, because they really defeated France and took all over Europe. I think without our help, the Russians would've fallen too, so it's something I'm proud of being part of, but would hate to have anyone go through the same thing I did.

Robert F. Kirk passed away at the age of 85 in May 2005.

CHAPTER FOUR

The Scout

Harold Leonard Bloom was born in 1925 in Rhode Island. The future rocket scientist remembers the early days of World War II as a high schooler, parting with a cherished treasure during scrap drives, and later finding himself on the front lines in one of the most battered divisions in World War II, certainly during the Battle of the Bulge, as a replacement soldier. Wounded in a minefield, he recalls lying exposed the entire day, only to struggle to crawl away at night, forced to leave a wounded fellow scout who had never before seen combat behind after he would not respond to Harold's entreaties.

"Charles, unfortunately, [instead] rolled over, and there was another tremendous blast, and the sarge, *going out there, saw it had killed Charles. So I got behind the woodpile, and I tried to figure out how I was going to get back…"*

He goes through his medals with his interviewer, one at a time.

"There's one thing about these medals that bothers me. I'm proud that I did some good and was recognized. The thing that bothers me is, I hate the idea of glorifying war, and I can't help thinking that when you show your medals, you're glorifying war. The last thing I want to do is glorify war. I hate war. Old men make war, and young men die. I hate that."

He continues:

"I've got to tell you, [after the war, and being wounded], I didn't think anything was due me. I think that what I did was a payback for what the country did for me. Both my parents… left Russia under tough circumstances, came to this country, and they found not only safety and peace, and a way to make a living, that I owe this country."

He sat for this interview in April 2012, four years before his death.

Harold L. Bloom, Jr.

I was born in Providence, Rhode Island, on April 7, 1925. I graduated from high school, and I went to Rhode Island State College, from where I was drafted in 1943. When I heard about the attack on Pearl Harbor, I was at home and I felt that we would get even. I guess I was more angry than anything else. I had no doubt that we were going to win at that time, so that's why I was angry more than afraid. Afraid didn't come until later.

One of the major things that changed was that there was a shortage of lots of things. Very quickly, there developed a shortage of metal. I didn't have much of my own, but when I went to school every day, I would see piles of metal on the sidewalk where people were collecting it and leaving it to be picked up. I didn't have much of my own, but I had one of something that was very precious to me. I had an old sword that my grandfather had picked up someplace and let me play with when I was a kid. When I got older, I simply took it with me and brought it home. And when the request for metal became rather strident, I took it, in tears, and I put it on the pile of metal in front of the house, and went to school, not very happily. My mother detected right away that I was pretty upset, and unbeknownst to me, my mother went and picked it back up and stuck it in my closet. Not until after I went to war and I got wounded, and came home and recuperated, and was back in school [did I find it]—one day I was looking for something in my closet, and my hand touched cold steel. I pulled it out and there was the sword, and I've still got it.

My father was alive, but he was already too old to be drafted or to join up. He was a butcher, but he had been a jewelry maker, and he had done lots of other things; my father was a jack of all trades. So if he couldn't join, he decided he'd volunteer to do some work to help the war effort. He went and took a course in torch burning of metal and went to work in a shipyard in Rhode Island where they were building ships. Kaiser was building ships there, and he went to Kaiser.[7] And he had all kinds

---

[7] *Kaiser was building ships there*-Part of the 'Arsenal of Democracy,' between 1941 and 1945, 18 shipyards were turning out cargo and transport vessels; over 2700 were built, with the fastest one rolling off the line in four days, 15.5 hours. Source: Zimmerman, D.J. *Henry J. Kaiser and the Liberty Ships,* Defense Media Network, June 7, 2012. www.defensemedianetwork.com/stories/henry-j-kaiser-and-the-liberty-ships

of guts. They used to use him to go all the way up to the upper mast on destroyer escorts, which are long, narrow boats. And while they were fitting them up, he would burn the holes in the mast so they could put communications gear down below, so he always remarked that the ship sitting in the water was so narrow, it would sway from side to side, so he spent half the time over the water. A lot of the younger men wouldn't do it, but my father would do anything, he would go up there and he would do it. That's the way it was all during the war: he worked there, and I was in the Army.

College Man to Rifleman

I got drafted out of college, Rhode Island State College at the time, which had gone onto an accelerated program, so we finished a year in eight months. No summer vacation, no other vacation, just steady. I finished my freshman year in August, and I was drafted in September of 1943. I took the AGCT test and I found out I had choices: I could either join the Air Force or the Army; at that time they had what they called the Army Specialized Training Program, ASTP. Their whole objective was to grow more engineers quickly, and that's what I wanted to be anyway, so I took that instead of joining the [Army] Air Force. Everybody who is drafted has to go through basic training. So they sent me down to Fort Benning, Georgia, for my basic training. I ended up, with some of the rough games that they play, with a broken shoulder. So I spent six weeks in the hospital, and meanwhile, my class kept on going and they were off to school. By the time I recovered from that, I had to join a different group of people, and they never got to college because at that time we were planning the invasion of Europe, so I was sent to Advanced [Infantry] Training in Louisiana. I became a rifleman. I did well, I made expert, and when I went overseas, they took us out as replacements because I finished up just about the time the invasion was over, and now they had all these replacements they had to have because there were a lot of casualties during the invasion. So I went over, it was a group of 1500 from Camp Livingston, Louisiana, over to Europe. And there in Europe they began splitting us up among the various divisions that needed help, replacing the people.

*

I went over on the *Queen Mary*. Let me tell you, it was very impressive. We went first to Fort Meade, Maryland, and they sent us out in all fresh clothes. We marched in one side of an open area, took off all our clothes, and they gave us all new stuff again.

The *Queen Mary* doesn't go by convoy. They were quite confident that they could go fast enough to outrun any sub, and when they got to what were considered dangerous waters, they would zigzag every seven minutes. They decided, in their own minds, that it takes a submarine seven minutes to sight on a new target, so every seven minutes they would zig and then zag. They took the northern route so when we went over to England, we were actually above England and Scotland. We went down the Firth of Forth, which was that big inlet that runs all the way down, next to Scotland. It was an interesting trip. There were 22,500 troops on board that ship. They had taken the staterooms they had, and they converted them to six-man bunkrooms. So you shared your stateroom with six other guys, and some liked to stay up and talk and others liked to snore, so I found that a lot of guys slept up on the promenade deck. So I took my sleeping bag and I slept, the whole trip, up on the promenade deck, which wasn't bad. It was enjoyable.

We landed in Scotland, I think it was Brulach, Scotland, some distance away from Edinburgh. And we marched from Brulach to Glasgow; I'm not positive of that. We went, I think, for four weeks to England, a place called Drew. The only distinguishing mark I could make of it was it had an old castle, a ruined castle, off on one side. We stayed there for about two or three weeks, and it was very crowded, lots of guys there.

The Repo Depot

And that's where we boarded a Belgian ship, the *Leopoldville*, which was the biggest ship they had at the time. It was later sunk by the Germans.[8] But

---

[8] *The Leopoldville*-On Christmas Eve, 1944, the *SS Leopoldville* was torpedoed in very rough Channel waters five miles off Cherbourg, France, at 5:54 PM, carrying over 2200 American replacement soldiers of the 66th Infantry Division. A cascading catastrophe of mishaps—the alarm was not immediately raised, only vague calls for help were issued, much of the Belgian crew abandoned the ship—went on as she took on water and slipped beneath the surface nearly two and a half hours later, leading to the deaths of 736 Americans.

they took us out to just north of France, and off France they brought these landing craft, LCIs and LCTs. LCIs are landing craft, infantry; LCTs are landing craft, tank. We took an LCI, and the way they operate is they load you on and then head for shore full bore in order to ground it. And when you get out there, they let down the leading edge of it, it's like a ramp that lets you off into the water, and then you get on to the shore.

You didn't get assigned as a replacement yet. But this group that went over on the LCI, they landed us at a replacement center—repo depot, they called it—and at the repo depot, you went by troop train from one repo depot to another, to another, until you finally got close enough to the front that you could begin to get taken on by various organizations. I went to about three repo depots, until I was picked by a sergeant from the 28th Division, and that was when we were already pretty close to the front. Once you get picked—there are about five of us he picked—we could walk and be on the front lines. It wasn't that long; it took only about an hour of marching.

That was October 1944. The first night, we were right up on the line there, and I've got to tell you I was pretty nervous, and I wasn't the only one. They put one new recruit with one of the old-timers there, and he was supposed to [show us the ropes]. The one that I was with said, 'Don't get out of this hole. If you go to the bathroom, do it in your helmet and throw it over the side.' And it's just as well, because all night long, grenades were going off. It turns out that most of the soldiers, when they heard any sound, they would throw a grenade. You didn't have to find anybody; you'd just throw a grenade. That was pretty scary, anybody could get killed that way. But I didn't.

The next morning, they organized an attack, and the sergeant decided the new guys were not smart enough to the ways of war yet to do much, so he assigned a bunch of us—five of us—as ammunition carriers. He stationed us on a hill while they made the attack, and when he wanted ammunition, he would call back, we'd have it ready to go, and they'd move us down there. Well, two of the guys were real gung-ho guys and they didn't want to carry ammunition, they wanted to be in it. One was from Louisiana and one from Texas. So after he left, even though I was supposed to be in charge of this little group of five or seven that's left, they're not going to listen to me and they took off to find the front and do some fighting. I'll never forget that, [and what happened]. Once we had cleared the town, we were supposed to go through all the houses and make sure that they were clear. We came to one house, and it sounded like crying inside. So I went in, and sure enough, there they were. They had been subjected to bombardment by our side, then the Germans bombarded [back at us], and this went back and forth till we got the town secured. So they had been bombarded by both sides, and they were just devastated [to the point where] they finally went back with combat fatigue. They were lucky they were alive.

The 28th Division moved into the Battle of the Hürtgen Forest.

I stayed where I was, and when my sergeant called me for ammunition, three guys went with ammunition down to where they were. They were in a village called Vossenack. Oh, by the way, I was at that time in the 28th Division, in the 112th Regiment, and Company F of the 2nd Battalion. So they had taken the village, and they were essentially hunkered down in the remains of a big stone house that had been hit pretty good; some of the walls were down, and it had a cellar in it. The whole squad I was in was in the cellar, and they sent one guy up to keep an eye on what's going on. We were, like, in reserve. It was very scary—the Germans had that thing you called a minenwerfer, a 90 mm mortar, and that thing was all explosive, and it's very effective against stone buildings, because it sets up a concussion wave, and the walls just give, and stone doesn't have integrity like that, just stones set together, so they were coming in. So even though we were in the cellar, the sergeant warned us that that could happen; you could either sleep outside and take a chance with that, or in the cellar. Well, we were lucky nothing happened there, and we were able to get out and fight from there.

We were located so we had a good idea where the opposition was. The Germans had an 88 up on a hill behind the lines, in a cave. When it was ready to fire, it was rolled out, and fire those things down. Those 88s are terrible, they've got a straight trajectory, and practically no sound, just [*makes whooshing sound*], and boom! With no warning at all. So the sergeant and the heavy weapons platoon got together, and they set up a .50 caliber in a corner outside of the house; around the corner so it can't be seen from the 88. And what they did, was whenever the 88 rolled out, you'd hear that gun go 'Boom! Boom!' [*Slaps fist into palm*]. It's a slow thing, but you had those great big shells in there, and they were able to keep that thing down pretty good, so we didn't get hurt by it.

*

Not far from a town called Julich, I think, we were getting some pretty tough spotting on where our troops were. And they finally decided that this tall building, which was like a church which had been sort of off limits to us [as far as targeting], had [Germans in it] who were spotting us. And we couldn't quite stop it. So after the first time we got real good air support, they called the Air Force and they got P-38s, and it was quite a sight to see them come diving down and they dive-bombed that thing, and they blew it pretty well apart. Finally, a group of combat engineers went in there—it's not their main function, to fight, but they can—they went in there and they were really tough. We could see bodies coming out the windows of this thing until they cleared it so we could advance. I'll never forget that. The Air Force earned my deep respect at that time.

And we went into Germany, the beginning of it, and we set up a line of attack at the Siegfried Line. That's just a tough place, you can't get in there. They have the pillboxes, these great big things with ten-inch walls and little openings for their machine guns, and all around their field of fire, the grass was no longer than two or three inches. There was no place to hide. Like any Army thing, they had a procedure for taking a pillbox. A platoon could do it. Two guys were assigned to carry the charges; two guys were assigned to cover the door for going in; I think four guys were assigned to hitting the embrasures, and so on. That's the way we did it, we took one at a time, with everybody assigned a job, taking care of two pillboxes, watching the third one, suppressed, and that's the way we went from one to another. It cost us some casualties, and I was lucky I didn't get hurt there. But it's a tough way to do anything.

*

  We had been in combat for some ninety days, or 180 days, or whatever it was, and they decided we could be in reserve. So my regiment was pulled back to a place in Luxembourg, which was considered a very peaceful area. Luxembourg is made so that it's tough to be concealed. All the forests are straight, all the trees are planted in a straight line this way, and a straight line this way [*gestures*], and the space between them there's a little room to walk, and all the branches of the trees are cut to about six or eight feet off the ground, so it's tough to be concealed. All the roads were right along the ridges of these hills, and I'll never forget how impressed I was at the fact that, when you look out, you could just make out a vehicle going down the road, you could see just where the wheels hit the road—that's how precisely they were located.

  So anyway, they put us in a section. First we went and took the big town Wiltz, but then they had us bivouac near a town called Weiswampach, and we had the side of a hill and the back of it, and in the good old Army way, they had two foxholes, one on the front end of the hill where they'd be firing, but another one to retreat to in the back side of the hill. We had a sergeant who was by the numbers, so the first thing we do when we're assigned to this area was to dig two holes. It turns out that that was the way they handled this concealment. Where the headquarters were, they had a big hole dug with bulldozers that looked to me like thirty or forty feet square under the ground, and the top covered with wood and then dirt piled on top of it so the headquarters were protected that way.

We had smaller holes of our own that we made, and we put our own cover on them, which was trees that we cut down. All we had to have was our bayonet, we cut trees with bayonets, and we put the dirt on top. It was pretty much a standoff; they would fire occasional shots over at us, and we dug trenches from one foxhole to another, so we didn't have to be exposed, and we were living that way.

This peaceful area was [fairly quiet]; they didn't want anybody to attack the other side, there was such open areas. We were required once a day to send a patrol from my platoon to company headquarters, report on what was going on, and they'd report back again to us; nobody shot at us and we had all this concealment. The company headquarters was being run like they were in the United States. They had a nice place to eat, they had their own latrines there, and this was on a section where you could see, right across the hills, to where the German lines were. We weren't firing at them at all, and they didn't fire at us.

'Combat Team'

I remember when I was on one of those patrols from my platoon to company headquarters, it was a nice walk. It was all concealed, and you could walk down there, and we were supposed to be looking out for Germans, but we didn't see any, so there was no problem. But [soon enough], when the Bulge occurred, that's when they came up and they hit us pretty hard, the whole regiment really got pretty well banged up; we had the whole division pretty well banged up. The 110th was completely captured, and they got our kitchen and other supplies from the 112th. It was pretty bad, so we had to retreat in front of the Bulge, and I guess the Army commanders had to assess the situation, because there wasn't any regiment that was big enough to operate by themselves. They replenished our regiment, except instead of being a regiment now, we were called a 'combat team.' And for the rest of the war, that's how we were used. Whenever they needed a live supply of shooters and defenders and so on, we got sent. Most of the time they'd get us there in trucks, although lots of times we had to walk.

Well, they did one thing [right], and it probably saved part of my problem. It was later though. Just before Thanksgiving, we were having trouble slogging through the mud. Those Army boots are nice, but they can't take a beating for a long time. They sent out a shipment of overshoes, all one size, 12. So I didn't like wearing a 12—I wear a size 8 shoe. You had to take one step inside before you could take a step further, but they kept your feet dry. Well, looking forward, when I finally was wounded, it may well be that that oversize boot saved my leg and maybe my life. By that time, it was late in January. Other things happened in between, but I'll tell that story.

The Minefield

We were doing a reconnaissance patrol in the Alsace region of France, that's where we had been moved the last time. We were sent to replace the 30th Division—not the whole Division, but part of the 30th Division. We had to get up one morning about 4 o'clock and where we were going, Alsace, is a very wild forest area, really forest. It had been occupied through most of the way by a lot of French partisans, and they didn't have much in the way of anything, guns or ammunition, so what they did is they mined a lot of the area there, and you had to be careful where the mines were. Part of the job everybody had was to note where the mines are and put up a ribbon or something where it was, so you wouldn't be killed.

I was part of a reconnaissance patrol to get information on the location of any machine guns, storage depots of the Germans, things like that. Lt. Christiansen had held up this platoon reconnaissance patrol. It started at about 4 o'clock in the morning, and we went pretty much toward the German line without spotting any trouble, and we came to a hill where there was a long, flat area, and there was actually the remains of a dirt road that ran out into this area, and along the side of the road was stacked cordwood, stacked in neat cords, which was what the Luxembourgians liked to do—everything neat.

I was first scout, and there was a guy assigned to go with me as second scout, a fellow named Charles. I had been in combat, then, about six months. He was new; he'd never been in combat before. But we were assigned this job, and you couldn't do anything about it. So we walked about 10 yards apart, out into this flat area, and the lieutenant was behind us about 500 yards, and every now and then I'd look back to see if we were to keep going. I wanted to stop, but he wanted us to keep going. So we came to this flat area in the road, and it had snowed the night before, everything was nice and smooth. We walked out into this, and I think we got about 100 yards and all of a sudden there was this tremendous blast and I went up into the air, and there was a second blast as I came down and was lying there, and I thought we'd been hit by a mortar. Turns out after I started to get my senses back, that I could look around, was lying there looking around, and I could see the German little antipersonnel mines from the pillbox, and when you step on one, the outer cover slips down and cuts the restraining pin and boom! It isn't much, it's like a quarter pound of TNT. Well, my overshoes must have just clipped the edge of it. Most of it went up here [*shows the area on his foot*] and took out the heel of my shoe and my foot. And the rest of it came up [the leg further] and there was shrapnel in my thigh, and one piece of shrapnel actually went through my scrotum. Later on, when the doctor examined me, he said you're one lucky guy, because it went through the scrotum and didn't touch anything else. Well, I lay there, and I could see the stuff around us, and Charles was thrashing around like crazy, and I was trying to calm him down, but I didn't want to roll any, I couldn't move. [So he set off] a second mine; our sergeant, Sgt. Lamming, got our squad behind this stacked wood because no minefield ever [tripped] by our combat group was uncovered without some kind of [accompanying small arms] fire; he figured that any minute [the Germans] would start shooting. Anyway, nobody is shooting at first, and I'm enough discombobulated that I was trying to do something with my foot, and I couldn't do it. I could see it was bloody, but I couldn't see anything else.

The sergeant was one brave guy, Sgt. Lamming. He came in, despite the fact that somebody was going to be [targeting] this. He found me, took a bayonet, and cut the boot loose and took my pack, took the sulfa out and dusted everything with sulfa, and then we stood up. At that time, there was no problem, nobody was shooting at us, but he couldn't get Charles to stop thrashing around, to see what he could do for him. It turns out, I found out later, Charles had a bad wound in his arm; I don't know how that happened. The sergeant tried to get us going back, and at that time, the Germans started firing initial rifle shots at us, and the sergeant dove back behind the stacked wood, and our people started firing back. So the rounds were going over our heads, so I yelled as much as I could to the sergeant, *'Don't...!*

'Don't Leave Us Here'

What happened was our fire apparently hit one of them; I could hear the guy hollering, 'Hilfe, Hilfe,' meaning, 'Help!' So I yelled back to the sergeant, 'Don't shoot at the wounded man, because if you shoot at him, they'll shoot at us!'

They hadn't been shooting at me and Charles. And that's the way it went. That happened probably 6 or 7 o'clock in the morning, and we lay there until it started to get dark, and about the beginning of dark, instead of firing rifles they started opening up with mortars. That's when I got worried, because mortars don't care about who's getting hit— they hit anyone who gets near it. So I heard the sergeant starting to talk about getting out, so I yelled to him, 'Don't leave us here!'

Now, two nights before, another platoon had gone out for reconnaissance, and they left their wounded men behind, and the sergeant said, 'We won't leave anybody behind.'

He said, 'If you can get safely over here to the wood, we'll take you back.'

So I yelled to Charles what to do. Where the explosion had been, it pretty much cleared, and you could see the mines there, so you could avoid them. I said to Charles, 'Don't roll over because there's mines right over here. Get up on one leg, jump as far as you can, and crawl across!'

He didn't answer me, but I couldn't afford to stay myself. So that's exactly what I did. I left my rifle behind, and when I was ready to go, I asked the sergeant to cover us—they were firing—and I leaned forward on my good foot and I jumped as far as I could where it was clear, and I crawled back and got behind the wood. Charles, unfortunately, did roll over, and there was another tremendous blast, and the sarge, going out there, saw it had killed Charles. So I got behind the woodpile, and I tried to figure out how I was going to get back, and Sarge said, 'I'll carry you.'

And he did; he put me on his back, and we went into the trees and started back. He knew where we were going, and the others were following him. And the Germans, of course, were trying to stop us, so there was firing going, and they hit a couple of other guys, not too bad, they were able to walk and so on. And I could see we'd been out since 4 o'clock in the morning, and the sergeant must have been terribly tired. Plus, they began firing mortars trying to locate where we were.

I thought, sitting up on his back, I was particularly vulnerable, so I said, 'Put me down, I'll crawl.'

And this is the technique he worked out. Two guys were sent out ahead to find a place where we could stop, that we could defend. And then as soon as they got going, I went behind them, crawling as fast as I could. I ended up using up everybody's gloves. As I wore out one pair of gloves, another one of the guys would give me his gloves, and that's what I did. I got over to where they were stopped, and the rest of the guys would come, and we went all that way back. I didn't have any idea how far we were, or even the direction to go, but the sergeant knew. So we came to a nice hollow in the area there, and he said, 'You guys set up a perimeter defense here, and I'll go back, and I'll bring back help.'

So we set up a perimeter defense, those who were still able to shoot, and we waited, and sure enough, after a little while, we hear this jingle of equipment and so on, and pretty soon, the sergeant shows up and he had a mule and a sled. They put me on the sled, and one of the other guys on the sled—I've got to tell you, those mules, they do a fantastic job. When we first got sent down to Alsace to replace the 30th, we were going up into one of those big hilly areas. The way we got up them, they gave us a mule and the first guy in line would hold the mule's tail, and the second guy got hold of the belt of the first guy, and it went all the way back, and that mule pulled us all the way up the hill, all the way up to where we could get to the foxholes the 30th left behind.

So anyway, they brought us back to battalion aid, and right away gave me a shot of morphine, so I was out of it. And so I was told then that Charles had been killed, and it bothered me because he hadn't had any combat experience at all, he was fresh. He should never have been given that job, but it could have happened to anybody, I suppose. So they took care of me at battalion aid; you know, it's not like *M*A*S*H* on TV—they take you and just keep you from bleeding to death and give you a bandage, and give you a shot to keep you quiet and get you back to wherever you're going.

Evacuation

They got me to a hospital train, which took us to Vittel, France, and in Vittel, the Army was operating a hospital. At that hospital, which was staffed heavily by people from the Buffalo General Hospital, the doctor there operated on me. He told me that I'd lost my heel bone, but he got out most of the shrapnel from me, told me what I had up here, and then from Vittel, we were there long enough that they had two hospital ships in Marseilles. So the train, again, they took us to Marseilles, and they got us aboard the hospital ship. The hospital ship I was on was the *Ernest R. Hines*, the funniest little thing. It was almost as wide as it was long, and it was slow as molasses. But there was another one, a much sleeker hospital ship, the *Cherokee*. So we left for the United States in the *Ernest R. Hines*. The *Cherokee* left 14 days later, and it got to Charlotte, North Carolina, the day before we did. But they were nice people on board, they really treated us good. The crew brought everybody ice cream, things like that, and we had to take a detour anyway. They were keeping us informed of all of the information that they were getting, and they told us that we were going to have to divert from the course because a Navy ship had reported that they had a seaman that needed to be taken off their ship and brought on the hospital ship. He needed medical attention.

So we went off to the Bahamas where this happened, and there they were going to transfer this wounded seaman to our ship. Damnedest thing you ever saw. The first thing they did was, the other ship, was to spread oil all around the other ships. It turns out that keeps the waves from breaking, so that made it easier. The sailors on our ship took a lifeboat, and they rowed across from our ship to their ship. Well, our ship was so wide we didn't have a lot of trouble, but this Navy ship was going back and forth like crazy. They brought out [a small vessel] to pick him up, and you could see it going here, and there, and here [*gestures up and down*]; now, how are they going to do this? So everybody out of bed just had to watch this whole thing. I had a pair of crutches, so I hobbled over to a porthole and watched that. Just amazing. They rowed over to that ship from our ship, and they placed themselves close to where the guy was coming down. And when [the basket] came over this way, they went underneath, and when it went out, they got ready to dump him out of the basket, and when it came down, our guys grabbed him and put him into our boat, and they did it successfully, and everybody was cheering like crazy. And then we found out the ins and outs of it. The sailor had been stabbed by one of his own shipmates, in the groin, and it cut an artery, so it was a pretty hairy thing, but he did survive.

*

We ended up in Charlotte, North Carolina, and stayed there a few days, just temporizing, until another train came down and I was sent to Utica, New York, the Rhoads General Hospital. That's where I fell in love with the Adirondacks. I'd never known how nice it was until I went up there. I'll never forget that. It was a nice hospital, the Rhoads General Hospital, and they treated us well. They had great food and things like that, and every day—of course I was bedridden—I and other bedridden patients were taken outside and it was like June, and the sun was nice, and they let us take our clothes off so we could get the sun. And it was the damnedest thing, we had a snowstorm in June! By the time they got me in, there was two inches of snow on top of my blanket!

I wound up in Cushing Hospital in Massachusetts, and that's where I was discharged from, when the war ended. They had a big celebration there, and I was enjoying that, too. The biggest thing was that the doctor at the Cushing Hospital said, 'We can send you to Valley Forge Hospital, where they do plastic surgery, and they can put more flesh back on the wound here. You can't get the heel bone back, because that was shattered in pieces, but we can at least make it look decent.'

And I said, 'Will it do anything to help me walk?'

And he said, 'It might, but you don't have the heel bone so it's going to be tough.'

I had already called the school where I wanted to finish my degree, and they were starting in September and this was August. So I said to the doctor there that if there's no guarantee that it'll make me that much better, I would just as soon go back to school. The fall term is starting.

'Well, it's your choice,' he said. 'You can always opt to have the plastic surgery through the Veterans Administration.'

So that's what I did, I went back to school. I started out using crutches to go from class to class, and I made it okay, no problem. The teachers were pretty nice about that. I was determined that I wanted to get rid of those crutches, so after a few months I started trying it with a cane. The VA gave me a cane, and I hobbled around with the cane for a while. And after a while I thought I'd see what I could do without the cane. And it was tough for a while, but I kept at it and kept walking; now I walk without a cane most of the time.

I decided not to have the surgery done. They couldn't guarantee a thing. They said, it's very likely to work, but I could never get anybody pinned down to say yes, this will do it. I'm just as happy I didn't. For a long time, I was walking three miles a day. I don't do that so much anymore. At 87, that's really more than I have to do.

*

I went back to school [with the GI Bill] and got my degree in engineering. I was an aeronautical engineer, and I ended up working on a missile program, and lots of space programs. I went down to the Cape to watch the launches. I worked on some of the stuff that was launched. I'm happy I contributed something to this organization.

*

Before I went into the service, I was a straight guy. I studied and I was going to get educated, and I didn't want to waste any time with women, and stuff like that. I took a couple girls to the senior prom from high school, and when I went to college, my older cousin, a woman, introduced me to a girl, a nice kid, but I wasn't interested. When I was in the Army, I realized that I could have died there, and never had the pleasure of love or a love affair or anything else, and I made up my mind that once I got out, I would have time for women, and I did. I saw lots of women, but I was lucky. I married the smartest one of all, in 1948. I graduated one weekend, and got married the next weekend, and went on a honeymoon the next weekend, and from that point on I was committed to go to work for NASA.

Rocket Science

I worked for a bunch of high-class people. I was the least, probably, qualified to work with these people, but I did my best. I finally learned something. If you're not the smartest guy in the world, you can be the hardest working guy. And I did. I put in more hours than they ever paid me for. And that's how I was able to keep up with these people. But the pay was government pay, it was not a big deal. So I decided at some point in time it was time to start looking for ways to get a higher paying job, and that's when I came to work for GE. And that was really satisfying; I enjoyed that, and it turns out that the things I learned while working at NASA stood me in great stead when I took the job with General Electric.

There was a fellow I was in the service with. He was the chief engineer for the international space station; he came in after I left already. But we had put to NASA many plans for a space station, at their request, back in 1966. They would go through various studies, and they would put out another request for a proposal, for another space station, a few years later. They kept reinventing the space station again and again. GE was actually awarded a $400 million contract to build a space station, and I worked on it for a while. I had to help put together a plan for its manufacture. I had so much fun doing that. I worked on all kinds of crazy things. GE gave me the opportunity to try anything new that I wanted, and I never had to go to work. I just loved my job.

Payback

[I never went to any reunions of the division], I'm not sure if they ever had one. They were nice guys, but there was so much that we didn't have in common, [being from different areas of the country]. We watched each other's back, and things like that, and everybody did their work, except those two from Texas and Louisiana, but we never really got friendly. They do have a museum of the 28th Division in Pennsylvania, but I've never been there, and I can't travel that far anymore. I sure would like to see if there are people there that I knew. I may get on the internet sometime and try to find them. I've got to say, I didn't feel particularly close to any of them. There were a couple guys from California that seemed to be nice guys; we used to, when we were in camp here in the United States, we used to go drinking together. But I never felt really close to them.

I never joined [any veterans organizations], and I'll tell you why. I just barely was discharged at home, and one after another, various veterans organizations came to see me. And they all had [the same pitch]—either the first thing they would say, or the second thing, was, *'We're here to make sure you get what's due you.'* And I've got to tell you, I didn't think anything was due me. I think that what I did was a payback for what the country did for *me*. Both my parents, and their parents' grandchildren, left Russia under tough circumstances. My mother described the pogroms where she came from in Ukraine. My father, his father, moved the family from Russia because he had left a job in Russia, and moved to what he thought was a safer place in Bialystok, in Poland. While he was there for a year or so, he heard about a pogrom just south of where he had come from originally, and he decided that that was no place to stay, that's why he moved. Following that, they came to this country, and they found not only safety and peace, and a way to make a living, that I owe this country. That's all I did, was to try and pay some of it back. So their arguments of what they were going to get me, bonuses and things, just hit me wrong, and I never did join. And that's all of them, I'm telling you, the Veterans of Foreign Wars, and the American Legion, one at a time I went through this with them.

There's one thing about these medals that bothers me. [*Displays his medals*] I'm proud that I did some good and was recognized. The thing that bothers me is, I hate the idea of glorifying war, and I can't help thinking that when you show your medals, you're glorifying war. The [last] thing I want to do is glorify war. I hate war. Old men make war, and young men die. I hate that. I'm not sure that those guys feel the way I do. But, all right. And that's about it, my life in a nutshell.

Mr. Bloom passed away at the age of 91 in November 2016.

PART TWO

MALMÉDY

Aftermath of Malmédy massacre. Credit: US Army

"I observed an elderly man with a little covered wagon. He was pulling it and going into a garage directly across from my tank. He had made several trips down the street and when he came back he stopped at my tank. Since I could not speak Belgian, he pulled the cover from the wagon. I have never forgotten the sight of the two children's bodies. There they were, frozen with the older child's arms around the other as they were shot by the SS troops—they were still frozen in that position."

— Soldier, 743rd Tank Battalion

CHAPTER FIVE

Men of Old Hickory

The 30th Infantry Division originated in the South and was nicknamed the 'Old Hickory' division in honor of President Andrew Jackson. Later christened the 'Workhorse of the Western Front,' it had a history that dated back to the trenches of France in an earlier fight against the Germans, and it had been fully committed again in the ancient Norman hedgerows after coming ashore about a month after D-Day. It was earning a fearsome reputation, particularly after the division's stand against a major German counterattack at Mortain in August. Now, as the main German spearhead unfolded in the south, the 30th Infantry Division and her attached 743rd Tank Battalion hurried in that direction and found themselves in a desperate struggle for survival as temperatures plunged to the coldest in European memory during the winter of 1944–45. The tankers and infantrymen had to stop the German thrust northward across the rivers.

Carrol Walsh had won a battlefield commission fighting in a light tank in the 743rd Tank Battalion's D Company as the Americans originally broke through the Siegfried Line and beyond to Aachen.

Carrol 'Red' Walsh

It was muddy and cold, but we were doing okay. Then the Bulge came. We were doing just great, and then December 16 came.

We came back out, waiting to cross the Roer River. The Germans had the dams up there and we were hoping to get across the Roer before they burst the dams. While we were waiting to do that, we were getting everything together, and we were poised [to attack] when the Bulge hit. They were trying to get to the coast, to take Antwerp, to split the British and American forces to the north with the American forces to the south. We were in the Ninth Army then. We had been the First Army until September, I think, and then we joined the Ninth Army. We were in the north, and they were going to cut us off and annihilate us, they were going to let us have it. We were at Malmédy, Stavelot, St. Vith, and La Gleize. That is when we fought in the snow and cold. It was cold, and we had no winter uniforms. We didn't have any overshoes, and of course we couldn't wear any overcoat on a tank anyway. And in the Bulge, we slept in the tank.

On the northern front of the German offensive, on just the second day of the attack, the spearhead of the ruthless Joachim Peiper's 1st SS Panzer Division captured 150 Americans. Herded into a snowy field, the unarmed prisoners were mowed down by the SS with their machine guns, their Tiger tanks blocking any escape. More than eighty men were killed, the Germans moving through the field, kicking and delivering coup-de-grâce pistol shots to the wounded. News of the Malmédy massacre steeled an unwritten American response: take no SS troops prisoners. The barbarity extended to the civilian population as well. In the nearby hamlet of Stavelot, where more than 20 men, women, and children had been murdered, Joseph Couri of the 743rd Tank Battalion recalled:

> I observed an elderly man with a little covered wagon. He was pulling it and going into a garage directly across from my tank. He had made several trips down the street and when he came back he stopped at my tank. Since I could not speak Belgian, he pulled the cover from the wagon. I have never forgotten the sight of the two children's bodies. There they were, frozen with the older child's arms around the other as they were shot by the SS troops—they were still frozen in that position.

Only days after this incident, the 30th Infantry and the 743rd Tank Battalion would repeatedly tangle with Peiper and their old SS nemesis from the battle of Mortain, regrouping and counterpunching as the tide of battle slowly turned. Peiper was denied his immediate target of Liège, on the way to Antwerp, having failed to breach the American line past Stavelot and Malmédy.

*

The original main German thrust collapsed by Christmas 1944 as the skies cleared and Supreme Allied Commander General Eisenhower brought to bear a quarter-million troops of his own at lightning speed. Although the Americans were now on the offensive, Hitler was bent on a war of attrition. In the Battle of the Bulge, the US Army would suffer most of its battle casualties in pushing the Germans back through the sub-zero cold and waist-deep snow, artillery attacks, and enemy mines. Tanks ground slowly in low gear along snow-covered roads in the mine-free ruts of previous vehicles, any uneven surfaces liable to send the tank skating sideways without traction.

Carrol 'Red' Walsh

Of course, it wasn't very comfortable being in the tank in that cold, on cold steel. You were not very warm. We would take our boots off sometimes to rub our feet so they wouldn't freeze. It was so cold, but we had no winter clothes. They hadn't figured on that, you see; winter clothes were not a priority when they got the ports because the army was moving so well that the attitude was, 'The hell with that, we're going to get through with this [the war] by Christmas.' And they put the priority on food and shells and ammunition and things like that, and so we had no overshoes.

I was lucky; I had an undershirt like a sweatshirt and I had OD pants, you know, wool uniform pants. I had a pair of coveralls and I had a sweater, and my combat jacket. And I found a scarf. We had gloves but they weren't warm. The funny thing was, my father was a leather sorter in a glove shop in Johnstown and he sent me a beautiful pair of heavy mittens and that was great. I wrote to him and I said, 'Gee, Dad, that was great. They're nice and warm… the only problem, no trigger finger!'

[*Laughs*] But the gloves they issued us were not warm enough in that climate.

Now some guys that came in later as replacement troops, they had more heavy clothes and they gave them overcoats. Of course they couldn't wear overcoats with the tank! You could not maneuver; you couldn't get in and out of the turret or out of the bow gunner's side door with a heavy overcoat! Oh, so cold... oh, man alive! I was never so cold ever in my life—ever! And it just stayed cold day and night. I mean, how are you going to get warm? The infantry guys were digging their holes—that was tough because the ground was frozen. Boy, they had to chop. That's where they lived. They lived in their holes and we lived in the tank.

George C. Gross was Walsh's fellow tank commander in D Company, 743rd Tank Battalion.

George C. Gross

The tanks were so cold, our breath would freeze into little icicles about an inch and a half long on the roof of the turret, and our hands and our feet would be cold all the time. Once in a while we would come across some infantrymen who had built a fire. We would get out and warm one side of ourselves on the fire and then turn around to warm the other side and get back into the tank and freeze again. Occasionally we would be able to go into a house and stay in a house for a day or two and be warm, but that would be it.

Carrol 'Red' Walsh

While we were in Malmédy, things had quieted in the latter stages of the Bulge. We would go out during the day—it was like going to work. About eight o'clock in the morning we'd be called and we'd have to go someplace, like to relieve troops.

I remember one day there was some infantry who had run into a firefight with some Germans. All infantry and, I guess, no armor, because they didn't want to send our light tanks against German tanks, because 37-millimeter guns were all we had on the light tanks, 75-millimeter on the mediums. Those Germans had the 88. That gun was the greatest gun that ever was, the 88. They used it for anti-aircraft, they used it for artillery, and they used it on the tanks, anti-tank gun, everything!

They could fire an 88 and I guess it could go two miles and still go through a tank! I think so; it was a long way.

Anyway, there was a group of Americans wounded and they were pinned down somehow. So we were told, 'You have to go up and clean out that nest of Germans and get those wounded back.' So we'd go up and we'd have our armored firepower and infantry, and then we'd give help. But then we'd pull back at night, and it got to some point we were able to pull back into Malmédy, and they said, 'Look, if you can find a place to sleep or stay, go ahead.'

We went to this house, three stories and everything. We went there and I can remember I could speak a little French from high school. We had our bow gunner at the time, 'Hot Lips' Havelock—he could speak some German, so we were in good shape. So I said, 'Avez-vous un lit pour quatre hommes?' (Have you got a bed for four men?) This woman was very nice and we stayed in her home. We hadn't had a bed in months! My God, she had those big comfortable featherbeds or whatever. [*Laughs*] When they could get rations to us, for the tankers…we could have 10-in-1 rations in a big box and they'd have things like bacon in one and some kind of meat or something in another. They weren't bad rations, [but sometimes] we could hardly eat some of that crap! Well, she was in bad shape because they didn't have much to eat in those areas and everything. So she would take that stuff and fix it up—she would fix it and cook for us, and we'd stay there. I think I can remember that she had two sons, and they were in the German army! Of course, that's where Malmédy was, that is, sort of on the border between Germany and Belgium. And I think that the two sons were on the Russian front, so you can imagine what that was like… But anyway, that woman was so nice to us, and we were nice to her too. And you know, we gave her as much food as we could get. We were there about maybe three or four days, I guess. Wasn't that something? There she was, taking care of us, with two boys in the German Army!

Lt. Frank W. Towers was the 30th Division's liaison officer with the light tank 743rd Tank

Battalion. In a less strenuous combat position after having helped secure the fall of the first city on German territory past the Siegfried Line, Aachen, in October, he relayed his memories of the Battle of the Bulge in the northern sectors of attack, putting pen to paper over 50 years later. Never a man to mince words, Frank's anger at the failure of intelligence to pick up the signals of the attack is evident, as is his horror and heartbreak in recounting yet another 'friendly fire' Army Air Force bombing snafu, a distressing 'déjà vu' hour for the men of the 30th Division and civilians alike, five months after a similar incident in Normandy. He offered up this comprehensive account of some of the fighting in the northern sector of the Bulge in 1998.

The Battle of the Ardennes: Malmédy, Belgium

16 December 1944 – 23 January 1945

Frank W. Towers

In early December 1944, the 30th Infantry Division was in a more-or-less static combat situation, with much aggressive patrolling going on, probing into the German defenses in the vicinity of Langweiler, Germany, just a little bit north of Aachen.

It was bitter cold, rainy and muddy, and the forward progress was very slow. We were still waiting for the build-up of supplies, to enable us to make the crossing of the Roer River as soon as possible, and to then be able to continue on.

All supplies up to this point were being brought to us from Omaha Beach – 450 miles to the west, so it was a slow process of bringing up adequate supplies, and replacements, to keep a division in a static position, and yet build up a reserve for future action.

In the meanwhile, all of our battalions not on line were being sent back to Kerkrade, Holland, to our rest center, an ancient monastery by the name of Rolduc. Each battalion rotated at this time, each one for 5-6 days, so everyone had an opportunity to get some badly needed rest, showers, clean clothes and limited entertainment, as well as good hot meals, and to enjoy hot coffee and donuts supplied by the American Red Cross girls.

Upon returning to the front lines again, each company received intensive training in tank/infantry tactics, learning how best to coordinate and communicate with each other, in preparation for the big assault that was to come 'momentarily.'

This continued on a daily basis, until Sunday, 17 December 1944. About noon, the entire division was placed on alert, and was to be ready to move out on a moment's notice. An unusual way to announce the beginning of a proposed assault across the Roer River, we thought, but we soon found out that the assault by our division had been called off.

All weapons, other equipment and ammunition were loaded onto our organic vehicles, and other attached transportation that had been provided, to enable us to move additional supplies, as well as the entire division's manpower. We then stood by for further orders, to direct the movement at a moment's notice.

The Attack

Unknown to us at this time, 1800 hours, the German Army had struck the day before, on the 16th, in a least likely area in the mountains of the Ardennes in Belgium. This particular defensive line, from Bastogne northward to Malmédy, was held by the newly arrived and green 106th Infantry Division, and the 99th Infantry Division, the rationale being that this would be a good place for them to get their initial exposure to combat experience, through patrolling and coming in very limited contact with enemy patrols. No one in their right mind would mount an attack of any consequence in a mountainous area in the middle of the winter. It would be too confining to the narrow and winding roads, which would be a prime necessity for troops on the attack. They would also have to maintain their supply lines and any traffic on these roads across the mountains and through heavy woods, which would impede vehicles and troops.

Guess what? That is right where the Germans mounted their attack!

*

It must be mentioned here that the 106th and 99th Infantry Divisions were stretched out over 85 miles of a defensive position, with little or nothing to their rear as reserve troops. They were stretched out there all by themselves! A big miscalculation by SHAEF Headquarters, and damned poor U.S. intelligence! They had been adequately advised of unusual activity to the front, but it was dismissed as rumor or hallucination and a few other reasons to downplay any reports of activity to the front.

How wrong they were at SHAEF, in their evaluation of these reports!

The German plan was to break through, capture some supply and fuel dumps of the 1st Army, then race on to Liège, thence to Antwerp—which had recently been cleared and made operational, thereby shortening our supply line from Omaha Beach. This would have effectively cut off the entire Canadian Army, the entire British Army, and the U.S. 9th Army. Hopefully, this would allow the Germans to sue for separate peace treaties with each of these Armies, enabling them to end the war in the west, and allow them to devote their full attention to the war in the east against the Russians.

That was the plan...

Axis Sally Reports

At about 1000 hours the night of December 17, our 30th Infantry Division was ordered to move out – to where, no one seemed to know. Just follow the vehicle ahead of you! Soon, we were able to realize, by orienting on the stars above, that we were moving south, but to where or why was still a big question.

Finally, in the early hours of the morning, with some of the men still being awake and partially conscious and listening to the American Forces Network on their radios, there was a break-in on that frequency by our nemesis and rumor monger, 'Axis Sally,' the major German propagandist, who informed us:

'The 30th Infantry Division, the elite Roosevelt's S/S Troops and Butchers, are en route from Aachen to Spa and Malmédy, Belgium, to try to save the 1st Army Headquarters, which is trying to retreat from the area, before they are captured by our nice young German

boys. You guys of the 30th Division might as well give up now unless you want to join your comrades of the 1st Army HQ in a P.O.W. Camp. We have already captured most of the 106th Division, and have already taken St. Vith and Malmédy, and the next will be Liège.'

We were stunned, as only then did we have any clue as to where we were going, or the reason for this sudden movement.

Malmédy

We arrived at the prescribed destination on the afternoon of the 18th of December, and light defensive positions had already been established all around.

Malmédy had not been taken, as Axis Sally had said, and we found that Malmédy had been our objective destination. Malmédy was in our defensive sector, but St. Vith was not, being just south of our sector. However, St. Vith had been captured by the Germans.

Prior to our arrival in Malmédy, it had been hurriedly occupied by the 291st Engineer Combat Battalion, which had hastily erected roadblocks on the most strategic roads and approaches to the town.

Col. Joachim Peiper was the commander of the 1st S/S Regiment, of the 1st S/S Panzer Division, the spearhead which was to attack Malmédy. Due to the many defensive roadblocks established by the 291st Engr. Bn., and the 120th Regiment, Peiper was unable to get into Malmédy, and then he opted to skirt the area to the south, and make a dash for Stavelot and Stoumont by backroads. The main incentive for this re-routing was to reach our 1st Army fuel depot at Stavelot, where there was over one million gallons of gasoline. Had they attained their goal, we could not have stopped them, and they would have been on their merry way to Liège and Antwerp. There were no reserve troops in this area to block his advance.

En route through this area, Peiper met up with Company 'A' of the 285th Field Artillery Observation Battalion, composed of about 140 men in over 30 vehicles, that were passing across the front of Peiper's advance at Baugnez, commonly known as Five Points, as they were en route to St. Vith.

Needless to say, they were all captured and herded into an adjacent field, lined up, and methodically machine gunned down. Following this, some of the German soldiers walked through the mass of bodies, and any that were moving or groaning were shot in the head. Thus, this became the noted 'Malmédy Massacre.' This was not an isolated incident in which this type of atrocity was committed.

Their reasoning for committing this act of atrocity was the fact that they did not have the men or vehicles to keep them as PoWs nor the food to feed them, and further, prisoners would impede their rapid advance so that they could not maintain their schedule.

This massacre occurred on 17 December 1944, in a field behind a prominent café, at Baugnez, and it was not until 1 January 1945 that the uneven humps in the ground—the bodies had frozen in grotesque forms, and were covered with 4-6 inches of snow—were discovered to be U.S. soldiers and were found by men of the 120th Infantry of the 30th Division.

A few of these men did manage to survive, one of whom was Bill Merriam, and his story, and the story of others, led to several of the Germans being captured later on and having to stand trial at the Nuremburg War Crimes Trial after the end of the war.[9] [10]

---

[9] *after the end of the war*-Mr. Towers continues: "A monument has been erected near the site of the massacre, and the name of each soldier that was killed is inscribed on a plaque along the wall, about 100 feet in length, and the U.S. flag flies there, day and night. It is well attended by the local citizens, and fresh flowers are laced at the monument by someone, nearly every day, and is one of the most highly visited sites in the area. Memorial services are held here frequently, particularly when veterans' groups visit the area on Memorial Day and on other special occasions."

[10] *having to stand trial at the War Crimes Trial*-Peiper and 73 other members of the Kampfgruppe Peiper were actually tried at the Dachau Trials, which took place from May 16-July 16, 1946. Peiper and 42 others were sentenced to death by hanging; the others received lengthy prison terms. The trial and subsequent appeals were embroiled in controversy, however, with lawyers for the defendants arguing that their clients did not receive a fair trial, a charge championed by then up-and-coming Senator Joseph McCarthy of Wisconsin, a state with a high proportion of voters with German heritage. As a result of this and 'under popular pressure in the midst of the Cold War between the western powers and the Soviet Union, all the sentences of the Malmedy defendants were commuted, including those sentenced to death. By 1956 all of the convicted had been freed from prison.' Joachim Peiper settled in France in the early 1970s. On the early morning of July 14, 1976, his house was set on fire. He was killed, yet for some he has become a cult figure; in fact, on Dec. 16, 2019, the 75th anniversary of the Battle of the Bulge, 'an official US Department of Defense Facebook account featured a picture of Peiper as part of its celebration,' apparently copied from a fanboy site. The DoD took it down and walked back the controversial post, noting it showed what American forces were up against.
Source for commutation quote: The Malmedy Massacre. Holocaust Encyclopedia. United States Holocaust Memorial Museum. encyclopedia.ushmm.org/content/en/article/the-malmedy-massacre

*

Later on that same day of the massacre, Col. Peiper's troops were passing through Ligneuville, they captured eight more Americans of the 9th Armored Division, and they were executed by a pistol shot in the mouth of each man. A monument is also erected here in their honor and memory.

Some of the most intense and vicious fighting of the entire war took place in this area due to the cold weather, lack of warm clothing, food, supplies and ammunition. Temperatures hovered below freezing during the day, windy and with snow falling on many days, and temperatures running as low as −20 degrees at night.

During this December–January period, we endured the coldest winter on record up to that time, according to local authorities, and although fighting was severe and continuous, we actually had more casualties from frost bite of the feet and hands than actual wounds from enemy action. This required an enormous number of replacements continually throughout these two months. The logistics of keeping us supplied with ammunition, food, and replacements was an ongoing nightmare for our Service units.

In order to assist Col. Peiper in the execution of the plan, the German 3rd Parachute Division was dropped well behind our lines, and they created havoc by cutting phone lines, turning road signs in the wrong directions, and even acting as MPs, and directing traffic in the wrong direction! All of the men in this unit were dressed in U.S. uniforms, and by devious means, confiscated many U.S. vehicles, and thereby gave the impression and credence to their being genuine U.S. soldiers, and authorized to be there. Little thought was given to challenging them, so far behind the front lines! Most spoke excellent English, which many of them had learned while living in the United States prior to the war, and they even knew our passwords of the day, which had been captured during the break-through from the 106th Division.

Pfc. Francis S. Currey, MOH

In this area, on the western outskirts of Malmédy, one of our men, Pfc. Francis S. Currey, engaged a group of German tanks, a half-track and two anti-tank guns, and he single-handedly—with a B.A.R., a bazooka, anti-tank grenades, a .50 caliber machine gun mounted in a U.S. half-track that had been knocked out and abandoned earlier, and a .30 caliber heavy machine gun—knocked out three German tanks (one of which had the markings, fake of course, of the U.S. Star on the turret and on the sides of the tank), two half-tracks, killed several German soldiers, and in the midst of all of this, saved the lives of five of his comrades from certain death or capture. For this Francis S. Currey was awarded the Congressional Medal of Honor, and the Belgian equivalent, the Belgian Military Order of Leopold II with Palm.[11]

'The 9th U.S. Luftwaffe'

In the meanwhile, the Germans had claimed the capture of Malmédy, and the headlines of the *Stars and Stripes* proclaimed this! Thus our Air Force partners, the '9th U.S. Luftwaffe' as we called them, came over with their heavy B-24 bombers

---

[11] *Francis S. Currey was awarded-* Along with the Medal of Honor, Currey was also decorated with the Silver Star, the Bronze Star, and 3 Purple Hearts.

on 24 December, and opened their bomb-bay doors directly over Malmédy.

Malmédy had been liberated in October 1944, with little or no fighting, as the Germans were on the run at that time, heading for their defenses along the nearby border of Belgium and Germany. So, Malmédy had been spared of any appreciable damage, and when we moved into the town on 18 December, it was a beautiful and picturesque resort town, where everyone was merrily going about their business as usual.

At this particular time, I was a liaison officer from the Division HQ, which was located in the Hotel des Bruyeres in Francorchamps, to the 120th Regimental HQ, which was located in the City Hall in Malmédy. I drove between these two points frequently, day and night, so it was prudent to find the shortest route between these two points. This led me to find an unimproved road up over a mountain to the northwest of Malmédy, and through the settlement of Burnenville, situated on the top of the mountain. This route saved me many miles of travel and hours of time.

On the fateful day of 24 December, as I was traversing this route, and was about to descend the slope of the mountain down into Malmédy, I heard the drone of planes to my rear. I told my driver to stop right there. We looked back and saw this great flight of B-24 bombers. What a wonderful sight to behold! I said to my driver, 'The Germans are going to catch Hell somewhere,' and he agreed. Little did we know at that moment that their target was Malmédy! In a few moments, we were appalled when we could see the bomb-bays of the planes open, and the bombs began to tumble out! It was total horror as we watched the bombs drop all the way down to their target, the heart of the City of Malmédy! Clouds of smoke erupted from this point, then flames reaching hundreds of feet into the air over Malmédy. I had a small camera with me, and I took a few photos of the planes, dropping their bombs, and then of the city shrouded in smoke and flames.

This suddenly changed the whole picture! Malmédy was a total disaster, with the entire center of the city laid to waste. Many civilians were killed and wounded, but we were fortunate in losing only a very few men of our own. [We thought our personal] biggest loss was our Christmas dinner, which was being prepared that day. Spam and bread is what we got! It was later learned that three of our 3rd Battalion kitchens had been totally destroyed, located within the City of Malmédy, and about 25 of our men were missing in action, all presumably in and around the kitchen areas, and no trace of them was ever found.

Of course, our Air Force 'friends' apologized, and they still could not understand just what went wrong. As they were apologizing, the Ninth Air Force again was on its way, to make sure of the knock-out, and they bombed Malmédy again on Christmas Day! This in spite of the whole city having been covered with our normal phosphorescent panels, to indicate that the area was occupied by our own forces.

As I mentioned, the entire center of the city of Malmédy was a total wasteland, and the next day, the *Stars & Stripes* proudly proclaimed 'that Malmédy had been retaken by our troops, due to the strong support of the Air Force, in stopping the German advance through Malmédy.'

There is some question as to just when this action occurred, as everything and everybody was in a state of chaos. Whether this action took place on 24 December or 25 December is questionable, but the fact remains that we were bombed on both days. All of the company's records were destroyed in these bombings, so all we have is the accounts written in the history books, and the recollection of others many years after the event.

*

We cranked up our jeep, and raced down the slope of the mountain, and crossed the bridge over the river on the north side of the city. That was as far as we could go, as there was debris from the bombing all over the streets, making them impassable. People were running around screaming for help and needing assistance. Knowing where all of our medical facilities were located in Malmédy, all that I could do was to direct them to the nearest medical facility, where they could get help. Upon reaching the Regimental CP located in the City Hall, I found that all of the phone lines were out, and radio communication with the Division HQ was not possible due to the distance and the interference of the mountain between the two headquarters.

I was delegated to race back to the Division HQ and advise them of the disaster that had just occurred, and to summon assistance at once. Almost immediately, as many of the Medical officers and staffs were summoned and dispatched to go to Malmédy to render any assistance possible to our own troops first, then to render assistance to the civilian population as needed.

Needless to say, the 105th Engr. Bn. was dispatched also, to render assistance in clearing the main routes through the city as quickly as possible.

It was remarkable to note that, although the entire heart of the city was destroyed, the St. Quirin Cathedral was virtually untouched! Talk about miracles!

However, we recovered from this disaster rather quickly, as most all of the necessary ground support was almost immediately available, since we were in the midst of the 1st Army supply depots, which had been abandoned by them on 16, 17 & 18 December 1944.

T/Sgt. Paul Bolden, MOH

In another action, in the small village of Petit-Coo, another of our 30th Division men, T/Sgt. Paul Bolden, earned the Congressional Medal of Honor. He charged a building housing 35 Germans, under the cover of one of his comrades, who was armed only with a rifle. The Germans had pinned down his Company for some time with heavy automatic weapons and small arms fire. His covering comrade was killed by this intense fire, but undaunted, he hurled fragmentation and white phosphorus grenades into the doorway and windows of the house. He received return fire, and was hit by 4 bullets in this action, then, despite his wounds and weakened condition, he charged the house again and sprayed it with a sub-machine gun. He waited for the Germans to come out to surrender, but none came out. Thirty-five dead Germans were in the house. None escaped. T/Sgt. Paul Bolden was awarded the Congressional Medal of Honor, which was presented to him by President Harry S. Truman in Washington, DC in September 1945, after returning home with the division.

Many more actions such as these two C.M.H. recipients occurred, but were never adequately documented, so those involved in these incidents were awarded 65 Distinguished Service Crosses, and an untold number of Silver Stars.

Finally, by the end of January, the Battle of the Ardennes had ended (more commonly called the Battle of the Bulge), and the front lines were nearly back to where they had been when the attack was first made on 16 December 1944.

Hitler's elite 1st S/S Panzer Division, the Adolf Hitler Leibstandarte, had been totally destroyed, and was never able to reorganize and come back into battle, as it had done before.

Around the 1st of February, 1945, our 30th Division was relieved in this area, and we returned to Germany, to nearly the same position that we had left in mid-December, and again prepared to attack over the Roer River.

This escapade of Hitler's cost us all very dearly!

Frank Towers passed on July 4, 2016, at the age of 99. Carrol Walsh passed on December 17, 2012, at the age of 91.

George Gross passed on February 1, 2009, at the age of 86.

You can read more about the experiences of these three men as Holocaust soldier-liberators in my 2016 book, A Train Near Magdeburg.

CHAPTER SIX

The Sergeant

He sits in the corner of a room, gesturing, telling his story. The youngest of five children, Bill Bramswig is telling the story of his life, interspersed with laughs and some emotion; he does not hesitate, or sugarcoat, the parts that reveal the horrors, the absurdity and stupidity of war—fraudulent medal awards, deaths from friendly fire, and the murder of prisoners in the heat of battle. A recipient of the Bronze Star, he sat for this 2001 interview at the age of 78.

"We had to go a hundred miles or more, and we're on big flat-bed trucks with wooden sides on them, and sandbags. It was all open and it was snowing, so up we went to Belgium somewhere, and we had to relieve the 101st Airborne Infantry. They were in white robes; I don't know if that helped anything. We came up and

they'd say, 'Hey, so-and-so, you're going to be relieved. The 87th is here.' And it was just, 'Okay, have a nice trip, I'll see you next Christmas,' and you were in their holes. That was Bastogne. There was no air support because there was so much fog and they couldn't get the airplanes up, which would have been very good.

We started to move out, then you could see the guys hanging out of tanks. Wherever they were, the Germans must have massacred them; they were trying to win the war."

William E. Bramswig

I was born in New York City, in Manhattan, Harlem, 130th Street. We lived in that neighborhood for about 30 years, and we were there when the war started. I had two brothers and two sisters, mother and father, and they were all older than me. My two brothers went in. One of them wound up in Iran, supplying equipment to the Russians. My other brother went into the Navy and was on a troop ship going back and forth to Australia most of the time. He always landed on the West Coast, in San Francisco, and when he was on leave, he used to borrow [money from] everybody so he could fly home for a few days. [*Laughs*]

At that time, you were supposed to check with your draft board every six months to find out what your status was. Different people in the neighborhood had sons that were in service, and when they met me they'd say—they called me Willy—'Willy, when you going to go in the draft?' One guy was flying a B-25 in Europe, he was home already. That's when it was 25 missions, at the beginning. So anyway, I had a half day off from work for Lincoln's birthday, so I went down to the draft board to check on my status. I told the girl my name and she's checking. She said, 'I have Harry here, that's your father, Henry, and we have your two brothers, John and Francis. We have no William.' She called her bosses over and they told her to make a card up for me. I thought I was going to be a big national hero by doing something like that; I could have not reported, and nobody knew I was alive. [*Laughs*] So anyway, two months later I was in the Army and they sent me down to Camp Stewart, Georgia.

I was in anti-aircraft for 14 months. In that time, we went to the West Coast for desert maneuvers.

They put us on big flat cars. We had sleeping accommodations on Pullman trains, but they took all of our equipment and tied it on, and across the country it went. In every state we stopped, we used to jump out and 'We're in Oklahoma.' [*Laughs*] We wound up in Yuma, Arizona, that's way down on the border of Mexico. When we saw it, we said, 'Water, give us water.' It was a barren place and you thought you were thirsty, but after you were there a couple days, you weren't thirsty. So that was pretty good, it's a dry climate. If you were in Florida, you'd be perspiring all the time, but out there, you didn't perspire that much.

I remember one particular night maneuver with blackout lights, and you had to watch the truck in front of you. Dust was flying around. When they made a turn, you were supposed to make a turn. All of a sudden, they made a turn and we didn't see them and we're driving for about ten minutes and nothing. We pulled over. We had to stay there all night long because nobody could find us. [*Laughs*] The next day they came out with a jeep and they found us. But that was it, we lost them with the dust. It was very good out there.

After that we went to Fort Bliss, Texas. At one time, Fort Bliss was used for the Mexican War and it was a cavalry place—all horses, no tanks. I think they put us there until they got an idea where they were going to send us. But I loved it, I loved all the traveling. It was a big thrill because I could never afford to get out of New York. The food was good, too. The food in the Army— [you understand], we were very poor people in the Depression. When we got down to Camp Stewart, we go in for breakfast and I see this big tray of sausages; the Army had all of that. Even in combat, they would come up four or five times a week with hot food. Maybe they'd miss one or two when we were doing some action, but they treated us really good. And you still find guys complaining; I would think, I wonder what they had in civilian life.

In Fort Bliss we had a very good setup, near El Paso, Texas. A notice came down that the Army was looking for infantrymen. I didn't like the antiaircraft, because we didn't do that much and all they kept saying was, 'Clean the gun, clean the gun,' every time the dust blew. I thought this was a good way to get out and see some action. You know, young guys, 20 years old. So I went to Fort Jackson, South Carolina. That was good, very exciting, a lot of people were coming in; they were making a whole new division. I was a corporal in the gun crew and when I got to Fort Jackson, they had no use for a corporal, they made me a sergeant. We were there maybe three or four months, it was October '44, and we were shipping out. That was after D-Day. D-Day we found out, one morning we woke up, 'We invaded Europe!' It sounded exciting but it turned out to be hell. [*Laughs*]

Overseas

We went across on the *Queen Elizabeth*. There were 13,000 [on the ship], and 90 of us were in the library. The funny part about it, I lived around the Hudson River area, I worked there all my life in that neighborhood, I worked on 56th Street and here was this ship on 50th Street. In fact, for a couple of years, I used to go down to the harbor and look at all these big ships. The night before we were going to leave, we had to meet an officer on 43rd Street and Broadway, it was an Italian restaurant. Sure enough, we met him at 12 o'clock at night and he said, 'I'm sorry to say, but you're not going home no more, we're going to ship out.' We got down to the ship. They go so fast, like 35 miles an hour or something, they don't need any convoy, thank God. To feed a crew like that, you went down for breakfast, they'd give you a hard-boiled egg, toast, an orange, and maybe coffee or milk. Nothing fancy and you only ate twice a day. We wound up over in Scotland, beautiful countryside, and they put us on some trains down to England. [At that point, I was in the 87th Division]. When I left anti-aircraft, I'll tell you—after all the fighting we did later in the cold and whatnot, that anti-aircraft outfit wound up in Hawaii. I kept in touch with them—they wound up in Hawaii. [*Laughs*]

Anyway, we were in England for about a month and we went across the Channel on a nice little steamer. They gave us only one bullet, going into combat, we landed in Le Havre and they gave each soldier one bullet. Too many people with guns; it happened to me one time, I had a round in the chamber and didn't know it. So we get to Le Havre and it's all flattened, all bombed out. When I saw that I said, 'That's good, they can make a new city.

Instead of having small little roads, they can make boulevards and everything from scratch.' Europe was bad for transportation, for big tractor trailers. They couldn't manipulate around the towns. I didn't see it, but sometimes they would just tear a house apart so they could drive through there.

We got to Le Havre and they put us on trucks, and we wound up in some apple orchards, all mud. We had our pup tents there. [It was] October. There was so much mud on your feet, the tent was behind you and you just plopped back in and took your shoes off because otherwise the blankets and everything [got messed up]. We were only there two or three days and we got some hay from the farmer's barn and put that in. It was good, warm and a little drier. The next day they told us that the farmer said we stole his hay that he needed for his cattle and so forth. We had to pay, we all had to go in like half a buck apiece. You have to go to war with some change in your pocket to pay your way. [*Laughs*] We had to give him 20 dollars or 50 dollars or whatever it came out to be. After that, a couple days, they put us on trucks.

I was a squad leader [in a rifle squad] and assistant platoon leader. The lieutenants were never there. They got wounded, they didn't get wounded from being in the foxholes, they were back in the barns or someplace with artillery. They always said that the war was won by sergeants. There were a lot of sergeants and they knew how to use their own noodle. The officers—nobody had any experience at war, even the colonels. Nobody knew anything about war, and nobody knew about front line troops, they didn't know anything like that. You learn by experience.

[We were part of the Third Army]; I was very proud. I feel that some of the other armies that were over there didn't get any coverage like General Patton did. They did things, but I don't think they were in the area where the real action was. So we wound up in Metz and that was a big fortification. Your anti-tank guns hit the walls and nothing, it was built 100 years ago. It was no man-to-man, just shooting at walls. Then we were near Nancy, France, and then the Saar, Saarbrucken, and then the word came that they were having trouble up in Belgium, the Germans were trying to break through. We didn't know nothing. All the time, we were just our little squad, maybe another squad, we didn't know what was going on. I read about all these towns, I never knew what towns they were and most of the time we were on the outskirts of towns, flushing out the woods. The colonel and everybody had their command post in town. So we had to go a hundred miles or more, and we're on big flat-bed trucks with wooden sides on them, and sandbags. It was all open and it was snowing, so up we went to Belgium somewhere, and we had to relieve the 101st Airborne Infantry. They were in white robes; I don't know if that helped anything. We came up and they'd say, 'Hey, so-and-so, you're going to be relieved. The 87th is here.' And it was just, 'Okay, have a nice trip, I'll see you next Christmas,' and you were in their holes. That was Bastogne. There was no air support because there was so much fog and they couldn't get the airplanes up, which would have been very good.

We started to move out, then you could see the guys hanging out of tanks. Wherever they were, the Germans must have massacred them; they were trying to win the war. That's why they say that Malmédy and what the Germans did—what were they supposed to do, capture prisoners? They were trying to go and go and go. We didn't like to capture prisoners ourselves either, because what are you going to do with them? Put them in your pocket? We used to just send them down the road when we knew people were behind us. In a lot of cases, the Germans wanted to get captured. They thought they could go to England. In fact, before we left the States, some of the camps we were in had German prisoners already, so they had a great time. They fought the war and they were eating the same food we were.

*

[We were not outfitted for the weather]; now, I can't believe in Desert Storm, these guys were going to war and they were taking a Boeing 747 [to combat]. They had the big transport plane, flying these guys over the ocean, all dressed in these beautiful uniforms. We got galoshes. They weren't prepared, the government. They didn't think they'd have a war or something! So we had galoshes, we had just regular dress pants, two pairs on, but the galoshes. They had combat boots, the kind that strap over, but we found out right away that they froze, and your feet were in there. That's why we had lots of the trench foot. With the galoshes, you could move your feet around. You had socks on your feet and if you could stuff straw in there, even better. At times, though, your feet would sweat. We used to have at least three pairs of socks, and the routine was you took them off your feet and you put them in your helmet liner and then from your helmet liner, you put them down around the stomach to warm up, and then from there back to your feet. You might have had another pair but that was the routine. That's why, in pictures, you see guys with their socks hanging out of their belt. [Sweaty feet will freeze]; some guys, I read after the war, actually did it on purpose to go back to have their feet treated. Some of them really had it bad, he toes turned black, no circulation; they just cut off their toes. We lost a lot of people, as many people, I think, as got shot. In fact, there were a couple of cases of guys shooting themselves, looking for that million-dollar wound. There was one guy in our platoon, and they said he did a lousy job, splintered his bone and everything like that. And they knew; they took those guys right out.

The 106th Infantry Division went across with us on the *Queen Elizabeth*. Sometimes it took three ships back and forth, it wasn't always the *Queen Elizabeth*, but there were different regiments and battalions going, guys with their artillery would go on another ship. So the 106th was with us and they put them [on the line], as a new outfit, they spread them out in the Ardennes over maybe 12 miles, because they didn't think the Germans [would attack there]. But that could have been us. They got captured, a lot of them did. I think one regiment got away because they were on the outskirts of the Bulge. The weather started to clear up, we started to get supplies in, we started to get more reinforcements and then we started to pound the hell out of the Germans. They were tough, but at the end, they wanted to quit. All the glory years they had; they could see that was the end.

Digging In

We were in foxholes and you only stayed there two or three days, and every day you stayed there, you dug it a little bit deeper, tried to make it a little more comfortable. We threw pine needles and leaves in the hole to keep your feet off the mud that was in there, and then you'd get the branches from the trees, the fatter ones; when you dug, you throw the dirt on the side—then we could put the wood across it, put the branches up and then after you did that pretty good, then you threw some mud on top. It helped you a bit, it kept the weather off you. You'd have two guys in a foxhole. There was a joke—two guys, you're supposed to stay awake for a couple hours while the other guy would sleep, but it was never like that. It was always, 'Hey, Willy, you awake?' You always thought the other guy was going to fall asleep. At night you couldn't get out of your hole—if you had to take a crap, you just did it somehow, but you couldn't walk around. Sometimes the Germans didn't even know we were there, and the patrol would walk in on us. We had like a wagon train, like for the cowboys and Indians, with all of us kind of around. They'd walk right in the middle of us and then somebody would spot them and 'Halt!'—and then there would be shooting all over the place, but the Germans were the only ones running around. That would last maybe five minutes and you'd stay like that all night long; nobody would get up to see what's what. The next day, beside rigor mortis, [the Germans we killed] were frozen, whatever position they were in. You never got to the point where it frightened you and that part about getting replacements—we used to get a lot of replacements—and before you even knew their name, they had to go back because they got injured, or they got killed.

Replacements

[Now, I think the replacements were treated] very good—it was the movies where they said you didn't get to be friendly with them because they might get killed and make you sad. But [it is true that] you didn't know their names. Let me jump to about two years ago—I got a couple of letters from these guys' sons, their fathers were in the service and they were in my outfit, the 345th, Company F.

They said, 'My father never talked about the war, did you know my father?'

They'd give me the names, and I never knew them. You would know about ten guys that came overseas with you, but anybody else, you'd say, 'Hiya, Joe,' or maybe, 'Hey, Burns,' but you never got friendly with them [just because] they'd get injured and they're gone; most of the time they'd never come back.

'Would you write to me and let me know?' That was another thing about the war. Most people didn't have any education and they didn't know how to write! They could maybe put their name down, but they didn't know how to write, nobody knew how to write before the war. They never wrote a letter, but when you got in the Army, to get a letter, you gotta write a letter. I don't think the Army took that into consideration—they weren't stupid, it was just that they never had an education.

I said, 'I'll call this fellow up, the son.' Now, I'm thinking to myself the soldier's son is like this [*holds hand at child's height*], but he was a man about 40 years old. One guy was a professor and I thought I was going to speak to a young son, his father had died in 1980 or something. I called him and he said, 'Mr. Bramswig, I didn't think you'd call, I thought you'd write a letter. Did you know my father?'

I said, 'No, it was hard to get to know anybody, they'd come and go and you're moving, moving, moving.'

He said, 'It's so nice of you to call. My father was a forward observer.'

The other guy, he said that his father got wounded and he was lying out in the field for a couple of hours and when he did get rescued, they told him it was good that he was out in the field with the snow because the cold weather healed up the wound a little bit. I was reading his mind, and I knew he wanted me to tell him something about his father, so I said, 'I want you to know that your father lying out in that field, the conditions, and besides that he was wounded—he was a hero.'

The guy wrote back to me and said, 'I told my mother what you said about my father, that he was a hero.'

This guy was a professor or something and he wanted to write a story about his father, so he wanted to know every little detail. He sent me a copy of it, it was about ten pages, and in the article he doesn't mention my name but he says, 'One of the soldiers from my father's outfit called me,' and the way he said it made me… [*trails off, gets emotional*] [He wrote], 'He wanted me to know that my father was a hero. I couldn't speak. That meant so much to me.' The guy was in my company, but I didn't know him.

But that was 1943 and I didn't do anything until two or three years ago. I didn't get in touch with anybody. I've never had to go to the hospital or ask the Army for anything, lucky. All the guys that got killed, they got wounded, they got captured, they got their feet cut off, they did so much, and I didn't get [wounded]. There must have been a lot of other guys, too, where the stuff was happening here and there, and you weren't [hurt].

That happened a few times to me. I always say it's like being a deer: I can feel how a deer is, but a deer doesn't know what's going on. We used to have to walk down roads at night, maybe by yourself even. One time I had to take a prisoner, somebody could have sniped me and the prisoner could have escaped. Most of the time the prisoners didn't want to escape. But a lot of people got killed like that, just from one shot. We were in this town on a hill and we looked down and there was this German soldier two or three blocks away, it must have been a couple hundred yards away. So I said, 'Maybe we could hit that guy.' So two of us knelt down, it was a two-story house, and two of us knelt down with our rifles and another two of us were over our shoulders with their rifles, so four rifles. I said, 'When I count to three, we'll shoot.' This [German] was walking on the other side of a little stream, like a roadway, and I counted to three, and we shot. In the States I couldn't hit anything on the rifle range—this guy was walking [and we hit him], and I think that surprised the hell out of us. He must have been dead, because he didn't move, but it was surprising that we hit him from that distance.

I was only in combat four months. I got three battle stars; it was 150 days. I tell my son that every day they get reports from 2nd Platoon, 2nd Squad or something, two men wounded or killed, and we'd have to get replacements for them as soon as we can, might take a week. But Sgt. Bramswig was here, Sgt. Bramswig was there. Nobody said anything about taking Sgt. Bramswig and sending him to Paris or anything. You weren't a guinea pig, but they were happy that you didn't get killed. Other guys that I went over with, one guy got wounded three times, Sgt. Wild, I correspond with him. Well, he got wounded three times, but it wasn't enough to keep him out, two weeks or something, and he got a Silver Star. But the thing was, a lot of those guys were living in the hospitals, getting treatment during the day and a good night's sleep, but guys like myself and a lot of them were in the holes every night.

*

I never knew the names [of the towns we took]. I knew Metz and Coblenz, but all these little, small towns of 500 or 1000 people, most of the time we didn't stay there where we could look at the signs. We were always on the outside. What would happen is the battalions and different companies would come in with their jeeps and trucks and cooks and the first thing they'd say was to get the troops out on the high ground, protect the high ground so nobody would sneak up on you. You could never make a fire; in fact, I didn't smoke at the time but if you wanted to smoke, you had to get down in your holes. They used to say that about shooting tracer bullets. If you wanted to tell someone where you thought the enemy was, you'd say, 'Watch my tracer,' and you'd shoot them. But at the same time, they found out where you were shooting from, so you didn't do it that much.

*

[We were up against principally infantry units], but we had a couple instances with German tanks, maybe in Schoenberg. The town was down a bit and then there were hills with Christmas trees I call them, pine trees. They had come to this German tank down the dirt road over there, half a mile away. 'Wow,' we said, 'he doesn't know that we're here. Get a tank destroyer.' They weren't too far away but they were never in front of the infantry, they were always in back of the infantry. Sure enough, the tank destroyer came up and they shot about nine times and they missed. The Germans were coming down the hill and there was a road, and he cut into the woods and got away. They told us that he was out of our range. I guess nowadays with the rockets we have, they would have got him with the first shot.

*

The first time we got overseas, you'd see a Joe Lewis type, or somebody [built] like that, you say, 'Wow, he'll never get killed, that guy.' And he got killed the first one, the physical education guy. And the little skinny guys like Audie Murphy, I don't know how he got all those medals. I don't know how he was in those spots all the time to get a medal. There weren't that many situations where you could stick out as one person.

The thing was, [the brass] came out one day and said we weren't using enough ammunition! And it was true; in the States they were always telling us to conserve, don't be wasting. But as we found out later on, the more you shot, the more the Germans kept going away. At the end, they didn't have the stuff to come back with. You have to shoot more ammunition so our colonel can tell the division, and he could tell the Third Army that the 87th, F

Company, is using ammunition, and boy, they're good. Then they said a couple of days later on, we're not giving out enough medals. We're going to give out medals? I always thought they came from Washington or something. What? We're going to give out medals? And that's the way it was. You had to tell the colonels and those people a story. 'Bill Bramswig, he went out there where that tank was and this and that and he drew fire'—you got a Silver Star or something. Even the officers, well most of them were never around, because they were wounded or something. We used to have to make up stories—'Oh, yeah, he crawled out there and the bullets were flying.' Not using enough ammunition and you have to make up stories for the medals so the division or the battalion can have [some recognition].

The Accident

[One time, we were in a house], and we were downstairs with the lieutenant, the sergeants and squad leaders, and a lot of the troops were sleeping on the floor upstairs. So the BAR man comes down and said he was having trouble with the

BAR; when he pulled the bolt back, it jammed. Sure enough, he had one in the chamber and it went off[*makes shot noise*], shocked the hell out of us. It went through the ceiling and before we knew it, they were flying down the stairs. One of our guys was shot dead upstairs. The guy who did it with the BAR, they had to take him out. It was bad enough that we were killing Germans, and here we are killing our own people. I know that happened to me in the States. We were on guard duty at an ammunition depot. It was just a formality, but you had a clip with bullets, and they'd take you by truck out to the ammunition depot, and you walked around, maybe a squad, 12 guys. After a couple of hours, they'd take you back and the truck would come with another 12 guys. And you'd go back to the barracks where they were keeping you and you'd put your rifle in the rifle rack. About 20 minutes later a messenger comes in and says that one of the guys minding the ammunition depot is missing a bullet. When you put the clip in, there were eight bullets, and one goes into the chamber, and when you finished, you'd pull the bolt back and the clip would come out but that one stayed in the chamber. I put that in the rack, I didn't notice. Then four hours later or whenever I went on duty again, I said, 'Everybody, the bullet's in here.' [*Laughs*] I had to take the bullet out and get rid of it. I never told anybody. But it can happen, so that story about, 'Don't let anybody point a gun at you that's not loaded'—It can be loaded, and then you're sorry.

Weapons

I wouldn't have wanted to fight the Germans at the beginning because they were trained and proud. They were real regimented. That was one fault they had, they would do anything that they were told, but if the officer got killed, 'What are we going to do?' They said the sergeants won the war for us, and it's true. A sergeant would just take over the situation, they'd say 'Take the lieutenant back' or something like that and then things would keep going on. But they said the Germans didn't do those things.

People always talk about the German 88mm cannon being the best for accuracy. Their tanks—they were prepared for this—their tanks had really good armor on them. Ours were like tin cans and the cannons weren't [that powerful]. I remember the .50 caliber machine guns from anti-aircraft, that's some bullet, that is. They said that they can go through a tree, powerful. We had four .50s on the half-track, they had them in the infantry somewhere, and you would look down the barrel through the [sight] and you could see a tree or a flagpole and you'd get this one gun [sighted] and twist it and lock it on, right on the top of that flagpole, and you'd do it with the four guns and if you fired it right, those four hit that spot with those .50 caliber bullets, that would scare the Germans. They knew the .50 caliber was a tough enemy to fight.

There were times that I threw hand grenades. You know how the roofs of houses would go? [*Makes peaked roof with hands*] Everything was houses or barns, and you'd go down and maybe there's nobody there—you never saw the civilian population, I don't know where they went, I mean sometimes you would on the small farms. When you would come down the side of a house or a barn, and we'd pull a hand grenade—people think you throw it like a baseball but you couldn't, you'd be throwing your elbow out, you had to push them. I pushed it. [*Mimes throwing hand grenade*] Do you know that thing went over the top by that much? [*Holds hands several inches apart*] It just as well could have come down into my lap or where some of our soldiers were! So you didn't do that too much. That was without thinking—you just thought you could throw it over and it would go over. And then a barn has that big opening in it to let the gas out from the animals; we were going down and I saw a barn and I thought I'd throw a grenade in there in case anybody is in there. I stepped back and the opening is [about 18 inches], where they took the bricks out. I stepped back and as soon as I threw it, I said to myself, 'Suppose it doesn't go in?' I should have been next to the hole; you'd think I was bowling or something. That was a scary thing. I'm sure people got killed by doing stupid things without thinking.

*

We got into the Siegfried Line and I think we were there in the morning; at night we were working our way there. They protected all those forts from the outside, they don't want somebody to come up and put a big demolition. We slept in one, one night; there was a big cement wall, you walked in and you stopped, you had to go this way [*motions left*], and then another way to get inside so you couldn't shoot [straight]. They were really well built because they were building them for 20 years.

Another time we were on patrol at night and we came down to a barn and this was like two o'clock in the morning and you can hear them moving around. The Germans had those boots that were made out of wood, they put nails in them so they wouldn't wear out, hobnail boots. We could hear some shuffling going on, we didn't know what to do. It turns out they were cows. But in our imaginations, scared, they were Germans. [*Laughs*]

The Prisoners

We were in German territory at the end. They didn't build foxholes, they had this one hole in the ground [as big as] this room and it must have dug down about five feet and then they put like an umbrella over it; the only purpose was to keep the snow from going in the hole. The place could hold twenty guys. Any time you could sleep indoors was like Christmas. So we're in there and Sgt. Riley, he was my assistant, there was an opening and he could stand there and look around, so I told him to stand there and listen. We were in there and fairly comfortable and all of a sudden Sgt. Riley shouted, 'Halt, halt!' The next words out of his mouth were, 'My gun is jammed!' I handed him up a grenade to throw, and he threw the grenade. Ourselves, we had to get out of there because all the Germans had to do was throw a grenade down there, and we were all confined, our eardrums would have [blown out]. So we all got out, and a couple of us ran down, one of [the Germans] was lying there on the dirt road. As a sergeant, you couldn't tell somebody else to go and see if he was alive, so I went out to see if he was alive, wishing I were a private at the time. [*Laughs*] I go out there and hit him with my rifle. He moved, I thought he was dead, I jumped back. [*Laughs*]. We made a prisoner out of him and then I had to take him, during the night, five or six blocks down in the woods.

You didn't know how to get rid of the prisoners. That Malmédy—we had the same thing ourselves. We were going to go into a town, and this must have happened lots of times, we were going to go into a town in the afternoon, about four o'clock. The Germans used to use the bazookas, [panzerfausts], on us, then they made some shooting and that was the end of it, [but] the lieutenant and this other guy got killed. After they started to do some shooting, two or three at a time, they came out surrendering. In the meantime, they killed a few of our tankers that were back, a hundred yards or whatever. They took them back there, and they killed them, they killed twenty-three. I went back maybe fifteen minutes later, and a Jewish fellow asked if he could go back and look. I said, 'Don't do anything, just look, because you'll have these things on your mind for the rest of your whole life.' One German got up and ran away, we had to chase him and kill him, otherwise he would have run up ahead. In the end, it was twenty-three. I found out a couple of days later, they just threw them into two-and-a-half-ton trucks, and when our general heard about it, 'Never happened,' he says. That was it.

One guy, a month or two ago, [I was telling him this story], he says, 'So you were responsible for that.' It must have been the guy that I sent back who said something. I said, 'Me? I had nothing to do with that!'

Across the Rhine

We went across the Rhine at night at Boppard. The Remagen Bridge, which they had captured whole, was only a couple of miles upstream. They told us we were going to cross the river, we crossed the Moselle, too. They said we're going to cross at night, send a scouting party over because you can't all go at once, you don't know if they have machine guns waiting for you. So we're going to go over at night and try not to make any noise banging the boat. This happened, and a week later we went across in small motor boats, we're hauling eight guys; anyway, we had to get on the other side very fast, sometimes we went slow and they'd be taking pot shots. But this was at nighttime. We had no problem. We got over there and the first thing you do is go through some houses, no Germans are there, and then the next thing, the rest of them came over. The same way with D-Day, I don't know how many thousands of guys were in D-Day. What they did when they came over a week later, they were in D-Day. The original bunch that went over, I think a couple thousand got killed, but after that, it all quieted down. D-Day would be the first 12 hours, you wouldn't want to be there.

*

The day [President] Roosevelt died, that morning they came up with breakfast and whoever was in charge said, 'Hey, Bramswig, they want you to go back to the company CP. They're going to send you home.' You talk about winning the lottery? That was really something. If you knew about it a week or two ahead, it was something you could think about, you're going back with the kitchen, you're going home. I went back with the kitchen. They had these tents where they were cooking so I knew them from just seeing them around. He said, 'Don't write any letters home, you'll get killed.' That was unbelievable. I was the third one they picked to go home, every month they picked about 50 guys out of the division. I had been overseas for six months, came back after four months. My brother was in Iran for three and a half years. So the first guy they picked was a small older guy—you know when you're 20 years old, a guy that's 32, he's an old man. Anyway, they needed somebody to go down and see if this little wooden bridge going across the stream was okay or if there was a problem. 'Anybody want to go?' He said, 'I'll go,' so they let him go. A week later they put him in for a Silver Star, it was a dangerous assignment, nobody wanted to do it, but he found out it was okay. A month or so later, another guy was going out. What we'd do, we'd take a collection. This first guy, who got the Silver Star, I gave him 150 dollars. There was no place to spend money. A month later, another guy was going home. I gave him 50 or something. He walked off with three or four hundred dollars.

Then when it came my turn—I wound up with like 200 dollars, maybe a little more. A couple of guys gave me their German Lugers and they said to see if I could get it home and they'll get in touch with me. I didn't want to get too monkeyed around with them, trying to smuggle a gun. I sold both of them for 100 dollars apiece. So that went with my 200 that I had in cash, and sure enough, when I got home, six months, five months later, I got letters in the mail, 'What happened with the guns?' I didn't even answer them. One guy was from Wisconsin. [*Laughs*] My son called a lot of the guys I was with, and one guy died a couple of months ago.

[In general, I'd say my experience in World War II] was fantastic, unbelievable. I try to write a little bit, and I think that [the film *Saving*] *Private Ryan* was nice and everything, but the guys who were actually there [should have] an Academy Award. See, *Private Ryan* and all that, they add a lot of baloney to it. It doesn't really happen that way with bullets and everything exploding around. I always thought the guys in Vietnam had a rougher time, especially with the weather and the fanatics, or even the [guys in the Pacific fighting the] Japanese.

William Bramswig passed away in 2007 at the age of 84. He was a recipient of the Bronze Star.

PART THREE

GUESTS OF THE REICH

"Surviving was all you thought about—you were so worn down you didn't even think of all the death that was

around you. I knew I'd go to heaven if I died, because I was already in hell."

– Jewish-GI survivor
of Berga am Elster slave labor camp[6]

CHAPTER SEVEN

The Artillery Spotter

Sydney Cole's service in World War II begins in Canada. The Buffalo, New York, native was anxious to join the Army Air Corps, but a series of incidents brought him instead to Toronto, Canada, to join up with the Royal Canadian Air Force. After the attack at Pearl Harbor, he managed to get released to return to try to become a pilot for the United States. He would wind up in the glider program, which he disliked; eventually he hit his stride flying 126 missions in Europe as a field artillery spotter. On his final mission, he survived being shot down and became a prisoner of war during the Battle of the Bulge; in his captivity, he became an eyewitness to the Holocaust.

In an interview in 1989, he emphasized, *'I wouldn't have come normally, but when you mentioned it would go in the archives of the Holocaust, then that just changed my mind completely. Now, this is something that I put in the back of my mind many, many years ago. I didn't want to think about it too much... but that's the only reason I'm doing this, because of the Holocaust. If one person in the entire world gets anything out of this interview, I'll be happy about it. Just one. I want people to remember what really happened back in the old Nazi days.'*

Sydney Cole

I was born on September 1, 1914. I attended grammar school in New York City, then moved to Buffalo with my family while I was young. My father did architectural maintenance on buildings, whenever they were in need of repair, and he got a call from someone in Buffalo for a mansion on Delaware Avenue that needed work, and that is how we got to Buffalo. I went to high school in Buffalo, Madison Park, and graduated in I think 1932. Then I went to Buffalo State.

I knew eventually, with war in the upcoming, that I would be drafted. I did not want to be a foot soldier. I wanted to be a pilot; I had just made up my mind to do that. I tried and tried to get into service and couldn't get anywhere; I tried to get into the Army Air Corps, but it was a big deal to get in; they told me that I'd have to go to New York City for my physical, just to be physically able to get into the Air Corps. I finally made connections in New York City. So I went to New York City. They had said, 'Go try to join a YMCA, get in the best shape you can,' and I went from there. I took the physical and there were about 70 people at that area from Buffalo, from New York, from New Jersey, and Pennsylvania. Just everybody trying to get into the Air Corps. I did pass the physical, and then they sent me to the University of Syracuse a couple of months later to take what they called a mental. Not your mental capacity, just your knowledge and everything else, and there again about 70 or 80 from different parts of the country. New York, New Jersey. And we all failed the test, couldn't comprehend it one bit the mental exam. But I didn't give up.

Canada

So, I went to Hamilton, Canada, [to see about the aviator program there]. They didn't know anything about getting me in, they sent me to Toronto. And I took the physical and the mental exam there in one day and passed everything, and I think it was a month later they called me. I went there, got sworn in and started, and graduated in their flight school training.

And then when the actual war broke out with Pearl Harbor, I, as an American volunteer, had signed a contract with the Canadian force that I could leave at my will. And later, they gave me an extremely hard time, because we had gone through this training which was very expensive. I had gone through it with a group that came from England, because they were bombing around London [before Pearl Harbor] and they were sending groups here to be trained for the Royal Canadian Air Force. I went up there and we checked into Manning Field, which is the exhibition grounds of the Canadian National Exhibition. And after many inductions and shots and programs and so forth, I didn't see an aircraft or anything for three, four months. It was all ground work. Then we started our fighter pilot training. We finished up with Spitfires, graduated with that Spitfire kind of training, and I finally got through with the paperwork and everything else. In the interim, when I was up there, I was called to the office one day, and because I had had two FBI men track me to Canada, and they thought I'd went to Canada to avoid the military, which [was not the case]. And they left with joy in their hearts because I was in the military, and that helped me get back into the American forces and get through with my contract with the Canadians.

When Pearl Harbor happened, I decided I wanted to come back to the United States. Being a volunteer with the USA patch on my shoulder, and the enlistment papers that I had signed when I entered the Canadian service, I could ask for a discharge at my will. Well anyhow, I put in for a request to be discharged from the service, and it finally came through after a few months. I reported to the United States, went to the draft board, and waited there because they didn't know what to do with me and that particular time, with the qualifications I had, just coming out of service. They weren't set up yet for any type of enlistment and so forth and so on. Then they called me and they asked me if I would be interested in taking glider pilot training. Now, in order to be qualified to do that, you had to have power shift training, which I had just completed in Canada.

So I agreed to it, I went into service here as an enlisted man. They sent me to Miami Beach to round up the thirty that were going to be the first class for glider pilot training in the United States. Well, from there we went to Santa Fe, New Mexico. We went to Janesville, Wisconsin. We rode flying power shifts right along, and then we were checked out by some of the Army Air Force pilots that came from West Point. They were a very, very small organization at that time. The complete thirty that took the first glider pilot training course did pass. There wasn't one failure. Now we went to Twentynine Palms, California, for our first glimpse of gliders. But from the moment I got into a glider, I knew I didn't like it. It was so quiet that the noise was deafening. I can't describe it, and I was always reaching for a throttle that it didn't have. I just knew that they wanted to use gliders in combat, and it would never work. I just knew it couldn't. Well anyhow, we graduated in 1942.

Field Artillery Spotting

One night I was OD, which is Officer of the Day. At midnight, a telex came through. They were looking for liaison pilot instructors. Now, liaison pilot people are ones that spot field artillery shells for field artillery battalions. They have forward observers that are on the ground, and they have them in the air. I felt that's what I would want to do because it's flying and not glidering. I went to my commanding officer the next morning, after reading this telex, and he refused to release me. I went over his head and finally made connections, and went down to Fort Bragg, North Carolina, which is one of the largest field artillery training camps in the United States.
They said, 'Fine. Your qualifications are fine, but you have to be a field artillery officer.' I was in the [Army] Air Force. I had nothing to do with a gun. I never took a basic training, where I had to march and go through all the other equipment that a

normal soldier does. Well, anyhow, I said I would, so they discharged me with the convenience of the government. They then sent me to Fort Sill, Oklahoma, which is a field artillery training camp, and that's OCS. It's a 90-day course. Everything is double time. I was in that group. I was probably 26 years old at that particular time. And I was in with a group of VMI students that were 21, 22, fresh out of school, and had to keep up with them.

I then became an instructor in liaison pilot training. After three or four months of that, I tired of it and asked for overseas duty, which they gladly recommended and okayed. I was assigned to a separate field artillery battalion, not with a large group or anything; we were by ourselves. We were sent where we were needed. We were like a SWAT team with a police department. Wherever there was a problem, our battalion went.

We got into combat in the middle of '44; I got to Paris right after the Germans vacated Paris.[12] We were waiting for aircraft. They finally came into Orly Field in Paris and then we went over, and then we were sent on separate missions, wherever

---

[12] *I got to Paris right after the Germans vacated Paris*-This was actually probably September 1944.

they needed us. That's when I started my combat flying.

Then we were assigned to the Battle of the Bulge. We had been around Bastogne in early December. The push started December 16th, and everything was amassed there.

The weather was horrendous. It was mid-winter. Incidentally, I'll never forget, I was sent out on a mission Christmas Eve, and when I came back, my special turkey dinner was gone; they had used everything up, there was very little food left, outside of C-rations and canned food. I missed Christmas dinner, I missed New Year's Eve dinner. I was out on a mission at that particular time, too.

The Last Mission

I had flown 126 missions. The last mission was the 126th, and that happened January 2, 1945. I had 125 missions with no parachute. We didn't have them available at that particular time; the shipments never arrived from the States. We were very short of materials at that particular time. Well, you see, we weren't fighter pilots or bomber pilots. I was flying in an observation unit. These were specially built with a large 360-degree cockpit, to see all around you. It was a low-flying propellered craft; the only thing I carried was a .45. That was it.

We could take off and land and be back in six or eight minutes, and that's considered a mission. That's why we acquired so many, that's how we could do it. But this particular mission now, January 2nd of 1945, I was ordered into the air at three o'clock in the morning. The temperature was hovering right around four or five degrees. The snow was [at least] eight feet high in drifts. The runways were completely blocked. We need runways to get off, we need a lot of room because of the ice and everything else, and we didn't have concrete. It was all mud and field, just open field. It was just done by the engineers in a rush, because everything was frozen. We just couldn't start the aircraft. We had to drain the oil out of the aircraft, heat it with blow torches, pour it back in, and finally take off. Now, with these types of aircraft, the only heat in the aircraft is a manifold heater, and that throws very little heat. You can't wear boots because the rudders and everything are small, and you have to operate with just your feet, and you have to wear very normal shoes. Luckily, that day I put on a bomber jacket, which was warm. Normally, you would wear just flight clothes, which was a thin nylon jacket and suit.

I was ordered into the air. I had been up around two and a half hours, and my fuel was getting low. We couldn't spot too many of the field artillery shells because of the snow-covered ground. We finally called for smoke bombs—when a shell hits the ground with a smoke bomb, it sends up a column of smoke. Then you can zero in and observe what you're doing and be able to get aircraft and field artillery shells where you want to put them.

At that point, though, there was so much confusion. Our own planes were strafing everybody. They were just letting bullets fly from wherever they could. Anywhere they thought the enemy might be, even on our side of the battle line. It was just a state of confusion. The Germans were confused, our forces were confused, but everything was going, you just couldn't believe what was happening there. My field artillery officer directing the ground fire would not let us come down.

When I told him our fuel was getting low, he said, 'Go within six minutes and try to get back.' And of course, we needed a lot more time. All of a sudden, our aircraft was hit by anti-aircraft fire. We are sitting tandem in the aircraft with a very small door. The parachutes we were wearing that particular morning, they were seat packs. Now, there are two types of parachutes. One is a backpack, but that puts you forward in the aircraft, where you can't control the aircraft too sensibly. The seat pack raises you up where your head is hitting the canopy. But we had them on, [although] our parachute training instruction was [just] two hours; they showed us how they fold the parachute and how to pull the cord. Period. That was my instruction.

When the aircraft was hit and I lost control, I had put it in a glide position; the engine was shot out, so I had no power, but when we were taking glider pilot training, our instructor would take us out five or ten thousand feet, reach over—he was in the back—shut the ignition off, and you'd have to land in a circle; that was part of the training to be a glider pilot. Well anyhow, it came in very,

very good stead with me, but to get back to the story, I ordered my observer out. Out of the plane, because we were both going to jump. We couldn't stay in the plane, it was disabled. So he had to go first because he was behind me. We opened the door, which was a very narrow door, and he got tangled up in his headsets and all these radio wires. He was leaning out; he couldn't budge at all. I took my foot and shoved him out. I saw his parachute open. In the three or four minutes between the time he got out and by the time I bailed out, he landed on the American side, and I landed on the enemy side. Minutes, just minutes, because we were right sort of in the center.

I was wounded by shrapnel and I saw the Germans shooting at me coming down in the parachute; I could see the holes popping up in the parachute. Now evidently, I was hit in my arm and I was hit in the leg. Now, I don't know if I was hit when the aircraft was disabled or when they were shooting at me when I was coming down in the parachute; I didn't feel it. When the aircraft was hit, I had a funny smell in the aircraft. I can't describe it, what it was, but it was not normal in that aircraft. After I bailed out and saw these bullet holes... You know, you can guide yourself coming down with the shroud cords, and anyhow, I got away and landed at the edge of a forest. Completely wounded and bleeding profusely. I grabbed the parachute, wrapped it around me, then I lost consciousness.

I woke up intermittently, back and forth. I think the second time that I woke up, I remembered my dog tags. The dog tags had an 'H' on them, for Hebrew. I knew I was in German territory; I knew that the Germans were starting to retreat through there, so I took my dog tags and just flung them as far as I possibly could.

Now, I passed out, and I was in and out [of consciousness], perhaps 36, 48, 72 hours. I have no way of knowing, but it may not have been more than 48 hours, because the Germans were retreating. There was a tank that passed by me, manned by German officers, and they were running for their lives. They spotted me, stopped, didn't take me into the tank at all, but threw me on top of the tank, just threw me on, without the parachute or anything, just physically grabbed me and threw me on.

The bleeding had stopped because the blood had crusted over, scabbed over. I was taken back to some small town or village. They turned me over to the Hitler Youth. Kids. They were in full uniform, with the Nazi thing across their chest, with the brown pants, with the brown shirts, with everything. They were just like you see in the movies, just like you see anywhere where they show in these horror pictures. These were anywhere from 12 to 19, 20 years of age. They started interrogating me, but they could speak very little English and not enough to convey anything that I would understand. When I didn't answer properly, every time I didn't give them a right answer, I would get hit. They never would hit me in the face, it was always in the body, in the groin, on the shins, and so forth. They were just so incensed they were [totally indoctrinated], being born and raised in that era. Their families, their fathers, their mothers, they just hated us, American [airmen] especially, because we bombed their cities, we ruined their beautiful Berlin, all the buildings were shut down, all their culture—they just had a hatred for pilots like you couldn't believe.

When they got through with me, they threw me down in a cellar, locked the door. Now, there were no windows in the cellars in the way these little houses were built in these German villages; you could just see the stone. It was extremely damp down there, and there was a mound of old, rotten potatoes, [and I had not eaten in probably three or four days]. The next morning, for some reason, I was thrown in the back of a truck, and taken to a Red Cross tent, where they were treating German soldiers somewhere in Germany. This German doctor was just treating the Germans first. When he got to me—I was, of course, the last one he looked at—he did wrap my arm and my leg with some paper bandages and gave me a tetanus shot. Now why I don't know, but actually, it helped.

From there, I was sent to some other place where they tried to interrogate me. I couldn't answer. I was put on a train and taken somewhere else, and they tagged me severely wounded. Of course, on the train, there was a bowl of soup. There was some food. On this particular train, there was an English doctor who was captured a long time before. He was a major, a medical man, but he had very little equipment. He had rusty tweezers, he had a little black bag with nothing in it, paper bandages, perhaps some Mercurochrome. He might have had some sulfur powder, I don't know, but anyhow, he was picking this shrapnel out of my leg. He couldn't do anything with my arm because the fragments were too small and they were embedded too deep—the shrapnel in my left arm is still there, 26 very small pieces of shrapnel, and the calf on my leg from my ankle to my knee had been split wide open—and he couldn't open up the scar on a moving train. And there were other prisoners on the train. There was no such thing in those days as pain pills or anything to alleviate it.

I went from camp to camp to camp. Everywhere I went, I remember lying somewhere for a day or two, in a large room with a wooden floor, and perhaps a hundred prisoners, just lying on the floor, awaiting orders, awaiting to be shipped out. And finally, I got to a stalag, which was a prisoner of war camp. The stalag was ironically named IV-F; I think it was on the German-Polish border, somewhere there.

In the meantime, they had wired a dog tag on me, a German dog tag, when I got to that camp, on my bad leg. It has the numbers that were assigned to me as a prisoner of war. Now somewhere, if the records are still available in Germany, it would show Stalag IV-F, a date I was brought there, my name and number. Now where, when, I don't know.

The Stalag

When we got to the stalag, there was a captain who was a senior ranking officer, and three other officers, including myself and two other officers. Of course, the first thing we did was to have a meeting of the officers to see how we were going to handle ourselves, and our escape routes, what would happen if we were ever liberated, what would happen if we ever overcame the German guards. We were split up into different battalions, and I was in charge of battalion three. There were possibly eighty prisoners under my command, mixed. There were English, Italian, American, and so forth. We were the only ranking officers there; the rest were enlisted men. Now, incidentally, anybody who was Jewish was called and taken out of this particular Stalag IV-F, and I never saw them come back, four or five, six at a time—Rosenberg, Finklestein, whomever it may have been; one day I asked the guard what happened to these soldiers that were picked, and he said, 'They are out doing work.' But they never came back. Whether they were killed, whether they were transferred to another stalag, I don't know. I presumed they were dead, executed.

Now I didn't go around saying, 'I'm a Jew.' I was as discreet as could be. I was in that camp possibly two and a half, three months. When I threw my dog tags away, when I was interrogated and they started registering my name, I told them that I was Protestant but they didn't bring up religion with me whatsoever, beyond, 'What is your religion? What's your age, your name, your rank, your serial number, where were you born? What outfit were you with? How many airplanes and aircraft do they have? How many tanks? How many field artillery battalions? How many infantrymen?' All those questions, which I did not answer, except the pertinent questions to my own personal views.

The treatment in the stalag was horrible. There was no hot water, there was little food, there was no medication, there were no showers. There was an outside pump with well water that was rank, filthy, rotten, rusty, smelly water. There was no shaving equipment. There was one in the morning, one at night, and both meals were alike—a potato soup with grass in it, anything they could make to try to make it a little thick. One of the German guards and I tried to converse, and we sort of got a little bit friendly. He brought me a loaf of bread. Now, this loaf of bread was baked in 1939. It was in a wooden box, completely sealed. It was a replica of a little coffin, and it was made out of wood, like balsa wood. It was very light, and you could just rip it open, and there was a fresh loaf of bread, four or five years old; they had produced maybe millions of loaves of bread. It was just amazing, how they had prepared all this, scheming ahead for food and so forth.

My mother did get an MIA telegram, and my sister still has it to this day. Everybody lost weight, and I went down to 95 pounds, from 145, in five months. They didn't ever issue clothes. My clothes were tattered, absolutely tattered. The bomber jacket I was wearing had been penetrated by fire. I was shot, I was shot in the leg and shot in the arm. My left arm, where I was shot, my left sleeve of this bomber jacket was completely tattered. The socks I was wearing were rank, the shoes, everything. And you know, you'd try to wash them, you'd try to do this, but you're using cold water. And it can't dry. It's the wintertime, too. You can't believe the cold; it's just almost impossible to describe the conditions there.

Liberated by the Russians

We had a formation in April, and the Germans did announce that President Roosevelt had died, they did tell us that. We had heard that the Russians were coming, by the Germans. [And] we knew that that particular night, that the camp was going to be vacated by the German guards. We had gathered everybody—nobody went to sleep, everybody was alerted—we were all awake, and we heard the Russians coming and they came in by horse-drawn carts, very few vehicles. The Russians came in like at 4:30, 5:00 in the morning, but the guards had left. Most of [the liberating soldiers] were Mongolians. The pots and pans were rattling on the back of the two-wheel carts. Just like the old days. You couldn't believe it, it took you back in history, it was primitive.

The first thing the Russians did was rip out all the barbed wire, the complete barbed wire encampment around the whole camp. And then, of course, we four officers were taken to meet the Russian major. The Russian major was a graduate of the University of Minnesota and could speak English. He took a liking to me. We became buddies, and wherever he went, I went.

Now, this is May of '45. April is when they announced that the president had died. The Russians came in with medical personnel also. They assigned a female doctor to handle me; they had perhaps three or four doctors with them and they were all female, incidentally. And this girl was very young. I assumed she was around 23, 24. She couldn't speak good English, but she examined me, she saw the condition I was in. There was a lot of infection there, which she treated. Then they went out and they slaughtered cattle, they brought in chickens, they brought in eggs and started cooking and having feasts and everything. We got excellent treatment by the Russians. I couldn't believe it. Now, the major also explained to us that we were going to be kept by the Russians approximately one to two months, to build us up, because we were the first Americans that were ever liberated in the Russian zone by the Russians. They were awaiting Russian prisoners liberated by the Americans to have an exchange.

'I Just Couldn't Believe What I Saw'

In the meantime, I had gained some strength. The Russian major and myself and a party went scouring the country; we needed medical supplies badly. We broke into pharmacies and just took what we wanted. That's when we ran into some of these satellite concentration camps where Jews were kept. And the first Jews I ever saw were in a barn, just inside the camp, away from the big dormitories and from the big compounds. There were yellow stars on them. They were in the pajama-type stripes. Of course, they start talking in [Yiddish], which I could understand. Then, of course, the Russian major knew I was Jewish. And then, of course, everybody knew I was Jewish after that. It didn't make a bit of difference, no, and I never denied the fact after that, because we were liberated.

I think there were possibly anywhere around twenty-five of these prisoners, the most horrible sight I ever saw in my life, with heads that had swelled up to the size of a soccer ball, or a volleyball. And their limbs, you can't describe it—they were just bones covered with skin, no flesh whatsoever. No flesh in the cheek, nothing on the hands, no flesh at all, just skin and bones. You could just see their groin just sticking out, the bones. They looked like a skeleton. I think [the Germans] put them wherever they could find room.

We tried to feed these people. We tried to give medication, water, hot drinks, whatever. No [effect]; they all died. They just could not consume food, they were too far gone. In other words, they were living death. They didn't want to shoot them because it would waste a bullet.

It was so confusing there... I think it was Auschwitz, and there was another one not too far from there—Bergen-Belsen, I was just going to say Belsen.[13] Now, I saw the trenches there. They hadn't been covered yet, with thousands, literally thousands of bodies, just helter-skelter, just thrown in there, and they were all skeletal-type people in there. I just can't even really describe it anymore. They had a grave at least two football fields wide and long with empty bodies in there—men, women, and children—both male and female, naked, lying there just like this one on top of the other. Unbelievable. It was a scene that I can't describe fully, and it just boggled my mind right to

---

[13] *It was so confusing there*-Mr. Cole was prompted to speculate that he may have been at Auschwitz, which was liberated by the Red Army on January 27, 1945, and then perhaps at Bergen-Belsen, which was liberated by the British Army on April 15, 1945, quite a distance from the eastern German-Polish border where Mr. Cole states he was held. Uncovered mass graves were indeed a spectacle at Belsen for a few weeks after liberation, but it is unclear if this is what he refers to; the author finds it unlikely that a Russian-held prisoner would have been in the vicinity of Bergen-Belsen, in the west, before the graves were covered. That is not to say that Mr. Cole did not witness these mass graves, just probably not at the most infamous mass grave site, Bergen-Belsen. See my 2016 book, *A Train Near Magdeburg*, for a more complete Holocaust liberation timeline/discussion.

this very day. The horrible, horrible conditions, and it didn't improve my [mental] condition much either.

These prisoners were now freed. There were no Germans around there, either, but these people couldn't maneuver, they were just too ill. You couldn't believe what you saw! You thought it was something that... I can't describe it. Emotionally, I was just gone, with seeing something like that, and knowing these people were all Jewish people, I just couldn't believe what I saw.

That was it for me, to just then realize how you were a prisoner there for five, six months, with this type of [perpetrator], and to come through it—I'm really surprised they didn't just wipe out the prisoner of war camp. The Germans didn't have enough food themselves, they didn't have enough water, they didn't have enough fuel for their aircraft, for their tanks, for their vehicles. They didn't have enough food for their soldiers, they didn't have medical supplies. Everything the Germans had was ersatz. There were no such things as gauze bandages, everything was paper.

In July [we left Russian control]. They had a tremendous ceremony with bands and music and speeches. It was like a light opera. There were Russian songs, Russian dancers, and there were American generals. Right after the ceremony, they turned the American prisoners over to the Americans, and the Americans turned the Russians over to them. I was flown right to Paris, to be interrogated by our own people, because we were the first prisoners to be liberated by the Russians. We were the first stalag to be liberated by Russians. They wanted to know what treatment we got, what the Russians did, how they acted, and everything. Of course, we were allies at the time. There were only good words for them.

I had built up my strength a little bit. There's no question about it. I wouldn't let myself lie down and say, 'I'm ill. I'm going to act ill and be ill.' I just fought mentally to keep my strength and to keep going.

After I was interrogated by the generals in Paris, I was sent to a camp to be built up some more, with the eggnogs and cocoa and all the medical things that you could think of. There were psychiatrists there, there were psychologists there, there were legal people there, there was a PX. Of course, they stripped me immediately, 'Go into the PX. Pick out whatever you want, as far as clothes are concerned.'

But there was no happiness there. It was a feeling of elation that I'm free, but how am I, really? How am I going to act? What's going to happen to me? I don't know. Because myself, being a POW didn't affect me as much as going into these concentration camps. That's what really set me off. I couldn't believe this was happening.

They had decided, me being one of the first prisoners of war liberated by the Russians, that they wanted to fly me back to get me back to the Pentagon to be interviewed by some of the generals about how the Russians treated me, an American officer, because we weren't really on good terms with Russia—there's still an enigma there. They put me on a liberty ship, instead of flying me—I could be home in twelve hours or whatever; it took seven days. They put me on the deck, 8:00 in the morning to 8:00 at night with the sun shining and bringing me eggnogs and milkshakes and sandwiches; the food was so rich I couldn't eat it, I would just toss a lot of it overboard, but drank some of [the liquids] trying to gain back some weight. Now, when I was shot down, my weight was 145 pounds. When I was liberated, I weighed 95 pounds. I never really got my weight back, right to this very day. My top weight was 120, right now I'm right about 115.

Home

My mother had gotten the telegram that I was an MIA, [and she did not find out I was alive until] probably when I was on my way home. 'Your son, blah, blah, blah, missing in action, we will give you further notice, blah, blah, blah.' And my whole family said, 'He's gone, he's dead.' They all believed I was dead! My mother was the only one who said, 'He'll be home. He's coming home.'

[We landed in New York], and there were people waiting for us; I was taken right down to Savannah, Georgia. I was still in bad shape, not in the greatest shape at all. I had to go be rebuilt; they treated me there for about two weeks, hospitalized and everything else. Then I went for my interview and was released home. I went back and they wanted me to hold PoW meetings with soldiers who were going overseas, and they kept me there for a while. How I was treated, how to be treated, how to treat the guards, how to talk to them, how to act if you are a PoW.

[I was discharged] at the end of 1946. I got a telegram and a letter and a phone call that I will be serving for the next 20 years in the Air Corps Reserves. Never called for duty or anything, but I kept up my flying status in the reserves.

I did not take advantage of the GI Bill because I had fulfilled one of the things on my mind when I was young—number one was medicine; the second was aviation. Once I had completed [my dream of] aviation, and given the condition I was in when I came out, I had no desire to go back to school or anything else. I just thought, what am I going to do with my life now? Of course, when I got released the first thing I did after I was out of uniform was to join the downtown YMCA for a fitness program to get back in shape. Mentally and physically I was still bad. Now this was in 1947, and I needed transportation. They were not making many vehicles then, the automobile business had been suspended, so there were no used car lots or anything else. I didn't know where to start and where to go, and I needed transportation. I couldn't take a bus; they didn't have any buses or streetcars. One day, I decided to take a bus ride to Lackawanna. I got off at one of the residential stations, and just roamed around the streets. I'd knock on a door of a house and I introduced myself and said I was looking for a used vehicle, do you know where I can get one? Because a lot of these people, their husbands were drafted, went into service, and a lot of them, of course, didn't come back. And one woman, 'Yes, we have a car.' I think it was a Chevy at that time. Flat tires, everything else. Her husband was killed in service. He worked at Bethlehem Steel, went into service, had a family. And they didn't know what to do with the car, but I knew what to do. Flat tires, no battery, won't start. In the meantime, I had lined up a mechanic that I knew, and I had the car picked up. They couldn't tow it, they had to put it on the lift, brought it in. In those days the tires had tubes in them, because you couldn't buy tires, you couldn't buy anything.

But there was an auto parts store on Broadway in Buffalo, and they had tubes. I put the car in shape, and cleaned it up, and used it.

One day there was a note on my car that someone wanted to purchase it. So I called this number, and I told him I wouldn't sell it right away because I needed it. Then something clicked, maybe this is something I should do. So I went back to Lackawanna, and through this woman, and I got her neighbor, the neighbor gave me another person. And I started buying cars, putting them in shape, and selling them. All of a sudden, it turned into a business—that's how I got started in the car business. I couldn't do everything myself; one of my fraternity brothers was back from service. I called him and asked him if he'd be interested in working for me. I sent him out to do what I was doing. And we started, and then I rented a lot on Franklin Street to store these vehicles. It was close to downtown, it was close to the YMCA where I was going every day. That's how I started my car business.

Then, of course, they started building cars again. Then I decided to go into the new car business when they did build the cars, and I acquired an

English Ford franchise. I flew to New York, met with the English people there and asked them about becoming a dealer for their English Ford. They said yes, they are contemplating opening up franchises in America. The English Ford was owned by Ford Motor Company, but it was all American-style parts and not English parts, metric and so forth. So I made a deal with them. They asked me, 'What's your bank, how are you going to finance, how are you going to pay for all this?' I said, 'Well, we got the price and everything else. How many can you put on a truck to transport now?' He said, 'We have a unit that has nine, we can put nine units on it.'

I said, 'Well, I'll give you a check for the first batch, the first carload.' I hadn't been paid for about three years in the service, [due to my MIA/POW status], and when I was released, I had little money. So that's how I started in the car business.

'I Had to Get On'

I have no idea what happened [to the fellow who went out of my airplane]. My entire squadron, every single one, including my major, my colonel, everyone else is gone now. I had no contact whatsoever with them at all, and now they are all passed away.

I went to a couple veterans organization meetings, but actually it depressed me a little bit. I could get nothing out of it. I did go through Post-Traumatic Stress, but that didn't help me at all. Just one or two meetings, and I canceled out; I did it all on my own. Oh yeah, I had my own problems. But [the Army] was more interested in knowing how the Russians acted toward me, if they were violent or anything else, or if they tried to get information out of me on how the Americans are. On a scale of 1 to 10, I would give the Russians a 10.

I had to get on. I was single, I was not married at the time. I just wanted to get on, to try to forget and put everything in the past.

And like I told you before, I wouldn't have come [but for what I saw regarding] the Holocaust, that this would be [read by] some person, somewhere in the future... If one person ever remembers this and gets some good out of it, then I'm very, very happy about it, because this is bringing back things that I didn't want to bring back—things that I put in the back of my mind, that I hadn't thought about in years.

Just remember, being a Jew is one of the best things that could ever... If you were born and raised as a Jew, stay a Jew. Never deny it. Be proud and remember. Remember there are people in this world today that I know do not believe there was ever a Holocaust. They think it's a fiction by the Jews. Believe me, it is true; [I saw it].

Captain Sydney Cole celebrated his 107th birthday on September 1st, 2021.

CHAPTER EIGHT

The Glider Paratrooper

Rosario Catalano was typical of many World War II veterans in that he left high school early in order to join up and maybe have a say in what his role would be in the war. He studied in the Army's Specialized Training Program for future junior officers, tried to qualify as a paratrooper, and wound up in the glider program, surviving a crash landing in the invasion of Southern France before deploying with the 550th Airborne Parachute Battalion to the continent from England during the coldest winter in living memory. And like many, he would have no say in the final outcome of his World War II experience—that of becoming a prisoner of war and slave laborer at the hands of the Germans. He spoke to his interviewers in 2003.

"Now, it's just about nighttime, eleven o'clock, January 4th. We could hear the rumbling of the vehicles around us, but we didn't know that they were dropping off German soldiers, and they were dressed in white. They had the white parkas, they were equipped for this kind of weather. We had called for tank support according to what I hear, and we asked for artillery support, but they couldn't give it to us for whatever reason. Naturally, you can't see. When I talk dark, we're talking dark. And that fire [in the town] was going on as a backdrop, so you didn't dare stand up. The Germans were dropping men off around that, so that it got to the point that I know a couple of [our] guys started to go over.

Captain Paxton came down and said that the situation is hopeless. He says we were ordered to break off radio communication and destroy the radio."

Rosario Catalano

I was born in New York City, down in the Village, on May 14, 1924. I'm referred to as Bob, but the name is Rosario. I was supposed to graduate high school; I did graduate, but my mother had to go up and get the diploma because I wouldn't take the student deferment that they were giving out, the six-month deferment at that time. My father said, 'You don't know how to kill yourself [fast enough]; I rushed right out, because they were going to draft me anyway. I was scooped right up.

[When I heard about Pearl Harbor], I had come out of a movie house, the Loew's Plaza in Corona. It was kind of a shock and you didn't understand why it was a shock. Everybody was talking as you went through the streets. I guess, now, in retrospect, looking at it, you didn't really take it very seriously. You were home, you were secure, you just think that 'It's not going to affect me.' It never even entered your mind that it might affect you. I think we were more interested in the movies that we had spent 11 cents to get into the movie house at that time.

I was in the service a while and I went to the ASTP, Army Specialized Training Program.[14] And I stayed there for a while, but they were dissolving the program. I was up in Ripon, Wisconsin, with

---

[14] The Army Specialized Training Program (ASTP) was a course of study and training designed to meet wartime demands for leaders with technical skills, including engineering, foreign languages, and medicine. It also helped to subsidize American universities but was criticized for drawing down soldiers available for combat as the war heated up.

a fellow that I had buddied with who had a big scar on his neck. He was at Pearl Harbor. I said, 'We can select the paratroopers, because they're going to assign us to an engineering or an infantry outfit.' I says, 'I would go paratroopers, that sounds nice.' And it was more for the extra fifty dollars a month and the jump boots, and at eighteen, you're misguided.

I went to Fort Bragg. It was a four-week program. And the fourth week, you made the jumps, the three weeks before was the rigorous training. It seems like they had all the time in the world just to donate for you to expand your lungs and run around the airport before breakfast and things like that. Any infractions, you were doing push-ups. 'Give me 20,' and, 'Drop down and give me 10.' By the fourth week, it was four day jumps and one night jump. They always used to tell you on the night jump, 'Be very careful. What looks like water, when it's shiny, that you slip out of the harness and dive in,' and they said, 'Be very careful, because the class before you, a guy mistook the highway for water.' I think they always gave out that same story, but that's one thing that stuck in my mind as possible, but I had failed on the third jump. I failed to get up because I had twisted my ankle. See, by way of qualifying, you had to say that you never broke any bones, wrists, legs, and arms. So, naturally, if you want to get in, you lie a little. And I had on record that I hadn't had any broken bones, but then they threw me in the truck and took me down to the doctors, and they X-rayed the ankle. Like any American boy, everybody had a broken arm or leg. I had a broken ankle at one time. And it showed up on the X-rays.

The doctor turned around to me and he says, 'Son, you have to be disqualified.' So, I said, 'Gee, I wanted to be in the Airborne.' He said, 'Well, I'll send you to the Glider Division.'

So, that's how I got in the glider program. I went Maxton Air Base in North Carolina. They took you up in a glider. If you didn't get sick, they landed on a nice, smooth runway and you were qualified for the Airborne, the Glider Division. From there, we had infantry training, actually, which is what you are when you come out of the sky. You're on the ground. We happened to be especially light infantry. We didn't have heavy equipment; the

550th Airborne Parachute Battalion was a mobile unit, but, as they say, once you're on the ground, you're infantry. We stayed there and then we shipped out of Virginia.

The *James Whitcomb Riley* was a Liberty ship with 550 men and officers in our outfit. We landed in Oran, Africa, took about twenty-one days. We zigzagged in a convoy. In three weeks, I think you could float a balloon across [in that time], but we landed in Oran, Africa, where there was no action; Africa was ours by then.

From there, we had the invasion of Sicily. We were just support, we weren't really doing anything, but I know that a few of us heard about the volunteering for the paratroopers, no questions asked. So, I went and a lot of us qualified. From there, we went over to Italy. We sporadically had contact with the Germans; Germans would hold a position for a while and then move. I remember Italy as mud. There was a lot of rain. The people there, they used to say, 'That's because of the guns firing. That's why all the clouds cover the rains.' I don't know if it's true, but the Indians used to believe that.

The Glider Crash

We were pulled off the line. It was more than a few days because August 15th was the invasion in Southern France. I went in on that and on the glider; instead of jumping into the invasion, they assigned me to a glider.

It was very difficult for that pilot because the Germans weren't stupid. They couldn't cover all the ground that they anticipated the troops would come in. They would put up poles in the fields and they put a mine underneath it so that when the gliders came in, if the wing happened to hit that pole, knock it over, the mine would go off. These poor fellows, the pilot and co-pilot, were trying to get themselves in the position for this field so that they could land, but most of them were interrupted by brick fences that the Europeans had constructed for centuries, and the moss and the age just made them as strong as cement. They would lift over as best they could a couple of times. Then, this one time, it just couldn't and hit this stone wall.

These American gliders are made like a lawn chair with aluminum and just wrapping. They had plywood for the floor. And I saw pictures of the British gliders, too, and they didn't fare much better, either. This one just broke after the impact, but we landed in vineyards. That's August, they were just about ripe. I remember reaching up and getting a grape or something like that.

There were about twenty-five of us, or something like that, and there was equipment in there, but as I say, it wasn't a jeep or anything like that. I happened to be sitting next to the pilot and co-pilots and I'd never gone in on an invasion before, so I was really concerned. At the [invasion of France], there was no runway there; we actually just crashed and finally stopped when we hit a wall. And everything came flying forward—the laws of physics, you know? Something hit me in the lip, hit me on impact—I was too afraid to stop and examine anything—I suppose it was a helmet or something that whacked me in that lip there. I don't know if you ever cut your lip. Boy, there's no stopping the bleeding. At that time, I didn't realize it because I suppose I was paralyzed with fear, would be the best way to describe it, [though] I hate to say that.

The pilot, the co-pilot, I happened to be next to them and they didn't move; I'm pretty sure they died. Of course, you have to get out fast because one mortar shell will take out everybody. That was the thing. Move! One lieutenant came alongside of me.

He said, 'Loan me the shovel when you're done, Catalano. How bad are you hurt?'

I said, 'I'm not hurt.'

I was digging away. Nothing like fear to motivate you to move fast. Something had hit my lip where my lip bleeds, my shirt was a bloody mess, and that was the adventure of landing in a glider.

[We were in combat in Southern France], I guess it was months. We went into the foothills of the Alps, where they have Barcelonnette and little, small towns where the German had dug in; their favorite place especially was a town that has a steeple—they always have a good shot up there.

A friend of mine named Bill Lees, we had to get across a courtyard. It's like the town just faces everything into the center. The animals live downstairs in some of these places and people live upstairs. It's cement houses, mortar or whatever. Every little town has a fountain or a trough or something for the animals. You have to get across that, what could be 75 feet, 60 feet. This one particular time, we had to get across. A couple of guys made it, some guys didn't. They were lying out there and this fellow Bill Lees went across and he had to stop at that fountain because it's too much of a journey across the courtyard. He had dived down. It happened to be snow there and when he went to get up, he couldn't get up. And he started analyzing. The way he tells it is very good. He says, 'Gee, my legs, I can feel my legs,' and he started assessing parts of his body. 'Why am I not getting [movement here?] What's holding me down?' To make a long story short, every time he tried to move, this German up in the tower was whacking away at him. What was happening was, he had dove down and there was barbed wire down under the snow and his gun belt and everything else had just gotten tangled up, so he [couldn't figure out why he was physically pinned down]. It sounds funny, even when he tells it, but at that time, you can imagine the kind of panic you're in. Somebody shooting at you. The full 'fight [or flight' reaction kicks in], that's in you, and the speedier you get.

My grandson, he was, I think, 17 at the time or 18. He's up there playing handball and he had beat some guy who had been on the court for a couple of games.

He said, 'Grandpa, you should have seen me. I was fast. I was over here, I was over there, I was everywhere!'

I said, 'George, you don't know what fast is.'

I said, 'One time, when I was running into a battle, a bullet came alongside of me and I just steered around it.'

He looked at me, then he said, 'Oh, Grandpa!' [*Chuckles*]I was fast when I was afraid, [you get the point].

The Battle of the Bulge

We had been shipped to England. Everything is rumor at that time. We were going to be shipped there, the States, to go to the South Pacific. Of course, that's about the time that when the Germans broke through in early December, they mounted the big offensive through the Ardennes, the same route that World War One, I suppose, had taken. So, that put a crimp in the plans of whatever the higher-ups had planned to do.

And then we were in an airport waiting for the fog to lift. I don't know how many days. It was Christmas, but I get memory lapses, but we were trucked into the area, excuse me, where Bastogne is, into a town where we were eventually captured at Grammont in Belgium. We were trying to break through to relieve the 101st that was in there.

We went in by truck. I don't remember exactly, but I know that we had a long truck ride after that because we're over by the English side of France and you had to get across France into Belgium. That was cold. Some areas had cold and some areas had snow and some areas didn't. Now, we did not have any winter gear, and that was the reason we ended up getting captured. I understand that the winter gear was going to be issued, but, well, rumor had it that the war would be over before that; it was before the breakthrough that the Germans made. It was General Bradley and those guys who figured the war will be over and there's no use in issuing gear because they were going to concentrate on the summer gear, whatever their thinking was. So we didn't have any winter gear. The Germans had winter gear. I know that. When I got captured, they took my gloves right away, my boots. So, that left me with a pair of galoshes or whatever they called them then and no gloves.

I had the overcoat, that brown overcoat, which is very, very obvious on snow. And it was cold. It was a cold ride. I had a bazooka and, of course, my rifle, and I had had a German Luger at the time. When I got captured, I had a German Luger, but the issue was the rifle and the bazooka and the ammunition.

A fellow, Ted Ronicki from Toledo, Ohio, he got wounded that day because we got captured that night on January 4th. He got hit in the hand, and like a good buddy, I said, 'I want to take the glove off.'

It starts spurting. We put the glove back on and put the sulfa back around the hand itself with the glove.

He says, 'I'm going to go.'

I says, 'Yeah. The battalion aid station is down that way.' And far as I know, he was one of the few, not the only one, of the guys to get out before we were surrounded towards evening. We had pushed ahead too far of the flanks; they didn't move up with us. No matter how you look at it, we were stuck out there just like one finger in an appendage.

It was B Company; I think Captain Paxton was right up with us. Captain Paxton, incidentally, he just died a few years ago. By this time, I don't think we had too many lieutenants left. He was moving around in different groups. We had taken the town. We'd lost it and we got pushed back. Then, we took the town again. By this time, that town was on fire. If you stand up in front of it, you're a silhouette, so you had to stay low and there's snow on the ground. It's frozen for a couple of months already; you couldn't really dig in to make a position for yourself. There was some used foxholes that artillery shells hit; they make a concave something or other for you to jump into.

But after we took the town the second time, now it's dusk. There was no sunset or anything.

The weather was bad. It was very cold. You didn't realize it, but your feet have frozen, but not to the point that you can't walk. They're just so cold and you're huddled together where it was feasible. Then, the other times, you had to move. I understand that Captain Paxton was with the group, three or four guys, that they had to just get out of there. They're running out of ammunition.

The Country Sharpshooter

Different guys had different experiences. I know that Bud Pratt was trapped up in a building that was isolated from the rest of the town and I don't know how, but he had an enormous amount of shells, ammunition. He was playing hell with the Germans. They couldn't get past that strategic spot that that house was in. He was up there, and this fellow was [wreaking havoc] ... He was a big, tall guy, about 6'3", 6'4"; it's amazing he never got his head shot off, he was so tall. He was from West Virginia with no address, he lived in the mountains, supplying food for himself and his family.... I spoke to one of the sons a couple of years ago. He never came to reunions because he had a scratch-of-the-land existence—just economically, he couldn't afford that, so he never spoke to his children about what he did, but he did a tremendous job over there.

This guy could cook a chicken in mud. We used to call it mud chicken. He would dig a hole and take a chicken. The head is off, the feathers are on, and it wasn't cleaned out or anything like that. Put it in there and cover it with dirt and then build a fire on top of it and everybody would cook potatoes or something like that. This is September after the invasion. When the potatoes were done, everybody had a stick or something like that, because we went to farms that had potatoes that were growing and would have been blown up, so then he kicked that fire over and dug up that chicken. He'd have it there and he'd whack at it. The feather and skin would just come right off that thing.

So, I mentioned it to the son on the phone. He says, 'Oh,' he says, 'we still do that.' [*Laughs*]

The word went around our guys that Pratt was over there. The Germans finally had to bring a tank up to take the building out to get him out of there. He got hurt. The Germans put him in a German hospital, I understand.

Surrender

Now, it's just about nighttime, eleven o'clock, January 4th. We could hear the rumbling of the vehicles around us, but we didn't know that they were dropping off German soldiers, and they were dressed in white. They had the white parkas, they were equipped for this kind of weather. We had called for tank support according to what I hear, and we asked for artillery support, but they couldn't give it to us for whatever reason. Naturally, you can't see. When I talk dark, we're talking dark. And that fire [in the town] was going on as a backdrop, so you didn't dare stand up. The Germans were dropping men off around that, so that it got to the point that I know a couple of [our] guys started to go over.

Captain Paxton came down and said that the situation is hopeless. He says we were ordered to break off radio communication and destroy the radio.

'I'm going to surrender,' he says. 'I think it's the best thing.'

I mean, look. He's got information I don't have. We all went. A couple of guys decided to break out and make it on their own, but they were cut down. I didn't hear of anybody that got out of there. So, we gave up and they searched us.

So back to the army overcoat. I don't know if you're familiar with an army overcoat, it has a pocket about 16 inches at least deep. You accumulated things. So, you have to get rid of a few, if you had any, German souvenirs or something like that, which, of course, you had to kill somebody to get, that's the German reasoning. So, I was making sure now that I didn't have any, and I find that in the bottom of my right-hand pocket all the way down is a hand grenade. You can't be like in the movies, I managed to get that grenade out. I dug a little hole and pushed it in there, [to hide it]. What do you got to say? One grenade is going to change the whole picture? The only picture that will change is you're dead.

And now they searched me. I know a guy took my gloves, [and now another wanted my jump boots]. They asked for the wounded to fall out, so I dropped out because I had gotten hit on the heel of my shoe by a piece of shrapnel. You know how you slice an apple and it's a clean slice. It just nicked the foot flesh. So, I fell out. I think somebody put a little bandage on it, anyway. And he says in pretty good English, 'Take off the boot.'

So, I took off the boot and I showed him.

He says, 'All right.' He says, 'Take off the other boot.'

I told him, 'No. It's just my right foot.'

He said, 'No. I want the boots.' I had jump boots. He gave me a pair of galoshes or something. They were kind of big. He left the wound untreated; it wasn't pouring blood or anything that bad.

Then, our artillery support came in and we had already surrendered and the Germans were taking us back. Of course, this big open field and our artillery opened up and we were caught right in the middle of that field. And naturally, the Germans went down, too. I hit the ground; I thought that the ground was going away from me. But what it was is, you had been picked up in the concussion from the explosion and dropped down. I guess I must have went up two feet at least and dropping down again. I remember that specifically. And the artillery was late. I don't think anybody got hurt.

They brought us to a barn, oh, maybe about a mile back, I suppose. I don't know. The thing was, they gave us onion soup, I remember that, with a piece of bread. That was great. I mean, you didn't feel the pinch of being hungry anymore. We never have hot soup when we're up on the line. And that was the best part of it, but then later on, it was a steady starvation diet. I don't know how it happened. I guess the luck of the draw, whatever it is. I got put into a labor force, a labor battalion, [separated from the others]. My best buddy Frank Parovich, he lives in Chicago. We're in constant touch. We see each other all the time. He and I and a number of the others got put in it. Maybe we were two, three hundred guys [to start]. You have to visualize, maybe you got some sergeant or lieutenant in charge, German officer, and somebody comes over that outranks him or has a need. 'I need twenty-five men.' You never see the twenty-five again because wherever they went, they went. So, in all that constant taking, I ended up alone. Frank ended up in [another] prison camp. I seemed like the Lone Ranger out there. You're working. You're not eating and I ended up at 92 pounds.

We were walking everywhere, although I did get shoved into a freight car, a forty-and-eight car.[15] They overpacked us; the way you went in, that's the way you stayed in. And you stay in there sometimes two, three days. Sometimes, American planes would spot the train and they don't know that you're in there. They would have strafing and then there's a need for bathroom facilities and everybody by that time has had diarrhea. You're in this boxcar and there's one bucket, which would slop back and forth because it was always full, so the floor was slick. The straw absorbed just so much and that's all.

They didn't feed you. They didn't open the door, even when they pulled over on the siding when I suppose a supply train or troop train or something has to pass it; you'd stay there for six or eight hours and then another train comes by, and then you would go when the track was cleared.

---

[15] *a forty-and-eight car-* World War I terminology; a railroad boxcar designed to transport forty men or eight horses.

Alone

It was all Americans, but from my outfit, there was nobody left, except a guy named Lemontina who was the last of the guys of the 550th. We were close together. I remember a plane strafed the column that one time when we were walking. The plane came down to strafe the road and everybody just whipped; you didn't have to be ordered to save yourself. Some guys went down, and some guys went up, including me, into this pine wooded area. So, this American pilot, whoever he is, he don't know [we Americans are there]. He took one bomb that he had and he dropped it into the forest. It made those trees like toothpicks just flying around and Lemontina got a five- or six-inch piece, pretty thick, right through his hand. So, then, he got put into a truck. I don't know whatever happened to him, but he was going to be taken to a hospital or a doctor. So, now I'm all alone, but it doesn't make any difference. We're all in the same boat, so we're friends here, all Americans.

Slave Labor

I worked the hardest at Limburg, Germany. It was a minor railroad center. They had to keep one track open, and they needed a lot of help. [An American plane might come in] before it got too dark and he'd see the condition of the track that we'd try to keep open. He'd drop on by and just make a hole and there goes the work you had done. The Germans would take a group of two, three hundred guys or whatever and bring them over to a wooded area where they had railroad tracks stored, another wooded area where they had the railroad ties, and the remainder of the group fell in the hole, all under the supervision of somebody who knew what he was doing. You talk about gloves. I got assigned to this only one time and I have no gloves and it's cold and metal is cold. You know the business about sticking your tongue? So, I got the track and they said, 'Okay. Let's drop it.' We dropped it, and this skin came right off my hand, but didn't bleed because my hand was practically frozen, between carrying the iron and the elements outside.

You work at that sometimes eight, ten hours a day. The barn you slept in where they gave out the soup, well, you missed another mealtime, maybe tomorrow you might be there. You ate snow in the meantime. Working in the fields sometimes, you would find rotten turnips that the farmers had no use for, or they used to store the vegetables in the ground, they had the turnips that were heartier at the top. So, the sun would come out and melt that over, and then it would freeze again, but the turnips on top there were what you managed to sit down near when they gave you a rest. You had a turnip, there were frozen turnips, rotten turnips, and that was a treat that you'd have to eat. Otherwise, we ate snow.

We were constantly moving. Sometimes, a truck would be stuck and it would take thirty, forty guys to get a hold and push it out. Manpower was a big thing. I was about 175, 180, but solid muscle. Muscle, you know? Ninety-two pounds at the end.

'Smart for Self-Preservation'

I was mistreated, but after a while, you get smart for self-preservation. Not to screw your buddy or anything. No. I slept on a shelf for a while. Coming off this detail, there was a warehouse and we would plop down on the floor, in front, because everybody was on floors. I mean, you'd have to crawl all over everybody if you had to get up. So, you plopped down on the floor. Then during the night, there's some guy the Germans wanted—fifty guys have to get up. They open the door. '*Raus, raus!* You just came in and you'd be out again.

So, one time I climbed over everybody. I got up on a shelf in this warehouse. Boy. I don't know. I got into it, so I slept there. Now, you got to understand, I'm cold and I'm sleeping. I got up the next morning, I didn't get up fast enough. '*Raus, raus!* And the guard whacked me with that rifle butt, caught me right on the bottom of the spine. Man, that hurt, but I think it was so cold that I couldn't hardly really appreciate the bruise that he gave me. [*Laughs*]

Collapse

[We seemed to be] walking from place to place. In fact, this is right up towards the end. Now, I got this overcoat on. It's a funny thing. The overcoat is warm, and yet it's not warm, because now it's accumulated rain and snow, melted in, wet, and the dirt. I couldn't walk with it anymore, so I took it off. I thought I'd be able to throw it at least three or four feet. I barely made the ditch. I thought I'd get it up on an embankment, [and try again]. I can still see that embankment, but then I went a little ways more and I collapsed. Now, what we had was one of these big vegetable wagons, a flat piece with two big wheels, if you can imagine that. We had to pick up anybody that collapsed, they put them on there, because if you didn't, there was a German in the back of the line coming forward who would shoot anybody that feigned [sickness or fainted]. The guys had seen the wagon and they had permission, I suppose, just to take the wagon for that reason alone. They picked me up and they put me on that wagon. In retrospect now, I know what happened. Then, I remember somebody saying, 'His eyes are fluttering. Okay, buddy. Come on. Get up. We got somebody else to put on there.' So, in effect, it was somebody saved my life because I just had gone as far as I could. The next thing I know, I found myself on that push cart.

Liberation at Bad Orb

That's when I was put into Stalag IX-B in Bad Orb and I stayed there for maybe five, six days. Now, you can see [flashes] at nighttime, the lines were getting close. The Americans were coming, or somebody was coming. [And sure enough], it was the American tanks. I don't know what outfit it was or anything like that, but we had woken up in the morning and somebody said, 'The guards are gone.'[16] They had jumped on bicycles, I understand; I didn't see. They took off out the back gate. The front gate was locked, but that didn't bother the tank. The tank didn't turn around and check or nothing. Just rolled right over them. I suppose they broke off into the groups, but the tank that came through, whoever it was, had cans of C-rations. They must have encountered other prison camps

---

[16] *I don't know what outfit it was-* On April 2, 1945, an American task force from the 44th Infantry Division broke through German defenses and went nearly 40 miles to Bad Orb, and liberated Stalag IX-B. Source: 44th Infantry Division History. 2010. Bad Orb was notorious for prisoner of war slave labor.

and saw how these guys were not fed, and we scrambled over, everybody did, like an animal just to get a can because they just threw them off the tanks. They went right through, [they did not stop]. Of course, they were on the attack, I suppose. They're not going to stop because there were other troops behind.

The Spoon

But I got this can, and I had me a wooden spoon. That's another story. I traded a slice of bread for a [wooden knife], which is a hard thing when you have the bread [in hand], but I was finding myself wolfing the slice of bread down. You take one bite, and then you take two, before you get your hand away [and it's gone]. So, I figured if I could get a knife, I can cut little small pieces [to ration myself], and I traded some bread for that with some, I think they were Polish guys who were also captured, they were on the other side of a fence. I traded the bread for the knife, and with that, I made a spoon. I know with the spoon, one time they opened the boxcars and the German guards went up on top and they had soup, big buckets of soup. What are you going to put it into? Dishes? No, but you got your helmet. But you had to also use that helmet when you had diarrhea. So, what could you do?

So, I got some soup. I scooped it up [with the helmet]. Watched everybody else, I wasn't the only one with that brilliant idea, but you had your soup. And I had that spoon.

You get flashbacks once in a while of the things like that. I know I can't [stand to see] my grandchildren [waste food]. My granddaughter will take the bread, she eats the insides [of the slice] and she leaves all the crust, as all children do in America, anyway. My wife cooks the meal, I clear off the table, but I can't throw that bread away. I will leave it for the birds or something like that, but I just [can't throw it away]. [After the war], I wasn't so wasteful anymore. I remember as a child, my mother and father would say, at that time there was a war and the Chinese and Japanese were fighting. She says, 'There's some child starving over there in China. Finish your spinach.' Everybody goes through that, but when you have a follow-up with it like me where you're actually deprived as a young adult, we don't waste food—just don't waste anything and that's the main thing.

[At the end] with the spoon, I took about two mouthfuls of that C-ration [the tankers gave us]—and it went right down and came right back up again. I remember vomiting, regurgitating. I was just to the point where I couldn't get up, I was on the floor, just weak.

When the [medical personnel] came, they put me right in the ambulance. I got flown to England. I stayed there for fifty-four days.

*

[I returned home sometime] in May, I think. I was taken right into Halloran Hospital in Staten Island. We came home on a plane, landed, I went right to the hospital. I later found out that only the worst cases came back that way. I stayed there. They try to fatten you up, so to speak. That was pretty good. By that time, I was in half decent shape, I got up to around 110 pounds. You had unlimited privileges for the kitchen; you could go into the kitchen and eat [anything]. You had a different kind of chart. They didn't care what you ate, so that's why I'm here to talk about it. That's the best part of it. So, after a while, we got a pass to go home. That's about the gist of it, anyway.

*

[I keep in touch with some of the guys]. One or two of the fellows have been back there a number of times; we [had liberated] a town called Le Muy in Southern France and they were treated royally by the French people. They put up a plaque in the town square. I have a picture of it at home. They made copies and sent it to all the fellows. The 550th has met each year for fifty-two years, I think it is, and one fellow has gone to every meeting. There's another fellow running neck and neck with him. He's just missed one meeting.

They met in New York for a number of years before I realized they were doing that. When they were coming to New York, it was in the early 1950s and it was very reasonable, but now they can't afford New York. So, we go to the smaller cities. We've been to Chicago, Cincinnati, I've been in Kentucky. The rates are better and there's a lot of things to see. So, we've gone to a number of places repeatedly, but the fact is that we're still meeting, and you can see, as my wife says, the lean, mean, fighting machine is getting kind of corpulent. [*Laughs*]

Roe Catalano passed away at the age of 94 in April, 2020.

CHAPTER NINE

The Survivor

Fred Dennin was midway through his undergraduate studies in upstate New York when he was called up for service with the 106th Infantry Division. Keen and alert at age 79 when this interview was conducted in 2002, he gestures and tells his story in a confident, flowing manner that has obviously carried him throughout his whole life. His combat days were short; he was literally captured on the first day of the Battle of the Bulge, but not without warning his commanders first of his simple observations.

"*I did talk another soldier into going outside a [captured pillbox that we were occupying], digging two foxholes, right on the road—the German lines were right down that road—and taking a bazooka. I figured that if they did choose to come up that road, we were in a better position to do some damage.*

Remember the rest of them are in the pillbox, this fellow and I are out in a foxhole out in front; we dug it. And I heard and heeded to all sorts of motorized activity that went on into the night, trucks, just about everything that was making an awful noise and an awful racket down that road. And I reported it... The battalion commander I knew came and interviewed me, along with the company commander. I dealt with the regimental commander later. I told them most explicitly what I'd heard. They were cynical about it. They said, 'Are you sure you weren't hearing recordings?'

I said, 'My opinion is that I was not,' that this was something that I truly had heard. I remember one of them asked me if I was neurotic and I'm not, I wasn't. Along with [me reporting it], a Belgian nurse had also come through that area and seen the build-up and reported it. And it was largely ignored. It was ignored, it was ignored...."

Fred Dennin's war was far from over.

Frederick S. Dennin

I was born on June 25, 1923, in Canton, New York, St. Lawrence County. I grew up in Lake Placid. I attended Lake Placid High School. I graduated from there in 1941. I had two years of college at St. Lawrence University in Canton from '41 to '43, prior to my entry into the military service.

[Pearl Harbor] was a Sunday afternoon, and it was right after I got out of high school and had started college. I was at my grandmother's house, I was born in that home, and I stayed there during my tenure. I did belong to a fraternity, but that's where I stayed. And it was a Sunday afternoon and I was just resting in the house at that time when that news came on. I knew it was momentous, I knew it necessarily [would have] an effect on my life. I listened to everything, I listened to the President and his speech, and I went to the fraternity house I belong to and we talked about it there, and we just knew it would have a significant impact. To what extent and how far it would go it was rather hard to envision at that time.

I enlisted at an Enlisted Reserve Corps that dealt gently with people in my category who were in college. That meant that the Army was free to call us up at any time. But until they did, we were free to continue with our studies. I actually finished that year and my second year, which would have been my sophomore year at St. Lawrence, and I was then called up into the infantry. And I reported, along with others in my similar category, to Fort Niagara and we were issued infantry gear and what-have-you, and we were then shipped during the summer of '43 to Fort McClellan, Alabama, for 13 weeks of basic training. My comment on Fort McClellan was that it was very well done. It was summer in Alabama, the cadre were professionals, the officers were professional; it was arduous but I'm glad I had it.

Infantry basic training was tough; a friend of mine from my class [was there who] attended the same time, and both of us said that after that, it made military life and what followed from it relatively easier than it certainly would have been without it. I think I was fortunate to get the full basic training at that time. Some went in later, when I was in prison camp, that did not have the benefit of that, and they were also younger than I.

So [reflecting on] that summer, I can't say I liked it, but I respected what they were doing. I remember some interesting episodes; there was some German prisoners of war at Fort McClellan at that time, who were from the Africa Korps. We were starting out the training close-order drill, rifle bayonet drill. These Germans were very elite soldiers, I'm sure of that; they were the Africa Korps. They were blond, husky, and they were really laughing at us as we're out there doing it; they looked very healthy, and you could see that they were elite soldiers, certainly compared to what I saw later. I concluded the basic training at Fort McClellan, and at that point, we took tests and what-have-you, and they put me and most of the others there who had been in college in what they called the Army Specialized Training Program, which was essentially a continuation of college.

I was, along with many others from there, sent to Auburn University, which is also in Alabama, not too far from Birmingham. Fine college, we were given really soft living compared to what we had been doing. We took over what had been a girls' dormitory that would have been two in each room; there were four of us. But the food was good, the teachers were high quality. I was strong on academics anyway; the other side of the coin is that we knew we were going to be shipped off soon and we were having a good time, more than you normally would have, because we pretty well knew that was down the road. But I did have some teachers there, during that winter, that I held in high regard.

Shipping Out

Probably in May, we were all shipped out, and many of us, including myself, were sent to Indiana and were made part of the 106th Infantry Division, which was at Camp Atterbury about 30 miles from Indianapolis. They had retained the cadre and the officers, but they had shipped out as replacements, all of the privates and PFCs, and we were all privates at that time. So we, in effect, filled up the ranks of the privates and PFCs, and took over the cadre that were there beforehand. They were fine, but they were not the same level as at Fort McClellan, Alabama, which was that training center. We had long hikes and we got into Indianapolis and we were waiting to be shipped out. The summer went fairly fast; it wasn't that tough after the basic training.

In the fall, probably in October, we were shipped out; we were shipped to Boston for transport overseas. We crossed on the *Queen Elizabeth*, as a matter of fact, which held I think as many as 15,000 troops going over. Other than being crowded, we whiled away our time shooting craps or eating lousy food.

[We did not go in a convoy]; we relied on the speed of the *Queen Elizabeth*; I remember thinking of that. We asked about it, and the theory was that the ship was so fast, that it could change directions from time to time. The thought did cross my mind if a German submarine was looking for a target that would have been a fruitful target, that would have been an ideal one to hit. But one, I didn't have a choice about it, and two, I had to think they weren't going to risk not just the ship, but 15,000 replacements plus the whole crew, unless they were reasonably sure, very sure, that it was going to make the crossing. But we had no convoy, no protection or anything on the way across. And I think the ship did it many other times and thank God for myself and others had always made it.

Anyway, we landed in Scotland, which was Edinburgh. We took a train down to sort of, it was near Stratford-upon-Avon, what did they call it, Sandywell Park, which was a training ground so to speak. This was the fall of 1944. Again, the weather was typical English weather, but we were having a good time. We could go to town, we'd go to these English huge dances, and we stayed there until about the end of November, and then we shipped across the Channel. And I believe we landed at Le Havre, which was flattened, it had been I think flattened by our own forces primarily at or around the invasion of Normandy at that time. I went over in a British private sailboat really, and this Channel crossing was remarkably rough for the short one; it was sort of a sailboat, had to have a motor on it too, the one I was on, anyway. It was the only time I got seasick in any traversing of that area. But it was a very rough crossing and I think that was fairly typical of the Channel at that time.

The Suicide

Anyway, we landed at Le Havre, I think on the 2nd of December. We were there a short while, and one experience there had an effect on me. We would play football like we did some at Atterbury, and it was fairly rough. And a fellow that I knew, although not well, was very artistically inclined, he would play a violin. But [while we were waiting], his temperament or modes seem to get messed up, he was not himself; I didn't understand it. And they would have us do guard duty. I don't believe there were any Germans near that area because we had to travel quite a while before we pulled into the Siegfried Line, and this was one of the first rough experiences that I somewhat encountered. I was doing this guard duty [with him] and it was at night. I noticed the fellow, and I thought he was cleaning his M1 rifle, but the M1 rifle was sort of pointed in a way... we'd all cleaned M1 rifles and gone through all that in basic. Instead, he put the rifle in his mouth and shot himself at the point when I was right beside him, or very, very close to him. And that was somewhat—that's, oh boy, this is really bothering some people even before we've really gotten into an area where you would expect it to.

Now it was in December, they loaded us in two-and-a-half-ton trucks and we moved across France and Belgium, and probably Luxembourg, through St. Vith. St. Vith is the last community we were in and I've been back to it since the war. But then we crossed into Germany at that point and we were to occupy positions in the Siegfried Line, which were [captured] pillboxes. Pillboxes may be a misnomer, they were really large, rather comfortable quarters with bunks and that type of thing in it. And this story is interesting because you know, my combat experience wasn't that long, those quarters were occupied by a veteran, I believe it was an armored division, a New York division, that had seen all sorts of combat. The pillboxes had sort of a long entrance into them, and they look very awesome to me and I said, 'How did you people capture these things?'

He said it was very simple.

I said, 'Well, please tell me.'

He said, 'We put a bangalore torpedo into the entrance, blew it up, and that's all there was to it.'

Now the pillbox that I was in with probably 15 to 20 other people was as far as you could get in the German lines. There was a road, it was a forested area in the Ardennes. There was a road that descended down, and the German lines were down there. We were clearly advised that this was going to be a very quiet sector and outposts were strung way out. The division of course had three regiments. I had been into the 423rd, shortly I'd been a scout, I'd been a BAR man, that's a Browning Automatic Rifle, and at the last minute, they shifted me to the 422nd where I was in a headquarters company, mortar, and the only side arm you have is a .45 at that.

And at that point, it got very cold, and that soldier's story about how they occupied and destroyed those pillboxes stuck in my mind. I thought, 'I'm not so sure it's the smartest thing to be inside that pillbox.' So I did talk another soldier into going outside, digging two foxholes, right on the road—the German lines were right down that road—and taking a bazooka. I don't know if we had one or two, figuring that if they did choose to come up that road, we were in a better position to do some damage.

'An Awful Racket'

What follows now is recorded in a book, I believe, which was *The Last Hundred Days.* This was the prelude to the Bulge. Remember the rest of them are in the pillbox, this fellow and I are out in a foxhole out in front; we dug it. And I heard and heeded to all sorts of motorized activity that went on into the night, trucks, just about everything that was making an awful noise and an awful racket down that road. And I reported it, and this was reported in an account of mistakes that were made in effect and not picking up this intelligence. The battalion commander I knew came and interviewed me, along with the company commander. I'm not sure the regimental commander came or not, but I dealt with him later; Colonel Devereux happened to be his name, who was the regimental commander.

I told them most explicitly what I'd heard. They were cynical about it, they said, 'Are you sure you weren't hearing recordings?'

I said, 'My opinion is that I was not,' that this was something that I truly had heard. I remember one of them asked me if I was neurotic and I'm not, I wasn't.

I said, 'I'm not neurotic!' I think I said, 'I'm probably the least neurotic of most privates in this Army!' Along with [me reporting it], a Belgian nurse had also come through that area and seen the build-up and reported it. And it was largely ignored. It was ignored, it was ignored....

Tiger Tanks

So we stayed there a few more days, then in the meantime, the Germans had cut through, and we were isolated in that position. So we then left the pillbox and sort of meandered around and it was really cold, it was at the Ardennes and [remember, it was mid-December]. All I had was the regular leather shoes, which were terrible, and I almost lost my toes, but I'll get into that later on; it was a night or two out there. Then the colonel got the regiment together, and it was a wooded high area, and he said, 'Now we're going to form a skirmish line.'

I looked at everyone that was there. We had no artillery, it was terribly overcast, there was no air cover. And now, we're going to move through these woods in a direction he set forth, and obviously the enemy is out there somewhere. And we did, and remember, at that time all I had was the sidearm, the .45, the pistol.

We went quite a ways and it was a full regiment to start with. I went with another individual specifically to a point where the woods stopped and there was a plain, an open field like a hill, but it was a grass field that went down to a road. And the road sort of wound around the promontory of the wooded area that we were on; there weren't many of us that had come that far. But at the foot of the hill where the road was, all of a sudden it was lined with Tiger tanks. I heard later that they got screwed up in the German transportation system, which was messed up, and they happened to be coming through. But there were lots of them, and they all had 88s on them and they all started shelling that particular point I was in, right at that point.

Wounded and Captured

My companion, I think, was killed; I was struck in the upper thigh with shrapnel, I was almost what I call an 'involuntary celibate by the sake of one inch' at that point. And you don't know how bad you're hurt, you're just bleeding. Then the Germans did... that was a fairly long hill, one lone soldier came up with a pistol. He was a kid and he wore one of... this is the first, I've seen a couple of dead Germans back where we were wandering around, but he had what they call a pistol. I don't think he was over 16 years of age. I was wounded and he was coming up to get whoever was in there out at that point. So he was taking some risk but there were very few of our soldiers there; the fellow beside me I believe was dead. So I did go out with my hands up at that point. [*Raises arms in the air*] He was stabbing me with the pistol and motioning what he wanted me to do, which was to go back in the woods, because they were still shelling the woods.

I looked at him and I looked at the woods and I managed to get back in there. And then I dragged myself up about another 50 yards and another

German soldier was coming up, an older one. And I limped out, surrendering to him, and he was great to me. We carried these sulfa packs with us, he treated the wounds, at that time at least with the sulfa, and helped me get down to the foot of the hill. Now at that point, I was put in a barn with other wounded people, many of whom were very seriously wounded, many of whom died that night. It was bitter cold there and I'm not really blaming the Germans, I think it's probably all they had. And my own experience with the German military, I think I was more fortunate to deal with them in that they did not treat me [as poorly as I could have been treated, had I been captured by] civilians. I could say something different, and perhaps I will, but they were all right with us.

Then next day, they marched us out, and my feet were terribly frozen. But they marched us to a hospital train, we that were wounded and still living, and we were put on the hospital train with German wounded, German nurses, German doctors, and we were treated there just the same as they were. My feet had turned black and they had to cut the boots and they were all black; the big toe, especially, was split. They talked of some amputation—I didn't want it done and they went along with [my wishes]. It worked out because I did save my feet, and I really had nothing special in the way of a foot problem. That really was a blessing to me, in many ways, because even though I was wounded, I did not have to walk out of that area. And with the foot problems I'd had, that would have been exceedingly difficult because it was brutally cold, and the ones that did do that took long walks.

*

They let me off at a prisoner of war camp on Christmas Eve, which was I believe near Hamburg. I was in two prisoner of war camps, XI-B and II-A, and I think this one was II-A. It was a huge one, there were some Russian prisoners there, whose lot was terrible. We were put generally with American prisoners. There were displaced people; we oddly enough got in there Christmas Eve, in a mess, although my trip in the hospital was not that bad, and they actually gave us a piece of steak that night, it being Christmas Eve, which surprised me.

I stayed there until early in January, it was a huge motley place, cold but you're in bunks; the food was terrible, but they didn't have that much themselves. Then around the 10th of January, when it was bitter cold, they shipped us out, and this is an interesting story here.

Strafed

We were loaded into freight cars. They were unheated, the door was then latched. There were no sanitary facilities; they gave us a loaf of bread and I believe a little water. They then locked the door. It was January '45 and history tells me that it was one of the coldest Januarys they'd ever had. It took us probably five days to complete that route. The sanitary conditions [were horrible], the food was terrible, there was just straw in there. And at one point, and this is quite interesting, the whole train was stopped and we were lying or trying to sit against the wall, and we were strafed then by one of our own aircraft; I believe it was a P47, which carries 8 .50 caliber machine guns, which were almost like eight cannons. It's interesting, the first strafing pass he took, we did not hear the plane, but the machine guns went off like eight cannons, and then he made two or three more passes. He did not hit our car, he hit cars further down, where there were all sorts of casualties. Then at last, the strafing stopped. The Germans then did open a door and gave us some water and pointed to what they said was a shot down aircraft over in a field alongside of it. It was somewhat surprising, but it was possible. It's hard for me to tell what type of anti-aircraft activity they had there, but the strafing did stop, it was very scary. Then you could hear the plane come down when it was going through [the strafing run], whether [the train was marked or not], well, those things happened in that time.

Anyway, the people I was in [that boxcar] with, we were okay. Then we came to a city and it was Rostock. Rostock was in East Germany, up near the Baltic Sea, it was. And at Rostock, we were unloaded from the boxcar for the first time and we walked through the streets of Rostock. We were a very sorry-looking outfit at that time. The civilians, they jeered at us and yelled at us and screamed at us and what-have-you, but they did not molest us physically at that time. We then walked to a prison camp, which again was a large one. The food was little or nothing, but we did get, if we were fortunate, some Red Cross parcels. One of the problems was the Germans didn't have any food at this particular point, and I believe the deal was made by the American government that through the auspices of the Red Cross, they would agree that these Red Cross parcels would be delivered; in theory, you were to get one a week. You wouldn't get one a week, but they were a lifesaver.

And as an interesting side note, I had never smoked before then and never had since, but they would send five packs of cigarettes, Camel cigarettes, and I would trade those for food. Invariably later on I saw a person starve himself to death almost to get those cigarettes. I wasn't in this place too long. Where I was with Americans, although I ran into some British prisoners, who had been prisoners almost since the start of the war, when conditions were far worse, I think much worse. I tended to admire them; they were very independent, self-reliant. They would never bother your goods or anything, and you better not touch theirs.

The most recent recruits [fellow prisoners] were the ones that came in with the recent replacements; they were only 18 or so of that time. Remember, I was only 21, but 21 was a little older than an 18-year-old, and I was going on 22. I'd had the advantage of more time and that really excellent basic training [than they had had].

The Estate

I was there a good deal of January and then a surprising thing happened. I was picked out, or my number was drawn for some reason or other, because they could work privates and PFCs; noncoms weren't supposed to work. And there was a small work group between Rostock and Stettin, they were both on the Baltic Sea, which was on the estate of a German, call him a squire, call him a baron, he also was high up in the Gestapo at that point. And he maintained this beautiful estate where the deer ran free, and it was beautifully forested, and this work group of probably 25 to 30 people worked those grounds for him. When I first got there, now you would go out with a crew, there was an old German sergeant named Braun, who had once spent time in the United States, who had been on the Russian front, and we all loved him. He knew it was coming to an end; he spoke pretty good English.

But we worked under civilian overseers and they were rough. We would plant trees, you'd get in a line and you go so far and you'd plant a tree and then go on, and we called this German, he was a Prussian, and they were tough people up in that agricultural area. And I know we called him [a nickname] because it reminded us of the train that some of the prisoners who had been there longer than I [had taken]. Remember, I was only picked out to fill the place of one person who had died, and they wanted to fill that group. I actually had a German guard take me on a German train to that site and walk with me to that particular small camp that night. And another interesting coincidence, in that small group, was a fellow named Joe Shuba who oddly enough had gone to St. Lawrence with me before the war. We had never met at St. Lawrence, he was one year ahead of me there, but we became quite friendly there and we probably had more college and more education than the [other prisoners] that they had filling that area. I got a bad back injury there because they had us planting his trees and I'd fallen off a two-and-a-half-ton truck, catching my foot on the gate; it acted up terribly. But fortunately it recovered enough so that I even went back, they put me back to work.

Now about this time it was approaching spring, it would have been in April, probably quite early in April, and we were not far from Stettin. We were hearing the Russian artillery. And one thing I remember so well, it was as though my ordeal was going to come to an end. The weather turned nice all of a sudden and I always remember we were not working one day, and we came back with Braun escorting us, and this young schoolgirl came along, was probably eight or nine years old, and she said, 'Heil Hitler!' Poor old Braun just ignored her completely.

So again there was a lot of barter going on, and I became the person who did a lot of the bartering with the French [prisoners] who were near us because of my high school French; their English was very poor. And I remember doing most of the trading and what-have-you at that time, especially in all of these Red Cross parcels. They would give you a can of powdered milk, and I always felt the powdered milk [was a good item to have] probably, so I was always trading cigarettes for these cans of powdered milk. And then I picked up the name the 'Sweet Milk Kid.'

The Gauleiter

Now, one other fascinating thing that happened there. One time the guards—we had some officer guards, but it was always Braun who walked us out—they said the gauleiter, or the squire, whoever was in charge, would like to see me. And of course, we were always told you only tell your name, rank, and serial number, and everyone said, 'Oh you shouldn't go there!' So, I don't know anything. And perhaps I was curious, and I thought, I have no information of an intelligence area that could possibly serve them, so I'll go. And I was escorted to this really palatial manor. He was educated and smooth and spoke perfect English, offered me a cup of tea, which I took.

He thought I was of German nationality. My name was Frederick, and at that point, the short haircut I'd had had not worn off. And he really was inquiring why I was over here fighting [against] the Fatherland, trying to get a feel on that type of thing. I did indicate to him that especially that the course that their leader was taking, Adolf Hitler, [was bad], and I'd seen this and his treatment of all sorts of minorities, especially the Jewish people, which I had personally seen, was something that the civilized world could not endure. And therefore, I felt that it was an evil that was part of my responsibility to be involved in [combatting]. He took no offense at that. It's just surprising, and he thanked me very much, had me escorted back to my quarters. I heard that after when the Russians were in that area, that they had executed him. I'm not sure that was so.

On The Move

Anyway, there came a time in April, when it was a beautiful day and the guns [could be heard], that Braun and another one or two, said, 'Why don't we all head westward; [the western Allies'] lines are that way,' and the Germans especially would much rather be captured by the [western] Allied forces than the Russians and for good reason, as I'll tell you later. So I always remember it was a bright sunny day and we started out and we're headed westward, and I took out a cigarette and smoked it and they all couldn't believe it. I didn't inhale, I never did, but they all couldn't believe I was smoking that cigarette. Well, we walked for most of that day and we came to the Oder River and the port was Peenemunde; the story gets very interesting now. At Peenemunde, there was the rocket base where the German V-2 rocket was developed. So we got down to the river, which was not too far from the estuary going out into the sea, and there was one small ferry boat taking everyone across and you had displaced persons in their striped uniforms all over, you had German military women in uniforms changing to get out of the uniforms, they were all deathly fearful of the Russians.

As we waited to see if we'd ever get across, on the other side of the river, a whole phalanx of American two-and-a-half-ton trucks came tearing up. And we thought it was our forces at first sight, on that side, but it wasn't, it was the Russian forces under Rokossovsky, I believe it was. And they all had machine guns on the back, and they were shooting and killing. We were with some French prisoners at that time, they were staying in that area and they invited us to come back while all this mayhem was going on and stay with them, which would be a rather secure place. Again, there were probably 25 of us, the same group that had left that area, and we did go back there, and we stayed there that night.

The following morning, it might have been the second morning, Shuba and I ventured outside. It was quiet, and then we walked, and very shortly we came to the headquarters at Peenemunde, the offices where the paperwork was done for this rocket base. There was no one there, no one there. We actually went inside, and papers were thrown all over and destroyed and as though they were trying to do something; whether the Russians had actually gone quite that far or what, [we did not know]—there was no one there. We left and then we came to, it had to be a dam, which went out into the Oder River right near where it went into the sea. And out on that were a whole flock of bicycles that had just been left there. My friend went out first, he thought maybe we would get a bicycle or something, then all of a sudden a Russian did appear, a few hundred yards away, and fired at him—and may have fired at me. He said he heard the trajectory go right over his head. Well, we made a quick exit from there!

We went back to the place where we were, and we tried to talk the rest of them into going back and getting these bicycles the next day. And then cycling as a group westward—assuming we could get across the river—but they didn't want to do it, except one other guy; Shuba later said that one went with us— my memory is fuzzy, it was always my recollection of Shuba and I [alone] during these next few days together. And I remember Shuba [telling them], 'If you stay here, the Russians are going to have you burying dead horses!' He ran into one later and that's exactly what they did have him doing.

Anyway, we did go out and the bicycles were still there, and we got the bicycles. We bicycled back to that spot where we were going to take the ferry over. The Russians, at that point, were on both sides; they were mostly Tartars and Mongols, you'll read of Rokossovsky's army in northeastern Germany being sent there almost purposefully to treat the Germans very, very rigorously, and they did. They were pretty good to us, either they had our equipment or, as an 'Americanski,' you got as good treatment as anything. Anyway, the long and short of it is that we got across on a small ferry, the Russians were there, we started traveling on the bikes along the road westward where we understood our lines were. We did see atrocities. I ran into German military who were just run over by tanks purposely, I saw several instances of rape along the side of the road. We would come to a German farmhouse, and when they saw we were Americans, they would beg us to stay over, because if we were around, they knew the Russians would not bother them, but otherwise they were in a terrible situation. I'm sure there were parts of Russia [where the Germans had treated those people the same way], but it was a terrible thing to see.

With the Russian army, they'd go into a pub or a place there and they bring out the liquor, they were always drinking; we drank some too, and we ate more than we'd ever eaten before. We then seemed to lose the Russians, we were in sort of a no-man's area, headed toward the Allied lines, heading towards Lübeck. And so we're bicycling into the German town, from the east, and the mayor comes out in a high black hat, and all of the townspeople, they're cheering us, they thought they were American Army coming in, you know, they were going to be liberated, because we still had our uniforms on, although I did not have a helmet on. Well, we disillusioned them rather rapidly and went on; later, I think we did have drinks and food with some Russians who were sacking that town at a pub somewhere.

Lübeck was intended to be in the Russian zone under, I believe it was the Potsdam Agreement, but it was occupied by a British unit of the First Army who had gone further than they were supposed to have gone. We suddenly came to where the Russian road ended, and it was British from that point on. The Russians were allowing no one across that zone, however, they did allow us across, being Americans. We went to Lübeck; Lübeck had been in German hands until very recently. A German sniper had just been holed out up in the tower and had killed several Allied soldiers, and I was there when they executed the sniper. War's tough.

Going Home

Meanwhile we were eating the British mess kits, and what-have-you, and I suddenly—fortunately, it didn't happen earlier—I got terribly sick to my stomach. It was just the sudden food, and that's where I lost Shuba, because I was terribly sick, but I was very fortunate in that they put me in a military hospital. The treatment was lining your stomach with chalk, feeding you reasonably well, and I was in with prisoners who were wounded and in far worse condition than I was. I only stayed there a day or two and then they flew me back to Brussels in one of those cargo planes. We were put up in wonderful quarters in Brussels, which had been occupied by German officers before. We were given $20 a day to be applied toward back pay—they gave me all my back pay, it wasn't much, I was only a private, but it seemed like quite a bit at that time. Brussels was a lovely, wonderful city to be in and it was in May, it was well into May by that time, it must have been close to June; I got in Lübeck around VE Day. I stayed in Brussels probably 10 days or so, and then they took us over to London, and we were given a place in London to stay and I ran into some of my initial comrades from both at Auburn and in Fort McClellan, Alabama. Two of them in particular I remember; we were invited out to an English country estate; they were just as interested in meeting us and I admire the British people very much. That was a fascinating experience, there were many Canadian soldiers there that weekend. And you could see the changes in the government coming; the Labour Party was about to win the election, there was some strong feelings about the American Navy and their Navy and which one was superior, and I probably said I think we probably have the more powerful Navy out there at that time. From there we went back to London, they shipped us back to the States, including a couple of guys that I had known way back, just by coincidence, and we shipped back on one of those Liberty ships, but because the war was over in Europe we took the gun crews' quarters and again the food was excellent, the trip across was uneventful. We landed in New York at night; we bar-hopped and what-have-you, and reminisced that night.

An interesting finale to the story is, I was then given a 90-day furlough, all prisoners of war at that point were given a 90-day furlough. I happened to live in Lake Placid, this was around the 1st of July, it was right before the 4th, as I recall. So I was ordered to report to Lake Placid at the end of the 90 days because they maintained a rehab center up there where the soldiers that had had the 90-day furloughs, who oftentimes were prisoners of war but not necessarily or severely wounded, would then report for whatever their destiny was to be from that point on. So that summer I was at my home, I got back a little later than some of the others, so many of the buddies that I knew were coming through Lake Placid at that facility at that time. And we got to renew acquaintances again; it was a ball, so to speak. The word was that we were planning on being shipped west then for the invasion of Japan. During that course of my summer there, we dropped the atom bomb on Hiroshima and then Nagasaki. I remember discussing it with a rather learned man who was staying in my father's house, and he really saw the consequences of what this was going to be. But I recall my immediate reaction was, as horrible as it is, it's going to end the war, which it did. And the invasion of Japan was, even I knew at that point, it was not going to be a picnic, and I've since ascertained from my study of history that they had envisioned tremendous casualties if they hadn't gone that route. Be that as it is, it was a wonderful summer. I was very fortunate to have met my wife that summer who was working up there at that time and staying at my own house. And at the fall they give you points that enabled you to get out; I was, I think, five points shy because my length of service wasn't quite enough, so they sent me up to Pine Camp for a month, at which time I would have the points at that point. When the war was over, they shut down the rehab center at Lake Placid just about the time that I went through it, and I came back. My future wife Helen and I were engaged at that time, though she had moved back to Rome. And at that point, I entered directly into law school under the GI Bill and the rest of it is different history. That's about it.

The GI Bill was very generous to me, I was able to get through law school in two years' time, because we went the summer. Remember, I'd had two years of college before the war. My academics were strong, and I took graduate work at NYU in tax law, and I had some wonderful teachers in tax law on that. And I tried that for a year and then we were married while I was in law school. I then returned to Lake Placid to practice law with an older lawyer who was sort of a gentleman's lawyer, who didn't have much practice. We had two kids, no car, I was on a $25 a week drawing account for a period of time and I owed him $1,000, and then everything turned good, at least as far as my career and everything else. I had a good law career, I had a good business career, and I was very blessed from every point of view and in many ways consider the war a rewarding experience for me.

A Survivor

I tended to feel that I was a survivor and I think the lessons I learned there—I also learned some foolishness there—but having said all that, I do think that the overall experience and the early years I had, and the training I had, and the life I had before, in sum total was a real positive thing. So I really felt that, in many ways, the Army did me a favor, but I also learned that I could survive in different [environments and circumstances]—but others had it infinitely worse than I did, don't get me wrong. I would much rather have been a prisoner in Germany than Japan, by far. But having said that, it was no picnic. And actually the ones that stayed in that prison camp, Stalag XI-B—remember, I said I was pulled out [to work on that estate]—they pulled everyone out and made them walk westward in the winter, and they had a tough one.

I always felt that my experience [in World War II] was positive, and I always felt very fortunate that I got out of it as well as I did, and the GI Bill was very helpful to me. I've also paid the government back a lot in taxes for sending me there, so I have paid for it. Significantly. [*Laughs*]

Fred Dennin died in June 2013 at the age of 89.

CHAPTER TEN

The Escapee

He sits comfortably in a leather chair at an armory in New York City. A native New Yorker, Martin Sylvester tells his story matter-of-factly, of his survival as a teenager from Brooklyn being thrown into the horrific battle of the Hürtgen Forest, of being a witness to the first onslaught of the Battle of the Bulge, and of being taken prisoner and escaping no less than three times, though a leg wound made movement painful. A retired psychotherapist, he does not put much stock in hyper-analyzing his own formative experiences; like many veterans, he was glad for the experience on some levels, but had no desire to repeat it.

He sat for this interview in January 2001. "*I know we're dying out very quickly, the rate of 1500 a day, I understand.*" At the time of this writing, we are swiftly approaching the day when there will be no World War II veterans left alive.

Martin was an eyewitness to a sight of terror in the early morning of December 16, 1944.

"It was my time for outpost duty on top of this hill where we overlooked the Germans, we had a little dugout up there. And there were three of us assigned to take turns. I think they were four-hour shifts that we would watch with glasses, binoculars, to see what the Germans were doing.

'Red, come here quick, come here quick. Take a look at this!' This was dawn. It was very cloudy.

I took a look. Thousands and thousands of Germans were coming across this river! They must have put in bridges, floating bridges, overnight. They were coming across in tanks. They were coming across on foot. And they were just flooding! We had a telephone to call down, and at the same time, we're hearing rifle fire. They told us, the exact words were, 'We're up to our ass in Krauts down here!', and our guys were getting hit all over the place. They said, 'You better get out of there while you can! And don't come down here! Get going!"

Martin Sylvester

I was born in Brooklyn and I grew up in Brooklyn and Manhattan. So I've lived in New York City all of my life, except the two years that I went to graduate school in Tallahassee, Florida, Florida State University. So other than that, I've been in New York and I'm a New Yorker.

When I graduated high school, I was about 17. I spent one semester at Brooklyn College. And then I turned 18 and two months later, I was drafted. I was for a short time in what they call the Army Specialized Training Program, the ASTP. I had taken the intelligence test and I guess I qualified for that. But that was a short stay. I think it was two or three months; they ended the program. And we went into the infantry and I went into basic training in Alabama, I think it was Fort McClellan. I'm not sure. But it was infantry basic. I think it was eight weeks or twelve weeks, and then we were shipped to England. I came in as a replacement in England, and it was in England that I joined the 4th Infantry Division. I know the 4th Infantry landed on Utah Beach on D-Day. I went in later, from England; we boarded the LSTs and we did land on the beach. We waded through the surf to get to the beach. And we walked up a path going alongside the bunkers. And then we went in through France;

I remember we fought in France. I remember hedgerows, but the thing I remember mostly through France was the dead animals, bloated and lying in the fields. And I did see dead Germans. The dead Americans, they seemed to evacuate pretty fast. The Germans stayed there a little longer.

[When we got to Europe and were sent to 4th Infantry Division as replacements], we were welcomed by the other soldiers, they were very nice, very good to us. [I thought we had had good training], I mean, I knew the rifle very well, I knew the equipment that I had. When I picked up the BAR, I knew exactly how to use it and what it did. I thought I was very well prepared. What I was not prepared for was how to avoid getting killed. And the guys really helped with that. They showed us how to maneuver through the woods. They showed us how to maneuver through a field. And we very quickly learned the sound of an 88 shell, and very quickly learned the sound of a German machine gun, and American weapons. And then it was positive in that sense. The guys on the frontline were very helpful and very nice.

The Hürtgen Forest

The [combat] I remember most of was in the Hürtgen Forest. When we got to Hürtgen Forest, I had been in my company maybe a few months. And within a short time, I was, I think, the seventh senior person in the company. Everybody else was killed. The trees were there to offer you some cover, you would go from tree to tree, but you did learn that you were not very well protected. Even in a foxhole, you were not very well protected from tree blasts, mortars coming in, or even 88s when they hit a tree and you got a tree burst. There's not much you can do. I mean, some guys would dig the foxhole and put logs across the top, and slide under the logs.

Sometimes you'd see shadows moving around, and you'd just fire at the shadows. It was hard to hit them. In the forest, see, you can tell where the fire is coming from, but you couldn't see anybody really. Most of the time, you're just firing blind, you're just returning fire—you saw a blast of fire coming toward you, you just fired back the same spot. And the other thing you learned was not to stay in the same spot for more than one minute. You got to keep moving.

I remember the mortars and I remember the 88s. I remember the shrapnel, being in a shrapnel barrage where there were tree bursts coming down on us. And I remember that I was trying to claw myself into the ground and couldn't get in there fast enough. Pieces of shrapnel were landing on my back and they were hot. And I remember them tearing through my pant legs. I thought I was hit; I didn't know how bad. But when [the barrage] stopped, fortunately, there was just some hot iron on my back and I had some tears through my pant legs and my legs were bleeding, [but only from] surface wounds, cuts. But I remember that barrage; we lost a lot of men. Guys were screaming for medics and guys were lying dead all around at that time.

The Battle of the Bulge

Now I can tell you where I was at the Battle of the Bulge. The 4th Infantry Division, when we got out of the Hürtgen Forest, we went to a town for rest and rehabilitation, a town called Echternach, which was a resort town on the [Sûre River, which flows into the] Moselle River. And we were there because we were really in shatters. I mean, when we got there, they told us that we would be there for several weeks; they took most of our weapons. They gave us fresh clothing. They gave back pay. And we were in houses. We had showers! We had hot food, and we were supposed to be there for a few weeks.

Now, this was early in December. The Bulge, if you remember, began on December 16. We had an outpost on the top of the hill overlooking the other side of the river where the Germans were; everything had been quiet for months, except for an occasional shell back and forth, but there had been no fighting along that river, and that's why they sent us there.

So they had taken most of our weapons, we were very happy. It was my time for outpost duty on top of this hill where we overlooked the Germans, we had a little dugout up there. And there were three of us assigned to take turns. I think they were four-hour shifts that we would watch with glasses, binoculars, to see what the Germans were doing.

So I was up there December 16. And I woke, I remember it was just about dawn, and I was ready to take my shift. I opened a box of K rations. I remember I was just having a can of, I think it was bacon and cheese for breakfast. They always called me 'Red,' I don't know why.

'Red, come here quick, come here quick. Take a look at this!' This was dawn. It was very cloudy.

I took a look. Thousands and thousands of Germans were coming across this river! They must have put in bridges, floating bridges, overnight. They were coming across in tanks. They were coming across on foot. And they were just flooding! We had a telephone to call down, and at the same time, we're hearing rifle fire. They told us that, the exact words were, 'We're up to our ass in Krauts down here!', and our guys were getting hit all over the place. They said, 'You better get out of there while you can! And don't come down here! Get going!'

We started to do that. But then we saw some guys coming up towards us. Turned out they were Americans, and they were medics. And they had a stretcher and they were carrying a lieutenant who was wounded. And they brought him up and put him in our dugout, and so we asked if we could be of any help.

They said, 'No. You better get out of here!'

They went back to get some more of the wounded, and we took off. And from that point on, I mean, we were dodging Germans all the way through. Fortunately, we were on the [southern] edge of the Bulge.

We kept running into Germans and running away from Germans. And finally, I don't know how we did it. We got to Liège, Belgium. Our men were scattered all over the place. We couldn't find anybody who knew where we were supposed to be. So, we spent like three days in Liège, I went to see a movie in there, *Custer's Last Stand* in French with German subtitles. Finally, we found an officer who was gathering up men, because they were expecting a German attack at the edge of Liège in Belgium, so we joined them.

Now it was Christmas Eve, and I'll never forget this. Christmas Eve, we were in foxholes about fifty feet apart. There were hardly any of us, and we expected a major German attack at dawn. I didn't think we were going to make it, none of us thought we were going to make it. There was just not enough of us.

'We Just Cheered'

Anyway, at dawn, what we saw was one of the greatest fireworks displays I've ever seen in my life. I mean, the Americans were shelling the edge of a wooded area. We were in the edge of an opposite wooded area; there was a field, and then another wooded area. And the Germans were in that wooded area. They were going to come across the field at us.

Americans shelled the woods. It was a spectacular display of shelling. And then all of a sudden, it must've been thousands of Germans came running across this field toward us. So we started firing at the Germans, but we knew we were going to be overrun.

All of a sudden, from behind us, fresh American troops came running through us! It was the, we called them, the 'Bucket of Blood' Division. I think it was the Pennsylvania division, [the 28th Division, because of the shoulder badge].

The fresh troops, they came running through, and the Germans were just dropping like flies; whoever was standing went running right back to the woods. It was the greatest thing I ever saw! Then a lieutenant came by and he said, 'Okay. You guys, come on back. Come back. You can leave now.'

They were rounding us up. But we just stood there, and we cheered. I mean, we watched them, and we just cheered. And that was an incident I'll never forget.

I don't think [I've ever been that cold again in my life]. But actually, it's interesting that even though it was very cold, you get used to the cold. And those woolen blankets were a godsend, because even if the woolen blanket was wet, if you wrapped yourself in a woolen wet blanket, you were warm. And we were always in wet ground, always on wet ground. And then there was a lot of trench foot.

Captured

I remember the attack on the town where I got captured. I believe the name of the town was

Fouhren. At that time, I was a runner and so I stayed close to the lieutenant. I remember a lot of arguing about going into the town, which was at the bottom of a hill. We were on the top of the hill, and we were supposed to go down into the town. We were waiting for tanks to escort us.

There were three tanks. There was an argument between the tank commander and the lieutenant, and the tank commander insisted that the infantry go in before the tanks. The lieutenant was insisting the infantry go behind the tanks for protection, because we had to go down an open field to get to the town. I heard they were Patton's tanks, and they were saying that Patton believed that a tank was worth a hundred men. So he wanted the men to go in before the tanks. So they argued for a while. And finally, they were in touch by telephone with their commanders, and finally it was resolved that we would go in behind the tanks, but the tanks would not go into the town. The tanks would stop at the edge of town and then go back, because they didn't want to lose tanks.

So that's what happened. We went in behind the tanks. We went into town. There was no shelling in the town, which made us believe that the Germans were going to put up a fight, because usually if the Germans withdrew, they would shell us as we came into town. But because there was no shelling, we figured they were in there.

And sure enough, the Germans were in town, and we had to flush them out building by building, which we did; they retreated, and they took off. I was with the lieutenant and a sergeant, there were seven of us. We went to the furthest end of town and into a basement. And the lieutenant was going to set up his headquarters in the basement.

Wounded

That's about when I got another leg wound. There was one house where we threw in a couple of grenades and flushed out a whole bunch of Germans. One of them was an officer. And we all looked to capture officers because officers had the good stuff on them. I mean, they had the daggers, they have the Lugers, some of them had the medals. It was souvenirs [we were interested in].

Anyway, I had seen this officer come out with his hands up, so I ran over to him to grab him. And sure enough, I got a Luger from him. And a buddy of mine came running up, and he looked so unhappy because I got to this guy first, because the prized possession was a Luger, a German Luger. But what happened was I was searching this German officer and I found a diamond brooch in his pocket, which I lifted from him and I put in my pocket. This buddy of mine, I gave him the Luger, and he was thrilled with that. He didn't know that I had taken the brooch. I figured it was a good trade-off.

Then the lieutenant was hollering for me to catch up with him, because he was going towards this house at the end of town, [where he wanted to set up a command post]. So I started to run, and all of a sudden, I got hit. It felt like a rock had hit me in the leg, it knocked me off my feet, and it burned. I went down, I just felt the burning sensation in my ankle. [I thought it was] like a bullet had hit a rock and whacked it into my foot.

Anyway, I got to this place where they were going to establish the command post in the basement, and we set up headquarters there. There was seven of us, and there was a wood stove, I remember. And the lieutenant said, 'Let's make a fire and have something to eat and relax.'

And I got a little nervous, because this town had changed hands two or three times, and I said, 'Tim, shouldn't we be waiting for a counterattack?'

He says, 'No, you don't have to worry about that.' He said, 'Heavy weapons is coming in. They're going to set up a perimeter around the town. And then we don't expect another attack for at least a couple of hours. So you can relax and take it easy. And you don't have anything to worry about.'

And I looked down, and my leg was all bloody. He looked down at my leg and he looked at me, and he said it looked like a bullet had gone right through my ankle, which it did. It didn't hit a bone, but it went through. It was a flesh wound.

And so he said, 'Jeez! You better take care of that ankle.'

He no sooner said that when all of a sudden, we heard, 'Come out! Come out! Raus! Raus!'

We looked up, and out of the basement window, there's a German standing there with a grenade. And at the entrance to the basement is another German who's standing there with another grenade.

We grabbed our rifles, because we could have gotten the two Germans—we could see them! And the lieutenant said, 'No. You better not. There's only one way out of this cellar, and one grenade will get all of us.'

So we filed out, one at a time, with our hands up. And we learned later that it was a German patrol that actually was sent in to take prisoners for information. If it hadn't been, we would've been dead, because all they had to do is drop a grenade and keep going.

Anyway, they marched us back, with our hands up. Finally, the guy, I guess he was a German sergeant, said, 'It's okay. You can put your hands down. Put your hands down.'

Then we put our hands down. I put my hand in my pocket. I had this diamond brooch, and I'm figuring when they interrogate us, if they see this brooch, they're going to figure I killed the German lieutenant, the officer. And it was not good. So I dropped the brooch on the side of the road in the mud. And then I had my dog tags, and they had the

'H' for Hebrew. And I'm Jewish. So I figured I better get rid of that, too; I unclipped the dog tags and I dropped them also on the side of the road and kept going.

Interrogation

We went through a barracks of Germans, and they took us to a farmhouse where there was a German officer who was going to interrogate us. And I remember he was upstairs. It must've been an old hayloft. And one at a time, they took us upstairs to interrogate us. And this guy, I don't know what his rank was, but he spoke perfect English, hardly any accent. And we went up, one at a time; when it was my turn, he was very friendly. He reached out his hand and shook my hand. And then he said, 'You can relax. You don't have to worry. Now the war is over for you.'

He said, 'Make yourself comfortable.' He gave me a chair. I sat down.

He said, 'You're from New York? I lived in New York.' He said, 'I lived in New York for 10 years. I was a geopolitics employee of the German government.' He said he lived on Riverside Drive overlooking the George Washington Bridge, and he was very friendly.

And then he started asking me questions.

He said, 'Who was the tank commander?' I didn't know.

He said, 'Who is the commanding general?' I really didn't know.

He says, 'Who is your battalion commander?' I really didn't know any of these things.

So I said, 'I don't know.'

He was getting angrier and angrier and angrier. Finally, he got so mad he starts screaming at me in German, which I didn't understand. And he had a Luger on his table, a little desk and a table. And he picked up the Luger and he came after me with the gun. And I thought for sure he was going to kill me.

But instead, he just waved it in the air and fired a shot. He backed me to the door and pushed me down the flight of stairs. I rolled down the flight of stairs to the bottom, but I really didn't get hurt or anything. I was just very relieved that I was still alive, and I joined the others.

Our lieutenant, they took somewhere else. I guess he went to a different POW camp, the officers' camp. And the six of us, they marched us up into Germany. It's a long story. I don't know how much time you want to take with this.

Well, the other thing that happened was I had a watch. They stripped us of all jewelry, rings, watches, everything. But when they searched us, I raised my hands, and I had a watch that slipped down from my wrist to my arm. And they didn't see it. So when they weren't looking, I took the band... This may not be important, but it was important to me. I took the band off the watch. I made a slit in the lining of my pants, right behind my belt buckle. And I slipped the watch in there, and I was able to keep that watch all the time that I was a prisoner. It was an important thing because my mother had given me the watch as a going-away present.

The First Escape

Going into Germany, we joined another group; we kept joining groups of prisoners until there was a long line of prisoners, and they were marching us at night along the road. We didn't march during the day because American planes were striking us.

So we were marching along. Some guy, I remember he was from [New] Jersey, we were talking, and saying that if we kept going in, the further we got into Germany, the harder it was going to be to get away. So we were talking about taking off and getting away.

It was a country road, and a very windy kind of country road. They had one guard every 20 or 30 feet. I figured out that if we stood behind a guard, and we had a curve in the road, the next guard would not be able to see us because we turned the curve and the other guy would be behind. So all we had to do was drop off into the brush, wait till the column passed, and then we would head back the other way. So that's what the two of us did.

I had told him my plan, and he said it sounded good to him, only I think he misunderstood what I was talking about because when we dropped off into the brush on the side of the road, instead of sitting there and waiting for the column to pass, he took off up the hill that led up to a field. I saw him running up, so I followed him up to the top of the hill, where we turned around to face each other. I heard this clang that sounded like a church bell, and we thought for sure we were [discovered], so we started running again. At the top of this ridge was a field; we took off running across the field, and nobody shouted at us, nobody followed us. So we were okay.

Later on, I found out that the guard saw us, and he aimed his rifle at us, but he decided not to shoot, he waved us off, and he said, 'Let them go.' The guards were Russian and Polish, I think he was Polish, and they were old people that they had guarding us, so they didn't really care.

We went across this field. We headed in the direction of the gunfire, American gunfire. We got caught in a shell barrage, American shells. It was one shell after another, after another—the shrapnel was horrible. We got down behind a couple of trees. And then I said to him, 'We have to run toward the guns, because if we stay here, we're going to get hit with shrapnel!' We had to go towards the guns, get under the public.

He said okay, so I started running towards the guns, but I notice he's not following me; I looked, and he was still there. I ran back to him. I said, 'What's the matter? What's the matter?'

He says, 'I can't do it! I can't do it!' He panicked. And he starts screaming and crying, 'I can't do it, I won't do it!'

I said, 'Well, you go back.' I didn't want to go back. I had this leg wound, and I was afraid it was going to get infected. I figured when I got back to our lines, [it would get taken care of].

He went back and I kept going, across more fields; I didn't know where the hell I was going, except towards the American gunfire. Along the way, I was picking up turnips and potatoes in the field, all kinds of vegetables from the farmlands, and putting them in my pocket.

Now, remember, it was at night, and it was getting towards daybreak. I saw a farmhouse, and there was a barn. I went to the barn. There was a pile of hay. I dug myself into the hay to spend the day.

I don't think I was sleeping there very long when all of a sudden I hear a commotion. And I wake up, and it is a bunch of women chatting, making noise, and a German with a rifle and a [lantern].

Apparently, what happened was that a woman came in to feed the cows and took the hay and uncovered me. And I was still sleeping. She ran out to call the German.

He brought me to his headquarters. Turned out that it was bedlam. I mean, the Germans were burning papers, they were packing up, because the Americans were advancing. And they were getting rid of stuff, they couldn't care less about me. They were getting ready to leave, so all they did was tell him to bring me to another place where there were other American POWs to join those POWs. And that was the first time I escaped. I escaped three times.

*

This time they took us to a labor camp, in a farming community. And we were housed in the attic of a one-room schoolhouse, we slept on the floor covered with hay. It was my first experience with lice—when we woke up in the morning, we were covered with lice. Anyway, we were slicing logs and chopping the log slices into chips, and they would burn the chips to run trucks. Are you familiar with that? I'd never seen that before. They had a big tank on either side of the truck, and they would feed in the wood chips, make some kind of a fuel out of that which would run the trucks. So our job was to cut the wood and make chips for the trucks, and that's what we did every day. We woke up in the morning, and they took us out to the town. And we would cut the logs, and make the chips. They fed us one bowl of soup and two slices of bread every day, a watery soup, but the bread was not bad, though two slices was not enough. We were all starving. I mean, it was very painful. I know I'd wake in the middle of the night in pain because of the hunger. It was very bad.

But there were some bright moments. One time, I was chopping my chips and all of a sudden I hear somebody hissing at me from one of the buildings. And it turned out it was a woman standing at the door, and she's waving for me to come over. So I go over to her. She grabbed me, pulled me in. I guess I was about 18 or 19 at the time, but I looked like I was 12. And she grabbed me, pulled me in, gave me a bowl of potatoes and meat and stuff, and pushed me in a closet to eat it, with the door a little bit open so there's enough light in there. I gobbled it down. I gave her the bowl. She grabbed me by the arm, went out to the door, made sure no guards were watching, and then she pushed me out to go back. So a kind gesture.

The Second Escape

I was in that labor camp, I think, for about a month. And then of course the Americans were advancing. And so, again, we were being marched away. And again, I had this plan. As long as we were being marched out at night, I'm going to try to get out again. And sure enough, I was walking with a guy—it's funny I never remember any of these guys' names, but I remember where they were from. He was from Texas, and he was tall. I told him about getting away the same way I did before, and that is to get behind a guard, and as we got around a curve, we duck into the brush. We got away and started back, heading towards the American lines, towards the sound of American gunfire. We were getting pretty close, but again, it was getting daylight.

We approached a town. Actually, it was a bombed-out town—it looked like they were expensive homes, but they were all rubble.

We went in to one of these homes. Each home was surrounded by a gate. And this gate had a wire around it. It's funny. The gate was intact, but the house itself was just rubble. We went in, and we managed to get into the basement of this house. We were going to go to sleep for the day and then continue our journey at night. And again, I must've been asleep an hour or two hours. All of a sudden, we were being prodded with a bayonet; turns out that the owner of this house would come to look at it every day or so to check on it, to look at his rubble, and he noticed the wire off the gate. We didn't put the wire back on the gate, so the gate was open. So he went in and he found us.

He went back into town and he got what they call the Volkssturm. It was like a people's army, they were all older Germans, they had pointed helmets. They had rifles from World War I. They came in, there must have been half a dozen of them. And they prodded us with the bayonets.

We tried to explain to them that we were lost, that we were Americans, that we were prisoners of war, we're trying to find our way back, we got separated, and so on and so forth. But they were very angry. They were pointing out the rubble, and they said, 'This is what the Americans did. They ruined our homes. They killed our people.' They were being bombed.

'We Are Going to Execute Them'

So they paraded us into town, and from what we gathered, they were going to shoot us as spies. They took us to a courtyard, and they were going to put us against the wall. The townspeople joined them as we were being paraded through town. I understood a little German by that time, not much. But I understood them telling the people that, 'We caught two spies and we're going to execute them.'

A German officer happened to be walking by, and he asked what was going on. They said, 'We caught these two American spies. We're going to shoot them.'

He said, 'Wait! You can't do that. We have to interrogate them. They'll have to come with me.

We have to take them to our headquarters and interrogate them.'

So they were disappointed, but he congratulated them for capturing us. And then as we walked away, he spoke English, he says, 'You guys are very lucky. These guys, it's a very crazy group of people you have here. So if I hadn't come by, they would've shot you.'

Anyway, again, they took us back to headquarters. It was a dugout in a kind of a trench. And we can hear rifle fire, we knew the Americans were not very far. But again, we were sent back to another camp with another group of Americans and joined them, it must've been about a hundred of us this time. We didn't know where we were going. It turned out we were going to a [real] stalag this time.

Now, at this time my leg was really sore. It turned out it was getting gangrenous. I had a swelling under my arm, and a swelling in my groin, which the doctors told me later was an infection.

Anyway, I didn't have to walk very far. That is the boxcar, the forty-and-eight boxcars. We were going to be taken to a stalag, we were packed in so tight that you couldn't sit, you had to stand, and guys were passing out. There was no water, and it was hot.

Strafed

We didn't travel very far when all of a sudden we were being strafed by American planes. The bullets were coming right through the boxcars, .50 caliber bullets, just rip you apart; in the boxcar I was in, two guys were hit with the .50 calibers. We tried to open the doors, couldn't open the doors. They were locked from the outside.

Finally, the train screeched to a halt. The doors opened. We all poured out. It turned out that a couple of the Americans, I don't know if they were officers or just leaders, talked the Germans into letting us get out and forming POW letters with our bodies to indicate to the planes that we were American POWs.

And that's what we did. We all took our shirts off, and we lined up and bent over holding each other's hips, and we formed the letters 'PW' in the field. And those were P47s that were striking us. And they came down, they saw, they tipped their wings, and they left. Actually, there was a picture of this in *Stars and Stripes* later on I had seen of this incident.

We got back into the boxcars, and the wounded were all moved to the last boxcar. And we went into the stalag in Limburg, Germany. Stalag, I think it was 12A—Stalag XIIA—and they just distributed us amongst the barracks. This place was surrounded by barbed wire, and it had Germans with dogs, the German Shepherd dogs running around.

Slave Labor

And I don't know how long I was in that camp, maybe a few weeks. But in that camp, that was like you see in the movies about the stalags, except that it was right alongside railroad yards, it was like a railroad terminal. And every few days, American planes would come over and they would strike and bomb the tracks.

The American POWs were sent out to repair the tracks, and the Germans would be in the dug-outs with their rifles trained on them. We lost a lot of American POWs who were killed.

At night, if you were caught outside of the barracks after 9:00, you were shot. The dogs were let loose at night. The barracks had three tiers [of bunks inside]. It looked something like what you see that the Holocaust survivors went through, giant barracks lined up with triple bunk beds. We slept on straw. There were several buckets in the corner of the room that we used as toilets because you couldn't go out at night. And again, we had one bowl of soup and two slices of bread daily. That was the daily ration. But fortunately, I don't think I was there more than a couple of weeks when again, the Americans were advancing, and they started moving us out.

The Last Escape

We went out, marching north on these roads. This time I was limping badly, and my leg was really getting bad, and I decided I had to do it again. It was getting towards the end, I was feverish. I didn't know that I had gangrene; I didn't know what was wrong with me, but I knew that I was feeling very weak. And I didn't know how much longer [I could last]. I had to make another attempt to get away. And I did the same as before, but this time, I went alone. First two times, I had partners. This time I told a guy next to me, and I told him what I was going to do, and he just said, 'Well, go ahead. Good luck.'

I dropped off on the side of the road. And the line continues to go past me; it was a long line, must have been 20-30 minutes before they all passed me. And then I got up and I start walking the other way. I'm walking south. But this time, no gunfire, and I was pretty far from the American lines. I knew that. I figured if I could find a place to hide, I could just wait it out and wait until the Americans caught up with me.

And again, the sun was starting to come up, and I see a town, a small farming town. But these were stone buildings. I mean, they were not farmhouses.

And I must've been at least a hundred yards from the town when I saw somebody standing there, and as I saw him, he saw me, and he started pointing in my direction. I stood still. And then he called somebody else over, two soldiers, pointing in my direction. So I didn't know what to do. I just stayed there, and I sat down; I waited and waited, and I didn't know which way to go, [but they did not approach me].

Finally, I just said, 'I might as well take a chance.' So I went towards the town. And I didn't see any activity, nothing—not a dog, not a chicken, cat, nothing. It was quiet. I went to this house, the first house I came to. The door was open, and I went in. And it was like a two-story building. And there were stairways going up on my right. And then in front of me, there was another door that looked like it might have gone into a basement. So I tried that door and it was locked. But just then, somebody on the upper landing started asking, 'Who are you? Who are you?'

A woman came out asking who I was. And she said, 'Russkie? Polski?' I guess I was unidentifiable because I didn't look like I had a uniform on anymore. It was just rags.

And so I said I was an American and I was lost, and I was looking for a place to sleep. Several other people came out, and they had a conversation in

German. She came down the stairs. She opened the door with a key, pushed me in. I went down a couple of steps, and it was a basement with a couple of bedsprings, no mattress, bedsprings. Anyway, I was feverish at that time. So I just lay down on the bedsprings and I fell asleep. The next thing I know, the same door opened, and a woman came in, and she greeted me like she was so happy to see me! And she brought me upstairs, welcomed me, gave me a bowl of food, gave me a [bath], and welcomed me like I was a long lost relative.

So I figured the Americans must be close by, otherwise, she wouldn't be acting like that. But there were no Americans there. I found out later that an advance armored vehicle came by under the window, and she saw it. So apparently she locked me in the basement, keeping me there for the Americans, if they came, or the Germans if they came. So either way, I would be bartered.

I also found out that the two guys pointing in my direction were SS men, that the building they were near was a one-room schoolhouse that was headquarters for the SS, and that they had moved out just an hour before, they had taken off. So if I had gotten there an hour earlier, I'm sure they would've shot me. The SS, they don't fool around.

*

I was there about three days. They fed me well, they treated me well, and the Americans finally came by, so I went down. I spoke to the commander, who was a captain. And he assigned a jeep to take me back to an aid station. And from there, I went to the American lines. And that's my experience as a prisoner of war.

I was in a hospital in Paris for several months. I had typhus from the louse, louse fever. It was typhus. Also had that infection, gangrene, and malnutrition. I was there on my birthday; it was April 4. I was there on the day that Roosevelt died, that was April [12]. I'll never forget that, I loved FDR. He was like a father figure to me. Everybody was sad when that happened, there was a gloom sitting over the entire hospital. It was as though no one expected it. But I grew up with FDR, he was the only president that I ever knew at the time.

I was there at the end of the war, VE Day, [VJ Day]. From there, they flew me to Halloran Hospital in Staten Island in New York, a 22-hour trip on a propeller plane. We stopped at Greenland for refueling and then Halloran Hospital, where I was for about seven months. I was in the hospital a long time.

Home

They treated me like a king. They gave me the GI Bill of Rights, so I went back to college. I was able to live at home; I had a car when nobody else had a car. After that experience, I lived very well. I went back to Brooklyn College and finished my BA degree in Brooklyn College. I started off in engineering, and it wasn't for me. So I went into the social sciences. And I graduated with a major in sociology and a minor in psychology. And then I went to graduate school. I got a scholarship for Florida State University. So I went there with a stipend and free tuition. And I was there for two years. And I got a master's degree in social work. And then I worked as a social worker in a state hospital. I worked with teenage drug addicts for about seven years. I became a director of an outpatient facility for teenagers with the Jewish Board of Guardians. Then I went into analytic training at the Postgraduate Center for Mental Health, a four-year training program in psychoanalysis and psychotherapy, and I became a psychotherapist. I worked privately as a psychotherapist for the last thirty years, and I retired last week! And that's why I'm going to Florida next week for two months to join all the older people in the sun.

[I think that my World War II experiences] really helped me, in retrospect. I feel that I grew up very quickly from being a teenager. And I was only 21 years old when I was discharged, but still, I felt much more mature. The Army taught me how to get along with people, and how to manage on my own. When you're at home and your mother does your laundry and does your bed, you forget what it's like to live on your own. In the Army, you have to do your own bed. You have to take care of your own foot lockers. You got to take care of your clothes. You got to take care of yourself. I think it's a maturing experience; for me, it was.

I was just so happy to be home and so happy to be out of the Army and out of danger and to be alive that everything was exciting to me. I just felt good about everything. [The GI Bill] put me through college. And it seemed like everybody was a veteran at that time. I mean, the people who were not veterans were very unusual. It was like people who didn't smoke in those days. Everybody smoked. If you didn't smoke, it was something unusual. Almost everybody smoked.

Antisemitism

[But in retrospect], the one thing that I didn't quite understand when the war was happening, was why I was volunteering for everything, why I was trying to make a hero out of myself. I mean, when we were in the Hürtgen Forest and the BAR man got hit, I volunteered to carry the BAR. The BAR weighed as much as I did, with the bandoliers of ammunition. And yet, I volunteered; I was always volunteering. Going on patrol, they needed somebody, I would volunteer. I don't know. I thought I was just being a hero. But maybe the gist of it was that I was Jewish, and there was antisemitism. And I was always afraid that people were going to tell me that I was a coward or that I was squeamish or that I was reluctant to do anything because I was Jewish. At times, people, I mean, the other guys, would look at me and say, 'Lousy Jew.' I didn't look Jewish, but my name was Jewish at the time; my name was changed from 'Silverstein' to 'Sylvester' after I was discharged. So when I was in the Army, it was Silverstein, which is Jewish. I remember one time I was with a couple of guys. We were walking down the street, somewhere down south, and some woman came over and said, 'Oh! Would you gentlemen like to have dinner with us?' Because they wanted to entertain GIs.

So we said, 'Sure.' They invited us to her house. And we're sitting around the table. And there were about eight or ten of us. And this woman was there with her children, she had some teenage children.

And then she asked us to introduce ourselves, our names. I remember one of them, his name was LaRue, Jack LaRue, or something like that. Another one gave his name. And then I said my name is Martin Silverstein.

And then she said, 'What?'

'Silverstein.'

She made a face. And I could almost feel a shudder around the room, and then one of her sons got up and threw his napkin down and walked out. I felt like I wanted to disappear. So I remember that incident. There were occasional ones, but they were there.

I didn't put two and two together. I figured these guys who were antisemitic, they were also anti-black, they were anti-Puerto Rican, they were anti-everything. A lot of them were anti-Catholic, if they were not Catholic. So I just thought it went with that territory... I mean, it was certainly unpleasant. But I didn't attribute it to the government or to the country. I attributed it to these guys who were like that. And most of the guys who were like that were pretty ignorant and uneducated.

The Saddest Thing

I had no idea where I was, why I was fighting, or where I was fighting. I had no idea. All I knew was that they'd tell me to go here, and I'd go there. And they'd say shoot, do this, do that. I knew my lieutenant, and I knew my sergeant. I didn't know who the commanders were. You don't know one day to the next. We had the saying that if a bullet's got your name on it, it's going to get you. And you just never knew; it was just luck and chance. I mean, some guys, a bullet would bounce off a rock and hit them in the head. There was one guy, he took a bullet in the shoulder blade. It hit the bone and it ricocheted that into his lung and killed him. You never know, you never knew. So we had that kind of philosophy that you don't know if you're going to be here today or tomorrow—whatever happens, happens.

[I would not have chosen to have the World War II experience]; I mean, I'm not unhappy about it—I think in strange ways, it was good to me, [but I don't have the feeling that I was a part of something 'bigger than myself,' or that I contributed to something]. Not really, no. The saddest thing about it all is that my brother was killed at the Hürtgen Forest. He was shot in the head about the same time I was there. I didn't know it at the time. I didn't learn about that until I was in the hospital in Paris. He was two years older than me, and he was killed. So I lost a brother. And it was really hard on my family, very hard, especially since they got two telegrams within a week of each other—one that he was killed in action, and the second that I was missing in action.

Martin Sylvester's older brother, Ernie, was fatally wounded in the head in the Hürtgen Forest at the age of 22. After completing college, Mr. Sylvester had a private practice in psychotherapy and psychoanalysis for forty years, and he joined the faculty of the New York University Graduate School of Social Work, retiring the week before this interview was conducted in New York City in 2001.

American investigators study corpses exhumed from a mass grave in Berga. Source: National Archives, public domain.

CHAPTER ELEVEN

Berga

Gerald M. Daub was wounded on the line in mid-November, 1944. A replacement soldier and scout with the 100th Infantry Division, he was told he had a 'million-dollar wound' and would soon be off the front lines of combat. As it turned out, less than two months later he would be captured, a Jewish GI at the hands of Nazi warders who had special plans for him as a slave laborer, boring holes for blasting and removing stone rubble for an underground armaments factory that would never be completed. Out of 350 American GIs selected for this slave labor, less than a third would be alive when liberated by American soldiers searching for them in the waning days of the war in Europe. 'Death through Work' was a German policy of annihilation reserved for their most hated victims; you may have been aware of this in your education about the Holocaust. Did you know it applied to Americans as well? Of the 350 GIs who were sent to Berga, only about half survived.[7]

In 2002, the author was contacted by Channel Thirteen/WNET New York. Would I like to serve as the educational consultant to a film they were working on? Could I work with them on some lesson plans surrounding a little-known episode of World War II? Midway through my teaching career and having recently launched my WWII veterans oral history project, I leapt at the chance. While I never met Gerald Daub, I became familiar with the story he shared later on. *Berga: Soldiers of Another War* premiered in 2003. Most of the survivors had never talked about their horrific experiences until summoned to bear witness for the filmmaker—himself a fellow World War II veteran of the 106th Infantry Division—or until the attention brought about by the airing of the documentary. Gerald Daub was one of them who spoke about his experiences a few weeks before the premiere. Near the end of his ordeal, the group was death-marched away from the advancing Allies:

"We marched down some roads, and after about a day or so, we came upon the [bodies of the] civilians who were from our camp. Apparently, they were marched out ahead of us and it appeared to me that it was almost the whole day [we were marching, and their bodies were] lining both sides of the road, and they were shot. Now, it might have only been an hour or a half an hour, but in my memory it seems like the whole day—I just can recall their bodies in these grotesque positions, [like they had been] pleading for their lives, and trying to get away from whatever it was that was happening to them. Apparently they were shot because they were no longer able to keep up with the march and were not doing well, or the Germans were just tired of marching them. I don't know."

Gerald Daub, the formerly innocent, unsuspecting 19-year-old kid from Brooklyn, New York, gave this interview in 2003.

Gerald M. Daub

I was born on January 26, 1925. I went to Brooklyn Technical High School and I finished one year of architecture at Brown Institute in Brooklyn. When I heard about Pearl Harbor, I was playing touch football in the street. It was a Sunday and I didn't know where Pearl Harbor was or what Pearl Harbor really was about, except that I was stunned to learn that the Japanese had attacked the American Navy in Pearl Harbor. My original feeling was, 'Well, they're pretty foolish and we'll just wipe them out in a very short period of time.' I had no idea that I might at some point wind up being in the service of the government. I had a few cousins who went into service very early in the war, but I really never thought that I would serve in that conflict.

I was drafted. I volunteered for a program called the Army Specialized Training Program, which would send young men to college or help them finish their college educations, and I was in college at the time that I received my draft notice, and I was deferred for my appearance in the Army for about three or four months to finish the year, my first year at college.

In June of 1943, I was sent to Fort McClellan, which was in Anniston, Alabama. I had basic training as an infantryman and I had the full basic training program, which I believe was about 90 days. I finished basic training in time to be sent from Fort McClellan to a college to study basic engineering. I was sent to The Citadel in Charleston, South Carolina.

It wasn't until late in the basic training period that we actually got a weekend pass to go to town. Going to Anniston, Alabama, was not too much different than being down in the main part of the post. Anniston was just full of soldiers walking around the street. There weren't too many civilians that we came into contact with. I had more experience with people from the south and the different cultures of the south when I was at school in The Citadel, because there I always had weekend passes and I usually had a pass to leave the campus one night during the week, so I had opportunities to observe the difference in the southern culture.

The Whiz Kids

At just about the end of what was the second semester, which I believe was late in March of 1944, and I believe in preparation for the invasion of Europe, the decision was made to close most of the ASTP programs down and to use most of the men who were in ASTP and were young 18, 19-year-olds to fill in as replacements in infantry divisions, which would participate in the invasion in the later campaign in Europe. So, in late March I was transferred from The Citadel, and I went to Fayetteville, North Carolina, to Fort Bragg, where the 100th Infantry Division was stationed.

The 100th Infantry Division had finished Tennessee Maneuvers. They were a division that was probably close to being ready to go into combat, and then the decision was made to take about half of the men that were in the division and well trained and use them as replacements for the invasion in Europe. So they refilled the division with young men like myself who were in the ASTP or Air Cadets, and those two groups then refilled the division and we spent the summer training and getting the newer men integrated into the division.

The older men were resentful of us. They called us the 'Whiz Kids' because we were from ASTP—that was a popular TV program at the time.[17] But I think in general, eventually as we performed and as we started to integrate into the division and show them we were fairly well trained and would make adequate soldiers to fight side-by-side with them, we were basically accepted as members of the division.

Toward the end of the summer, we were alerted that we would be going overseas, although we weren't told where we were going. In late August, or maybe early September, we were loaded on a troop train and came up to New York; I believe it was Camp Kilmer that we were at for maybe a day or two. We got a weekend pass and I had an opportunity to visit with my family for the weekend. I didn't know where I was going but I knew I was going overseas.

---

[17] They called us the 'Whiz Kids'- Mr. Daub is probably referring to the popular radio program, 'Quiz Kids,' a radio and later television series of the 1940s and 1950s [later changed to 'Whiz Kids'] featuring academically inclined children with high IQs answering questions.

Then, when we all came back after the weekend, they took us on ferries and barges over to the port of embarkation in New York Harbor and formed a large convoy. We were on a very large troop ship called the *George Washington*, which I believe was the largest troop ship that the United States had. We went in convoy about 10 days, very rough crossing, and through the Strait of Gibraltar. We knew where we were going by that time and landed in Marseilles. That was maybe three or four weeks after the original, initial landings in Marseilles.

We debarked and the division formed up and got ready to go into combat. In the beginning after we left Marseilles, we boarded trucks and actually we were chasing the Germans up the Rhine Valley. I believe that particular German army had prepared positions in the Vosges Mountains while we were chasing them up. We really had no combat experience with them while going up the Rhine Valley after them, although we saw a lot of wreckage of German vehicles along the side of the road from air attacks.

Eventually around Baccarat, we went into the line and we replaced the 45th Infantry Division, the Thunderbird Division, in very mountainous, snowy terrain. We had winter uniforms and I had an Army field jacket and OD sweater, with a little shawl collar as I recall it, and a little woolen OD cap that I wore under my helmet. Basically, yeah, we had winter gear. After a few days, I think, we were issued shoe packs to replace the leather combat boots that we had brought with us. I think probably the men who were in the division who had been at Tennessee Maneuvers in the wintertime were adequately trained for that, although most of the training that I had was in Fort McClellan, Alabama, in the summertime and it was a pretty warm climate. The late winter in Fort Bragg was cold but certainly not as cold and snowy as it was in the Vosges Mountains. We learned to adapt quickly, and after all, I was from the Northeast so I was used to the climate, although not used to sleeping outdoors in it, or digging a foxhole in it every night.

'The First Scout is a Target'

My job was the first scout out of the second squad of the first platoon of F Company, of the 100th Infantry Division, 397th Regiment. On many days, it was my job really to be the first one to move out. We were only in combat maybe three or four days and really hadn't had any firefight experience yet. This particular day was not my day to be on the point, it was November 12 to be exact, and we were near a town called Bertrichamps, and our objective was a small hill or a mountain. I basically was walking out in this snowy woody area ahead of the rest of the company.

When I got the job as first scout, I thought that was an honor or a privilege because I was fairly athletic and a good runner and I guess I was a fairly good shot with my rifle. I later found out that basically the job of first scout, he was just about a target. If I was out there and somebody saw me first and shot, then the rest of the company knew something was going on. That was generally what happened.

Anyway, on this particular day, I saw some movement in the trees up ahead and I dropped to the ground, which was the best firing position, and apparently, that person saw me just a little bit before I saw him. We both almost fired at the same time, and I just felt this burning pain in my neck. I don't know what happened to the other person. But fortunately, I turned my head to the side to shoot, so that kept me from being shot in the head, and the bullet went in here and went down my back and out just below my shoulder blade [*points to left side of lower neck area with left hand*], where it touched nothing vital. Absolutely nothing.

But anyway, I lay there in the snow and then the rest of the squad came up to me and somebody helped take off my pack. I was told that I had the million-dollar wound and was going home. Unfortunately, it wasn't the case. So toward evening, a medic came by and they had marked my place by sticking my rifle in the ground and putting my helmet on top of it, and the medic came by and helped me up and looked at it and cleaned the wound a little bit and the two of us, he helped me walk back to an aid station. From there, I went by jeep to a station hospital and I spent about two and a half weeks at station hospital.

I was pronounced fit for duty after that period of time. So, I was asked if I would like to go to a replacement depot or go back to my company. Of course, I wanted to be with the guys I knew. Maybe wasn't the wisest decision. I probably would have spent a month or so in a replacement depot, but anyway, the next morning they put me on a truck, and I was back again in combat with my guys.

Basically combat was this same kind of routine, moving out almost every morning. We were advancing all the time through wooded terrain, through the snow. Toward evening, digging a foxhole, getting in it for the night. Sometimes we experienced shelling or tree bursts. Most of the air attacks were American, fortunately, but once in a while we were attacked by German fighters until around just a little before the first of the year, after Christmas, I think. We were up just about at the Maginot/Siegfried Line in a place called Bitche, which is a fairly large city in Alsace. Our advance by that time had stopped and we were in I guess what would be considered to be the Winter Line. Actually, the Battle of the Bulge had already started [below] in the Hürtgen Forest, and we were on the other side of Luxembourg, actually.

Patton's Third Army was pulled out and was sent up to reinforce the Battle of the Bulge and we spread out to cover the Third Army's territory and our army's territory. I was in the 7th Army. Around just New Year's Eve, the Germans launched a big counterattack with tanks and infantry. It was very celebratory, very pretty at night, and all the flares were going off and there was a lot of noise and excitement. Then, we were moved into a small town called Remlin, which was at a crossroads of apparently some roads and highways that the Germans considered to be important.

'Not me, Howard. I'm Jewish!'

And we were cut off in this little town. We had two companies in there, E Company and F Company, which was my company. We were attacked by the 17th German SS Panzergrenadier Division. Basically, we controlled the town in the daytime, and they would come in with tanks at night and more or less take over the town because we had no tank support. They would withdraw the tanks in the daytime because the tanks were subject to being attacked by our air power or because they would be visible in the town, so just around dawn, they would withdraw. They would try to leave infantry behind, and we would spend that day taking the town back and either capturing, wounding, or whatever, the troops that they had left behind to try to hold [the position].

There was a lot of house-to-house fighting. On this one particular night, the night that I was captured, was January the 8th. Another scout from my [platoon] and I were assigned to go up to the uppermost part of town—the town was on a hillside—and to observe the German massing and what they were sending into town. It was basically our responsibility to get back to company headquarters to report what was coming into the town that particular night.

So, this other gentleman, Howard Hunter, and I found a very nice house at a bend in the road facing up the street, up the hill. We got into what, I believe, was a second-story window, and as night fell, we saw the outline of a German tank coming down the street. There were infantrymen behind it, crisscrossing the street behind it. Howard and I shot out the window at them and they saw us and started to shoot back at us. Suddenly, the tank rolled up right to the house and put his muzzle right in the window we were in. We decided mutually that it was time to leave the house.

We ran down the stairs out of the house, opened the door, and as I said, the town was on a hillside, so we jumped over a garden wall and landed right in the middle of a squad of German soldiers. We, two, maybe there were five or six of them. Howard hit the German closest to him with his rifle butt. I grabbed him by the arm and we dashed into the first house that we could find. And we got into the house and we headed toward the other end of the house, and it was our expectation to get through the house, out the window, and head back down to the company headquarters. As we got into the house, we realized that the windows were boarded over, solidly boarded over.

We got into a room called the kitchen and smashed at it with our rifle butts and couldn't get the boarding off, and we could hear the Germans come into the house. Because of all the fighting, there was a lot of shelling and this floor was very sandy, so we could hear their footsteps on the floor. As they would pass a room, they would throw a hand grenade into it. The two of us turned over a big wooden table, which was probably the kitchen table. It was dark, so not easy to see because the windows were boarded over, and we got down behind it and we heard the Germans come to the door of the room we were in and they tossed a hand grenade in.

The table bounced up and down, but we were not hurt. The table stayed together, and Howard said, 'I think we better surrender, Gerry.'

I said, 'Not me, Howard. I'm Jewish!'

Howard was a good guy. He stayed with me behind the table and they tossed another hand grenade in, and we didn't do anything. Then, we heard a machine pistol cocked at the door and we knew that that table wasn't going to resist that, so I recall saying to Howard, 'Howard, discretion is the better part of valor. I think we better surrender.'

I don't know which one of us said 'Kaput, kamerad,' but we both threw our rifles at them. The

German soldiers grabbed us, of course, as we came out and searched us and brought us back to this tank that was out in the street.

They had a very badly wounded soldier lying next to the tank. They ordered us to pick up the soldier and put him on the tank and to get on the tank and hold him on. Howard and I got onto the tank with the soldier, who was in great pain, and crying for his mother. Then, the tank took off and headed back out of town again with the infantry riding on the other end of the tank and some of them walking behind the tank.

As we headed out of the town, I can remember hearing this soldier's terrible cries of pain and suddenly he stopped crying and I said to Howard, 'Howard, I think he's dead.'

We were in deep 'what-cha-ma-call-it.' So, the tank stopped, and we were ordered off it. The tank commander waving his pistol, and I thought surely, they were just going to shoot us and leave us there. But he turned around and he pointed at a shovel that was on the side of the tank, so we knew that he meant for us to use the shovel and try to dig a hole for this soldier who was dead.

So, we chipped away at the frozen snow; it was very hard to dig anything through this icy snow. We dug a shallow hole, and he said, 'Okay, that's enough.'

We rolled the dead German into it and covered him over with snow again and then marked the spot, and they ordered us back on the tank again and the tank took off as the sun was coming up. And this tank was going right across the ridge line, I'm thinking to myself, 'Boy, we're going to get blown up by Americans.' But nothing happened. We finally arrived back at a barn, a little house which must have been their headquarters or their command post, and then Howard and I were ordered into the barn, and after a short while, somebody came in and got me and took me into a little room at the side of the barn.

Interrogation

There was a German SS officer, very well dressed and well-polished looking. He was sitting at a table and he had a couple of *Reader's Digest* magazines of fairly recent issue. Assumingly, it was meant to impress us that he could read English and speak English, and he spoke English very well. He asked me a few questions and I gave him my name, rank, and serial number, which is what we were told we had to do. Then, he told me that I was a member of F Company, 397th Regiment, 100th Infantry Division. I had no insignia on. I was stunned to hear that he knew so much about me. I didn't realize until later that somebody else must have been captured earlier and maybe was frightened enough to tell him what he wanted to know.

He told me the name of my company commander, Captain Stallworth. He told me the date that I landed in Marseilles. I said, 'Well, I actually wasn't with the company when they landed in Marseilles. I'm a replacement and I haven't been here very long, and I don't really know too much about what you're telling me, but it's probably true, but I really don't know.' He looked at me with disdain because I was dirty, smelly, looking like an infantryman, haggard, unshaven, and he said, 'You're Jewish, aren't you?' I'm really not proud of this, by the way, I said, 'No, I'm not. I'm Lutheran.' My grandparents were German, and I knew that they had friends who were Christian and they were Lutheran, so I said I was Lutheran.

He said, 'Take your pants off.'

I said, 'If you want to see whether I'm circumcised or not, that really won't tell you anything because almost everybody in the American Army is circumcised.'

He said, 'All right, all right. That's all.' [Incidentally], I had hidden my dog tags in my boot. It's interesting because your dog tags gave your religion. In all the times as a prisoner of war, I don't recall anybody really looking—except on one occasion—for my dog tags or looking to see whether they said H, P, or C on them. Certainly when I was first captured, nobody did, and this officer didn't either.

He motioned me to leave and the guard took me out. They called Howard in. They probably gave him the same kind of questions that they gave me. The next morning, which was January 9, the rest of my company appeared. They had surrounded the company command post, pushed everybody back into the command post, and captured the remnants of the company; maybe there were 25 or

30 men. Among them was this guy, Bob Rudnick, who I had been a kindergarten companion with back in Brooklyn.

They then questioned the rest of the company, and the next morning, I'm not sure whether they loaded us up on trucks or marched us out, but we somehow got to a railroad siding and they loaded us in boxcars.

Bad Orb

There were soldiers from other companies that they had gathered together, and they had about a trainload of American prisoners of war, and we went into this boxcar of I would guess about maybe 60 men to a boxcar. They gave us a loaf of bread and locked the boxcar up, which had no toilet facilities, and I can recall we took turns sitting or lying down because it was so crowded. Eventually, we got into what I later found out was Frankfurt am Main, and it was the night the British Air Force picked to bomb the marshaling yards in Frankfurt am Main.

The Germans did not let us out of the boxcar during the night when the bombing went on, and the next morning, they opened the boxcar and the rails were all twisted and messed up in the railyard. They surprisingly already had gangs of people working to put the rails back in order. They marched us away through the town, through German civilians who were very unhappy with us; they were yelling at us and they looked and acted very angry.

They marched us to a very large prison camp in a place called Bad Orb, which contained a good part of the 106th Division. [They were] in the camp before we arrived, and there were also French, English, Serbian, some Indian soldiers.[18] We were in that camp I guess for about a few days. We were reexamined and re-questioned again.

In that camp, I put my dog tags back on again, and as I passed by one of the benches, somebody did pick up on my dog tags and looked at them. In any event, we were in that camp for just a few days when the Germans announced that they were going to separate the Jewish prisoners and put them in a separate barracks. We were all, of course, basically privates, because the officers were separated

---

[18] *a very large prison camp in a place called Bad Orb*- Stalag IX B, discussed in this book previously.

almost immediately after we got to the camp and sent to a separate camp. The non-comms were also sent to another camp in a place called Ziegenhain. So, our 'man of confidence'—the man who was appointed to be the head of the camp—was instructed to tell us that the Jewish soldiers should stand forward at the next formation, but our barracks leaders told us that we should not obey that order, that it was improper for us to be separated from the rest of the American prisoners. So the next morning when we were called to step forward, nobody stepped forward. That night, the man of confidence and the other barracks leaders were maybe abused, and they were told that the next day, the Jewish men would have to step forward. So they came back to the barracks and told us that the next morning, we should step forward when we were told that the Jewish men should do so.[19]

---

[19] *we should step forward*-Other sources state that the Jewish prisoners decided to step forward themselves, that next morning: "The commandant said the Jews would have until six the next morning to identify themselves. The prisoners were told, moreover, that any Jews in the barracks after 24 hours would be shot, as would anyone trying to hide or protect them. American Jewish soldiers had to decide what to do. All had gone into battle with dog tags bearing an H for Hebrew. Some had disposed of their IDs when they were captured, others decided to do so after the commandant's threat.

'Step Forward'

The man who was the leader of my group, of course, was a member of my infantry company and knew that I was Jewish. I was resentful of the fact that they were so willing to give me up. I mean, it was silly because as events later turned out, the Germans would have separated us in any event because that was their intent. So the next morning this fellow, Bob, and I stepped forward when we were told to and we were marched to a separate barracks. In a sense, the Germans were true to their word. They had said that we'd be treated like everybody else and given the same food. The food, of course, if you've spoken with some prisoners of war, you know that the food was fairly meager to start with. The food was identical in this separate Jewish barracks. The big difference was that the barracks was in a barbed wire enclosure and we could no longer mingle with the rest of the men in the camp.

Approximately 130 Jews ultimately came forward." Source: Bard, Mitchell G., *Berga am Elster: American POWs at Berga.* Jewish Virtual Library. www.jewishvirtuallibrary.org/american-pows-at-berga-concentration-camp.

We stayed and we were in that particular situation for about another week or two. I actually remember the date, it was February 7, and it was announced that the Germans were opening a separate camp for American prisoners of war, and at random they would choose some barracks to go to this separate camp to get it started. They chose the Jewish barracks and another barracks, where men who had committed minor crimes [lived]. If you can picture what the prison camp was like, then you would expect there would be some thievery. Men who were pushed into very uncomfortable positions and might be tempted to steal somebody else's bread or clothing if you left it around. As a consequence, everybody slept in all their clothing and their boots.

A shipment of 350 men was put together. I understand that some of the people in the shipment were men who were picked out at random, who looked Jewish or who had Jewish-sounding names. And of course, we were loaded back into these boxcars again in a similar situation for another week's voyage. And when the train stopped—and of course, we didn't know where we were going or what the situation would be—it stopped in a very quiet, nice little German village. It looked pretty good. The boxcars were then opened. We got out, and as we marched through the village and into the countryside, we suddenly came upon this camp surrounded by barbed wire.

Berga

We marched into the camp and we noticed that the camp was basically filled with civilians, not prisoners of war, and the civilians were wearing blue and white striped pajama suits. They were obviously concentration camp victims. We marched to a barracks and went to sleep for the night, and the next morning when we were wakened, we were marched through the camp and over a little foot bridge to a work site, and the work site was a large mountain that they were digging tunnels into. We didn't know what the tunnels were for and what the material was that we were taking out.

Basically, the mountain was rock mountain. We were divided up into little groups and each one assigned to a tunnel, and in each tunnel was a civilian German miner who oversaw the operation. The

German guards basically left us there, so there was no military supervision. We worked 12 hours a day. We worked the 'night' shift, which was part daytime and part night, and the political prisoners worked the other shift. Food was basically the same as it was in Bad Orb. For breakfast, a cup of tea or coffee or some kind of an herbal mixture hot drink. Lunch was a bowl of soup, and for dinner, we got a loaf of dark brown bread to share with about six or seven men.

We had gotten one Red Cross package in Bad Orb before we left. It was a package to share with four men to a package. So, we took turns at selecting things from the package. I recall that Bob and I decided although we did smoke, we would not select cigarettes. We'd select food. And we selected a bottle of vitamins, which was a pretty good choice as I look back at it now. We were very careful about eating. It was 'One-A-Day' vitamins and we each took one a day. We did have an incident when we were in the second camp at Berga Elster. In the very beginning, five or six men I believe were pretty sick after the train ride and they were sent to a hospital, a German hospital. I believe some of the medics who were with us went with them. Apparently, it was mostly English prisoners of war at that particular hospital, and in some way they found out about how bad it was in the camp we were in, and in some way they managed to ship some of their Red Cross parcels to us. They arrived maybe halfway through our time in this mining operation, but the German officer who was in charge of that group called us 'bandits,' said we were dirty and unshaven, and that he had Red Cross parcels for us, but he wasn't going to give them out until we were properly shaven. Now mind you, we didn't have toiletry kits! A couple of men had managed to hold onto razors. They used to come in a little black plastic box. I don't know if you know what the shaving kit was like. It was a razor that you screwed the handle on to the head and you could put a blade in it. Several men had them, so in our off time at night, we managed to get just about everybody shaved after about two or three days, and then those Red Cross parcels were also given out and we shared them, again, one to four men. Those are the only two Red Cross parcels that we got in all the time that I was a prisoner of war.

The Germans' 'Final Solution'

Also, when we were in Bad Orb, by the way, we got an opportunity to write home. We wrote a letter and a post card, and my parents got both of them after the war was over.

I had a cousin, as I said my family was German, and I believe he was my father's mother's sister's son. In any event, my parents signed some kind of a formal statement saying that he would not be a burden on the government of the United States, and he came as a refugee. I was about 13 or 14 at the time, so it was before we were in the war. He lived with us until he went into the service. He was about two or three years older than I was. He and his brother, his brother went to somebody else in the family, they came to the United States and they had two other children, a boy and a girl who went to what was then Palestine. The parents never got out of Germany, but I heard a lot of stories about how the Jews were being persecuted in Germany during those early Hitler days. I don't think anybody outside of Germany was aware of the total impact and the totality of the Germans' 'Final Solution.' No, we couldn't see it, but we could communicate with the civilians who were there. In fact, if you get an opportunity to read that decision by the United States State Department, one of the people who was interviewed was a gentleman who was in that camp as a civilian. He was shocked to learn, and he says so in the statement, that there were American soldiers when we came in. And, he was also surprised that they could communicate with us because a lot of the American soldiers who were Jewish and spoke Yiddish—that was a language that was almost international, so these people from all over Europe apparently understood Yiddish and could communicate with us. I couldn't speak Yiddish, although I knew a smattering of some words of German from just hearing my grandparents talk, and my buddy Bob had studied German as a language in high school. So, we could communicate a little bit with them, but we didn't have too many opportunities to stand around and talk to anybody, frankly. We worked long hours and when the day was over and by the time we got our meals, attended to our personal needs, we just would drop off and fall asleep.

In Bad Orb, we were issued what appeared to be a half of a gray blanket, each one of us, so between Bob and I, we had almost a full blanket together. On these bunks we slept two men to a level, in each one of these compartments. Bob and I chose to sleep together, and we basically were able to keep each other warm with those little half blankets. We were supplied with these burlap mattresses to put in these wooden slat bunk beds. The straw was full of lice, and so were we. As time went by in this place, some of the men became sick. Diarrhea was prevalent, and once they got sick, they usually died. You could see that somebody was going to be dead the next day at nighttime, or whenever it was that we went to sleep. People would have this look of a mask of death about them, and we knew that they were going to die.

Outside the barracks, [for a latrine] there was a large hole with a log over it and that was it. Men who escaped and were recaptured—and so far as I know, nobody ever fully escaped—they were given the additional duty of having to clean out this latrine pit. That was usually a fairly fatal assignment.

The guards were similar to our ages. They were soldiers. They were soldiers who were no longer able to fight because they had been severely wounded in some way. I recall a guard who we spent most of our time with had one arm that was stiff, couldn't bend at the elbow. It's my recollection that he was injured at the Russian front. The guards really were basically following orders and didn't do anything outward on their own. The gentleman who was in command of the group was mean and did the most that he could to make us uncomfortable.

Slave Labor

The first prisoner who escaped was a man by the name of Goldstein, Jerry Goldstein, and he was captured and brought back and shot through the head. His body was displayed for three days in the compound, obviously as a lesson to all of us that it was not a good idea to try to escape. But some of these people were so desperate that they tried to escape anyway. The three men who were the 'men of confidence' in the large camp who had refused to turn over the Jews the first night, were sent with us [to Berga], and so they became our leaders in this camp. The three of them were non-Jewish so far as I know. One's name was Hans Kasten, one was Joseph Littel, who I know is the son of a minister, and the other's last name was Sinner, and I don't recall his first name.[20] The three of them escaped. They spoke German very well and we didn't really know what happened to them because they didn't come back, but we found out later that they were recaptured and sent off to some other camp and kept in solitary confinement for the rest of the war, but they were not shot, which was good for them.

*

As time went by and we just got weaker and weaker, death became more frequent. In the beginning, maybe just one man died and then after a few days, somebody else died, but then after a while it became almost every morning somebody

---

[20] *last name was Sinner, and I don't recall his first name*-The third man was Ernst Sinner. They escaped during an air raid, were recaptured, and sent to Buchenwald. [Berga an der Elster was a subcamp of Buchenwald].

would be dead and had to be taken out, and we had a regular burial detail by that time.

We didn't know at the time what we were mining or what we were doing at all. The work in the mine [was brutal]; I think there were something like seventeen of these tunnels in this mountain, and they were about a story and a half high. We were drilling with a large drill—about a six-foot bit—holes in the face of the tunnel, and then we would all leave the shaft. The fellow who was the experienced miner, the German, would attach dynamite into the holes and attach fuses. We'd all leave the shaft and he'd blow the face of the shaft and then we [were sent back in] to pick up the rock by hand, and put them in these little carts, on the side of the railroad. We just pushed the cart along there until it came to a little switch-off at the bank of the river and dumped the stone into the river.

Since then, I've been told that actually we were digging some kind of underground munitions factory.[21] We thought that it was perhaps launching

---

[21] *we were digging some kind of underground munitions factory-* "Each day, the men trudged approximately two miles through the snow to a mountainside in which 17 mine shafts were dug 100 feet apart. There, under the direction of brutal civilian overseers, the Americans were required to help the Nazis build an underground

tubes or tunnels for rockets, but anyway, I've been told since then that it was some sort of underground factory that they were building.

The Death March

One day, we were told that we were not going to work that day, and we were marched to a little building and told to take our clothes off. We wondered what was going to happen now. We were told to put our clothing in a little pile. And then the door to a room opened and it was a large, tiled chamber. We were ordered into the chamber, the doors were closed, and it was a shower room, and we got our first showers, our only shower in fact, our only washing in the time that we were in this place. In fact, I had maybe taken one shower after I got out of the hospital when I was in combat between then and the time I was captured, so maybe

---

armament factory. The men worked in shafts as deep as 150 feet that were so dusty it was impossible to see more than a few feet…. The Germans would blast the slate loose with dynamite and then, before the dust settled, the prisoners would go down to break up the rock so that it could be shoveled into mining cars." Source: Bard, Mitchell G., *Berga am Elster: American POWs at Berga*. Jewish Virtual Library. www.jewishvirtuallibrary.org/american-pows-at-berga-concentration-camp.

this was the first shower I had gotten in five or six months. You see, we had no bathing or washing facilities. If you wanted to wash, or clean your hands or your face, you had to do it in your tea or coffee water that was supplied in the morning. So, you can just [imagine] that in this stone-working operation, with the blowing up of the stone face in these mine shafts, that we looked like concrete statues, really—we were just totally covered with stone dust. Of course, after the rock was blown, we were ordered back in to pick up the rock; it was a pretty choking place down in this tunnel, so not really a good situation.

In any event, after the shower that I mentioned, the doors were opened again and we went back into the room where our clothing was, and told to put our clothing on again, which was of course the same clothing that we had been wearing in combat, and by this time, every seam was just full of louse eggs. Our bodies were covered with sores from the lice that we had living on us. Then, we went back to the barracks and the next morning when we woke up again, the gates to the camp were open and we were marched out. All the civilians who had been in the camp before us were gone. We didn't know what happened to them, or where they were, but there were no civilian prisoners at the worksite anymore.

We marched down some roads, and after about a day or so, we came upon the [bodies of the] civilians who were from our camp. Apparently, they were marched out ahead of us and it appeared to me that it was almost the whole day [we were marching, and their bodies were] lining both sides of the road, and they were shot. Now, it might have only been an hour or a half an hour, but in my memory it seems like the whole day—I just can recall their bodies in these grotesque positions, [like they had been] pleading for their lives, and trying to get away from whatever it was that was happening to them. Apparently, they were shot because they were no longer able to keep up with the march and were not doing well, or the Germans were just tired of marching them. I don't know.

A fellow Berga survivor, medic William Shapiro, offered his description of the same murderous action:

On April 15, we resumed our march along the road to the 'next' town. This phrase was always repeated by the Guards in some measure to reassure themselves as well as to prod us along. They were also suffering by the continued walking. Fortunately, the weather was warm, but I did not discard any item of clothing. You become very possessive of all your belongings no matter how fowl smelling, tattered or unnecessary on a warm day. I carried or wore all my ragged clothing.

Sometime during our march, we came upon the most frightening and horrible scene that I had ever seen. I could bring up that scene in my mind with no difficulty. To my mind it is worse than seeing the photographs of emaciated bodies piled high like wood in recently liberated concentration camps. It was infinitely worse that the hangings that I had witnessed. We knew that the political prisoners from the concentration camp annex were also on the road, guarded by SS troopers. They were many miles ahead of us and could be seen in the distance as the road curved or we were atop of a hill.

As we approached a steep hill, I saw the most gruesome, cruel, barbarous, inhumane acts that I have ever seen in my entire life even to this day. As we climbed the hill in the road ahead of us and caught up to where we had seen the political prisoners in the distance, we saw on each side of the road hundreds of dead Jews. Most of them were in the kneeling position, many on their side in a fetal position and all were dead by obvious gun shots behind the head. Many heads were blown open by the force of the shot and the brains were splattered about. It was ghastly. It was indescribably frightening. It was unspeakable. It was so shocking to look at the very recent awesome destruction of human beings, presumably because they could not continue the march up the inclined road. I can still clearly visualize that scene of Jews in their black and gray stripped pajamas in a kneeling position, many facing away from the center of the road and all shot behind the head.

It was unbelievably frightening to me and I am sure to my buddies walking up the hill. What was in store for us? Is this the manner in which it will all end? There were heads blown apart as a result of a close-range murder with a rifle or pistol. The horror of it reflected onto me and my overwhelming despair. After all the suffering that these Jews had encountered, so close to freedom, their inability to climb the hill resulted in instant death. I was engulfed by the same persistent thought of what if I cannot continue — this is what happens if you do not continue. I was exhausted and just dragged along, fearful of stopping until we were told that it was time for a break. I became an automaton. As we continued to walk through them and past them, we came to another group of political prisoners in similar positions. As we ascended the steeper part of the hill, there were more and more victims. You became immune to the sight, you expected it, it was walking into a hell. The 'trees' lining the sides of the road to hell were dead Jews. I could never imagine anything as macabre as this massacre. As we were catching up to the civilian prisoner march, we began to hear the firing of machine guns and burp guns in the woods a short distance from the road. We could not see the Jews, but we knew what was happening in those killing woods among the pine trees which blocked our view.

These barbaric inhumane acts were exemplars of the evil German mind created by Nazi preparation, inculcation, and philosophy. They were Hitler's willing executioners. At this point in the war and on this death march to nowhere, there were no lines of command to the private German soldier carrying the guns. I know that there was no 'on the spot' communication with higher ranked officers in charge. No one was observing, standing over the troops, directing or commanding their actions. These were self-motivated heinous actions by barbaric indifferent people with no personal forethought or concern about what they were committing. They possessed no feelings nor conscience, therefore, had no governance on their inhumane actions.

From that point on, I believe my fear for my personal safety began to grip me. I did not know whether I would be shot at any time although I saw that our guards would only prod the men with their gun butts to get them to move on. I thought that I was going to die. I have absolutely no recollection of the march from about April 16 until my liberation on April 23, 1945. I was socially dead. I kept to myself, probably walked like a 'zombie' – the walk ascribed to civilian prisoners in the camps who were close to death. I suppose that I ate and drank but it is all a blank in my mind.[8]

Gerald Daub

When the guards were asked what happened to these people, they said that the American planes strafed them, which of course was untrue because they were all shot in the head, but in any event, that was the story we were given.

As the days went by, we would be marching and sometimes they had food for us and sometimes they couldn't get food for us. Sometimes the guards were able to get potatoes from the farms and sometimes they were able to get a shipment of bread, which we then would divide.

As an interesting aside, we had a way of making sure that each of us got a fairly equal share of bread. If we had six men, we organized into a group and somebody would have a knife. Some people are surprised to hear that we did manage to have a knife or two amongst us, but you had to have a way to cut the bread. We would appoint a different person, we would rotate the person each day who was called the cutter—'der Schneider' in German—the bread cutter, and he would get to pick his slice last. So, he did his utmost to make every slice equal, because he got the last [cut, which could] be the smallest one, if he were a poor judge of cutting, or didn't do a good job that day. Your punishment was to not get very much to eat, so it was a very good way of everybody getting their equal share of the bread slice.

The marching went on and eventually as days went by, more men weakened and died. Of the 350 now, one of the medics had tried to keep track and keep a dog tag if there were some available for each prisoner who died. So, this man by the name of Acevedo, he had a count of 70 men out of the 350 who died.[22] Now, mind you, these were combat infantrymen. Healthy, young men of 18 or 19 years of age, as I was by that time, and basically in the prime of health when we got there, because we were infantrymen and had training and were hardened, and I was taken prisoner on January the 8th. I was liberated on April the 23rd. We left Bad Orb

---

[22] *this man by the name of Acevedo-* Anthony Acevedo (1924-2018). "A Mexican American who served as a US Army medic during World War II. He was captured by German troops during the Battle of the Bulge and held as a prisoner of war (POW) in the Berga subcamp of the Buchenwald concentration camp. While there, he kept a secret diary of his experiences. Throughout his ordeal as a slave laborer, Acevedo maintained a secret diary of his experiences and recorded the dates and causes of his fellow soldiers' deaths. He knew he would be punished if he was caught keeping the record, but he later explained that it was his 'moral obligation' to document the names of those who had died. Tony's fountain pen lasted throughout his imprisonment, and he later remarked, 'God gave me that ink to last.'" Of the 350 GIs who were sent to Berga, about half perished. Source: Anthony Acevedo. *Americans and the Holocaust.* United States Holocaust Memorial Museum. https://exhibitions.ushmm.org/americans-and-the-holocaust/personal-story/anthony-acevedo.

and went to this work site on February the 7th, so February, March, April [*counts*]; no more than two and a half to three months that we were working, and in that time, one out of every five of them died. So, it was really a perilous situation.

'My Bittersweet Day'

As the journey progressed, I can recall one night, the guards were acting upset, or differently. We were told from people as we marched through towns—farm workers and oppressed laborers—to hang on because the American Army is very close by. And we could hear firing; we just seemed to be marching ahead of it all the time. This one night and the next morning, our guards were all gone and there were different guards. Very old men, looking like they really didn't know one end of the rifle from the other. As we woke up in this straw in the morning, there was this young man by the name of Jack Bordkin, who didn't wake up. Instead, he seemed to be gasping for air, having difficulty breathing, but it looked to us like he was still breathing. With everything in disarray, and with the new guards, I said to my friend Bob, 'Why don't we see if we can just walk out of the barn with him and maybe the column will go on, and they won't even notice that we're gone, and it'll be over.' This other fellow, Joe Mark, Bob, and I, the three of us went over to the corner of the barn where there were some poles stacked in the corner. We took two poles and button Bob's overcoat over the two poles to make it like a stretcher and put Jack on it, and we walked to the door of the barn and we said to the guard at the door, 'This man is very sick and there's a little hut over there. We'd like to take him into the hut and see if we can revive him and rest a little bit.'

The guard said, 'Yeah, yeah, yeah. Okay, go ahead.'

So the three of us trundled over to this little hut and went inside with Jack. The hut had obviously been some kind of a kindling hut because it had a goose egg in it. We took the egg and made a little hole in it and tried to get Jack to suck it, and he wouldn't. Or just couldn't.

Just as we were doing that, there was a sound of what to me was unmistakable as an American tank! So, I threw open the door to the hut and over the rise of the hill came this tank with a big white American star on it and behind it a jeep flying a Red Cross flag on it!

I stumbled over to the guy in the jeep and it was a medic. I said, 'There's a man in the hut who is very sick.'

And he said, 'Yeah, we've been looking for you guys for days!' He said, 'I'll go in the hut and see.' He said, 'And by the way, there's a lot of food in the jeep. Take whatever you want.'

I can remember going in the jeep and pigging out and getting sick on it, by the way. [*Chuckles*] He went into the hut and he came out and he said, 'He's dead. I can't do anything for him.'

He said, 'What you see is moving through his mouth is probably rigor mortis. He's probably been dead for a while. His mouth is going up and down.'

So actually, I describe this day as being my bittersweet day. And so we were liberated; the ordeal was over. The men in the barn were all coming out and everybody was all excited and happy, and then some trucks rolled up and they took us back to a little German hospital and I can remember there were nuns in it, and I remember just trying to crawl up into this bed with sheets. They deloused us with kerosene.

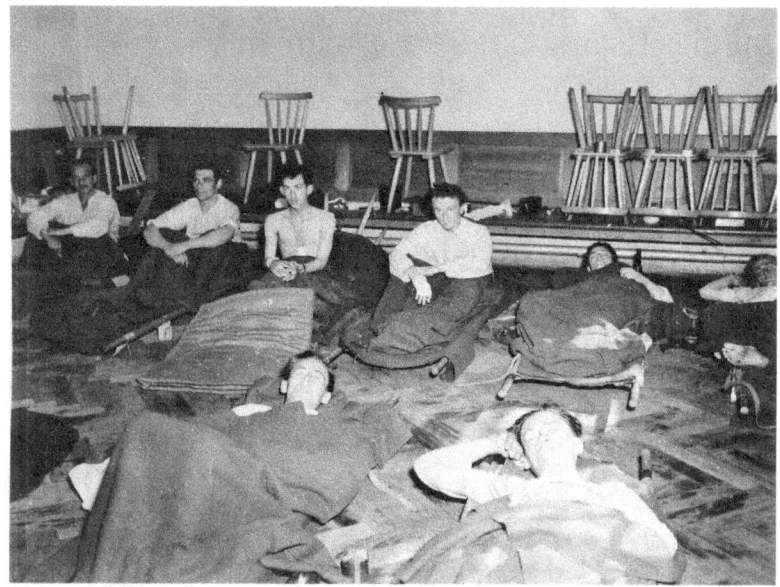

Berga death march survivors recuperate. Gerald Daub is third from right. Source: National Archives, public domain.

We stayed there for a while. An Army doctor came over and then they put us all back on trucks and they took us to this place—here I am, able to sit up—it was some kind of a school or something. They had us all in separate rooms; it's about three or four days later and I'm fairly cleaned up by then. This dog tag that you see is my German dog tag, not an American dog tag. My number was [*points to himself in photograph, recites a German number*] and it's one of the few things I can remember to say in German.

We were in this place for about maybe four or five days. My buddy Bob was terribly sick; he probably was on his last leg. He was diagnosed as having double pneumonia and so they took him away to the hospital right away, and after a few days of being here, they put me on a hospital plane too, and flew me to England. I was in England until early June, and then I flew back to the States.

*

I was in Army hospitals then for just about the same length of time that I was a prisoner of war, for four and a half months, until I gained my weight back and got over this persistent dysentery. When the ordeal was over, I was sent to a rehabilitation and reassignment camp in Asheville, North Carolina, and I was pronounced fit for duty and sent back to an infantry division at Fort Jackson, South Carolina. It was the 32nd Division or 23rd Division; I can't remember now what it was, but they were preparing to go for occupation duty in

Japan, and fortunately I was there a day or two when they put the list up on the bulletin board of points—that was the way you were eligible to be discharged, by how many points you accumulated—and I had enough points to get out.

I was discharged and went home. I got home in time for Christmas and went back to school and was back in school; there was a separate law from the GI Bill for disabled veterans because of my wounds. So actually, when I finished college and got my degree, I still had all my time left on the GI Bill and I went to school in Europe for a year.

'Justice'

One of the prisoners who died had an uncle who was an attorney. He formed us into a group here in New York. We could go to give testimony and they tried Sgt. Merz and his next in command. One was Metz and one was Merz.[23] The one who shot

---

[23] One researcher described Erwin Metz: "Erwin Metz, who was the German in direct command of the US GIs at Berga, was something quite extraordinary. Metz had been a petty criminal before the war. But war, as you know, is not only hell; it's also opportunity. And this mediocre criminal rose to a level where he was in command of the Americans. And when, after a week or two, they started complaining of sickness and weakness, what he would often do would be to empty a bottle of ice-cold water over them to see how they would react. How they would react would very often be to die within

Goldstein was sentenced to death by hanging and the second in command was given 20 years in jail. Their sentences were later appealed and found to be excessively harsh, and Metz's sentence then was changed to life and the other guy's sentence I think was changed to five years, and then later [General] Lucius Clay declared some kind of an amnesty and Metz's sentence was reduced then to time served and I believe after six or seven years, he was free to go home. I didn't follow his career, so I don't know really too much about it, but I did give some kind of a deposition for the court in that trial. None of us was called to come to Europe to identify him, to participate in the trial in any way, but they were tried.

Bob came back home by hospital ship; he arrived a short time after I did. I was at Halloran General Hospital on Staten Island in New York when he showed up. He went back to college, became a lawyer and an accountant. We both married. I had two sons, he had two daughters. We lived in Bergen County at the time, lived maybe three or four

---

the next day or two." Source: Roger Cohen, interview, 'Soldiers and Slaves'-A Saga of Jewish POWs, Morning Edition, NPR News. May 10, 2005.

miles apart, were friendly all through our lives. Bob died about four years ago.

'They Thought We Were All Dead'

I think [my ordeal] affected me; maybe I had a lot of bad dreams about it. I talk to [psychologists]. And I still see some of these men or I am in communication with some of them. Oddly enough, the large prison camp, Stalag IX-B, the one that was at Bad Orb where most of the 106th Division was, has had an annual reunion, and they include the men who were shipped out to Berga. By the way, they thought that we all were dead. They had heard that we had gone 'to the salt mines' and the Germans had killed us all. They didn't really find out about us until maybe seven or eight years ago, and they included us in their reunions.

I've been to maybe four or five reunions around the country with them, and some of the men who were in Berga an der Elster would show up. Handful of them, maybe six, seven each time.

[Of the men who had suggested we step forward], one of them has passed away. I had seen him at several infantry division reunions later on.

And one of them I saw at a division reunion. He was really not an officer, but he [became] a good friend. In fact, he was the other person who was with me the night I was captured. I mean, I was angry, I was upset, but it was not something—I came to realize that it was something that was out of their control, really. That they were not doing it out of meanness. That's what they were doing and that's the situation that they were in, and I was in the situation that I was in. It took a while to realize that.

Now I'm very active in American Ex-Prisoners of War, the Hudson Valley Chapter. I didn't join any things like the American Legion, or the DAV, or anything like that. In the beginning, I really just didn't want to have anything to do with my Army experience. And then as the years went by, Bob and I went to a few division reunions, and then we started to go every year, and at one of the division reunions, one of the principle topics was prisoners of war; they usually liked to have a theme at a reunion. So, a gentleman from the American Ex-Prisoners of War talked about the fact that they had an organization and they could be very helpful to [former] prisoners of war, and he suggested that everybody join, so I did. Bob and I both joined, and they were very helpful to us with helping us to get treatment for Post-Traumatic Stress Syndrome, helping us to increase our disability compensation. I regularly go to meetings. We meet at West Point once a month, a Saturday luncheon, and I enjoy the company of them and their wives.

Gerald M. Daub passed away in January 2006, at the age of 80.

Jack Blanchfield holds up a newspaper headline, 'PEACE', after his liberation and repatriation to the USA. Source: Jack Blanchfield

CHAPTER TWELVE

The Interpreter

Jack Blanchfield was a replacement soldier with the 5th Division. Although he was wounded and taken prisoner in November 1944 before the Battle of the Bulge, his time in captivity gave him an opportunity to witness related developments that puzzled him, such as having his uniform taken away from him—which his captors would later use to infiltrate American ranks during the battle. In sharp contrast to the previous narrative, he also held many of the Germans he encountered in captivity with high regard—including the guard responsible for him at the end of the war.

"I think I learned so much more about humanity, about giving people a chance to show who they really *are. That relationship is the basis for maybe sixty years of written conversation with Kurt and his family. Besides the horrors that I saw, that I had to be part of, to really sit back and take a look at that relationship is something that means an awful lot to me, to meet a man who was my enemy and become great friends for sixty years has meant a lot. I hope our kids, and grandkids, and great-grandkids know."*

The war, of course, affected everyone. His memory of Pearl Harbor and his friends' reactions to the news become all the more tempered as he leaves his listeners with this:

"I lost five friends [who were on that corner when we heard about Pearl Harbor], killed in WWII. So many—Bill Hoppe, Andy Hopkinson, Johnny English, Tommy Krone, and Bill Hill—I could go on, they were all killed in different places. I came back."

John J. 'Jack' Blanchfield

I was born in Schenectady, New York, on March 10, 1924. Eighty-five years old now, soon to be eighty-six. I am the oldest of five boys. My father was with the *Union Star* newspaper in Schenectady. We moved to Amsterdam, New York, where I spent the rest of my life.

My father's latest job was circulation manager for the *Amsterdam Recorder*. My mother did not work; she was a housewife, the third of six children. Her parents came over from Ireland in the late 1800s, and my father's parents came over from Ireland, also in the late 1800s. So, I am of Irish background and my parents were the first American citizens. Both were wonderful people. [Later, when I was shipped overseas], I was put aboard the *Mauritania*, which was an English liner. My grandmother Blanchfield said she came to the United States in 1870-something, on the *Mauritania*.

Growing Up

I was quite young [during the Great Depression], but I knew what was going on. My father—working for a newspaper—his office was right adjacent to a railroad station and very frequently he would bring home somebody that had just got off a train, but I really didn't feel any impact. I was aware of what was going on because it was in the thirties and I remember my father bringing these men in for supper and maybe they'd go out and clean up the garage or stay overnight. With five boys it wasn't unusual for three of us to bunk in one bed, and someone who was hitchhiking on a train to stay overnight. That's about my only awareness. We were not hurt financially, thank God. My father was able to work all the time. My father worked and the kids kept coming. Being the oldest of five boys was very interesting because I always got the clothes. When another boy was born, I got new clothes and I passed them down. I never saw a young lady grow up until our first child was a girl. I had a lot to learn and I'm still learning from it. [*Laughs*]

*

I graduated from St. Mary's Institute in Amsterdam in 1941. I entered Niagara University in the fall of '41 and of course Pearl Harbor took place in December '41. [Pearl Harbor] was a Sunday and I had gone to the movies at Niagara Falls with four of my buddies—classmates—and as we left the movies that afternoon, we stopped, waiting for a bus in front of Walgreens Drug Store on Falls Street. Somebody came up to us and said, 'Did you hear what happened at Pearl Harbor?' And that was our first knowledge of it. We were quite startled. We were all ROTC units—we had to take ROTC at Niagara. We were startled to hear it and we didn't know what was going to happen to us. We went back for supper that night. Being Sunday, we just had cold cuts and salads, and it was deadly quiet. Some of the fellas knew that they were going to go. Professors were leaving. It was an all-male school. There were a lot of pensive people at that point. What's going to happen? What can we do? And it was pretty much the demise of male students at Niagara until after the war.

I was not eligible for the draft or anything until '42, at which time in May I registered for the draft. Then in December of '42, a recruiter came to Niagara, and if we enlisted at that point in time, they would guarantee that we could finish the next semester. I enlisted on December 8, 1942. In May of '43, as I completed my second semester of my second year at Niagara, I received notice that I was expected at Camp Upton.

'All Safe 'Til Peace'

I went to Fort McClellan, Alabama, for 13 weeks of basic infantry training. And at the conclusion of that I took a test for OCS or ASTP, the Army Specialized Training Program, as we called it. Some other people called it 'All Safe 'Til Peace.' I was then sent to Clemson College in South Carolina where I stayed for about a week. I met a fellow there whose name was Ritchie Johnson who was a famous Negro baseball player. From there I was assigned to North Carolina State College in Raleigh and I started courses in engineering in the fall of 1943. I completed two semesters by March of '44 when ASTP was disbanded. I think I heard that there were about 40,000 of us in different colleges throughout the country, either studying to be engineers or doctors or medical people. From there I found myself in Fort Jackson, Columbia, South Carolina, with the 87th Acorn Division and that was of course prior to D-Day in 1944.

We were getting ready for something. As an infantryman, you used various firearms and so on and I was with them a short period of time until just after D-Day. I had a ten-day furlough and I came back to Amsterdam—my hometown—for ten days. And on the way back I met Sergeant Kirby who was our sergeant of our Company C and he said, 'You've been listed to go over as a replacement.' He said, 'You will be packing up your duds and you'll be out of here,' which took place then in the summer of '44.

Through various stops, I finally ended up at Camp Shanks, which is down in Orange County I believe. I was stationed there for maybe a couple of weeks or so. I had some time to go to New York City. My mother and father came down. They knew I was shipping out; it was the ocean liner *Mauritania* and it was jammed with GIs. I slept in a hammock and we had a half an hour a day to go up on deck. It took us seven days. There was no convoy, we were by ourselves. We were a speedboat—just seven days to get over there.

I ended up in Liverpool, disembarked and was sent to a place called Delemer Park. The trucks took us there, which was someplace in the area of Liverpool. I was there about a week when I got notice that I was going to Southampton and then headed to France. At Southampton I was put aboard a ship from the Netherlands called *New Amsterdam*, which was kind of surprising that I was on that kind of ship. We went across the channel that night and we were off the coast of France the next late morning when they threw all the ropes over the side of the ship. We climbed down into an LCI—landing craft infantry, I think it was, rather than an LST—which took us to the shores of Omaha Beach and there was a metal ramp that was in the water. It was high tide and we had full field packs and we had gas masks—the whole bit. So over the side I went into this LCI and went towards shore, and the front came down and we started walking off and I found out in high tide—I was about 5'5" at that point in time—I damn near drowned. The water was up to my chest. The guy in back of me grabbed me by my tush and said, 'Keep walking, keep walking.' By that time I'm spitting water out, couldn't swim, and I thought to myself when the Germans see me as a new secret weapon coming out of the water, they're really going to be in for a time. [*Laughs*] So I walked up Omaha Beach and the first thing we did was throw away our gas masks. There was a rise from the beach itself which we climbed up and at that point in time they were just opening up the new graves. It was probably around the first of August; it had been pretty well cleaned up by then except for the gravesites. They were just beginning to put crosses and Stars of David on them. I found out later one of my classmates from St. Mary's in Amsterdam had been killed on D-Day and had been buried there, which kind of shook me a bit.

From there we got on trucks and were sent to a repo depot—replacement depot. We were there for ten days or two weeks or so when my name was called and I was ordered to report—I was being shipped to Company C of the 11th Regiment of the 5th Division, which was part of the Third Army. The 5th Division had been in Iceland and then to North Ireland and then into France, so I was being sent to them. We were put on trucks and taken to Company C, the 11th, and at that point in time they stenciled a red diamond on my helmet. And then from there we took off.

The Third Army had not been in existence very long. Patton was our general. He was a heck of a good general. A little bit wild, I guess, because all we did was run like crazy. And we had the Germans on the run. In fact, we didn't see much combat for quite a while. We got stopped periodically at the remains of various towns and so on. I just remember the first time I had an 88 shot over me and with all the training and everything I had, the only thing I could do was just hold on to my helmet and say, 'Hail Mary.' Scared me to death. And the first shot I took was—we were held up outside of a small village, so we were behind some little bunkers and the sergeant hollered over to me, 'Shoot, shoot.' I hadn't shot my M1 yet. And I shot it. I hit a house. I thought, 'Boy I'm really doing a good job.'

We kept going east at a fast pace and our tanks were everything; they had the Germans really on the run. Periodically we would get stopped by a small group of Germans and then they'd fire at us for a while and they'd disappear. If we came to a village that we'd stay overnight, why that was fine. If we came to a village once in a while, we came down for a while, and the next morning everything was quiet—they were gone.

The tanks were doing well until we got close to the Moselle River and this was probably already mid-September. Then we were ordered to dig foxholes. We'd been sleeping in slit trenches every chance we had. Then they said start digging deeper. The question then was why, because we'd been on the run and we had the Germans on the run. The answer was that the tanks had run out of gas. We had stretched our lines of what we needed. Once the tanks were stopped, why, we were stopped.

We were there for a while and then in early October the rains came. It rained and it rained and it rained.

'We've Got Company'

Our object at that point was to take the city of Metz, which was on the Moselle River. Periodically, we sent out patrols—I would go out on patrol—periodically sent out to outposts. Metz was pretty well fortified by what was known as Fort Driant, which was part of the original Maginot Line. But Fort Driant was more than just one fort. There were a number of forts. Periodically we'd go out and make an attack, maybe twice, and we were always right back.

In the middle of October they took us off the line and we went in a rest area—went back up to a little village—I think it was Vierzon. They took us back there where we had a chance to clean ourselves up a bit and get some heavier clothing. We were relieved at that point I think by the 95th. At the end of October, we went back up on the line, and on the 4th of November, the sergeant came to me and he said, 'Company A got hit pretty hard a couple of nights ago. They are going to need some help. I want you to go over and report to them temporarily.'

So I went over and reported to Company A, which was just a little bit south of where I was. It was Saturday, the 4th of November, and they said, 'Okay, the first thing you are going to do is go to an outpost.'

I met a fella who I was going to go up with—his name was Cootch, from Vermont. So we went up to the outpost, which of course was ahead of everybody else, and we were supposed to be in charge of reporting any activity. They said no patrols were out at that time. Cootch and I were in one hole and to our left flank, maybe just ahead of us a wee bit, were two other guys. And as usual on outpost [assignment], you sleep two hours, and stay awake two hours, just flip flop. So I went ten to midnight with my tour. Just shortly after that, I went back to sleep, but Cootch said, 'We've got company.'

Captured

Well, we knew there were [none of our] patrols out, so it wasn't anybody that we wanted to see right then. Right behind me, our phone line was cut; I tried to use the phone and it didn't work. I knew somebody was behind us because the phone was gone. Yep, he was right; it was an enemy combat patrol that hit us—we had a pretty good firefight and Cootch was killed. We just had our M1s, and they gave us a pretty good battle; as I said, Cootch was killed. And the next thing I knew, I heard somebody say, 'Raus, komm, raus, hands up!' I had been hit with some shrapnel, one of the potato mashers as we called it. But it was as close to combat as I had ever expected because we were just a few yards away from each other. The fellas in the other hole, I do believe, got killed also, because I know there was a lot of firing over there, too.

Thinking back about it, I always wondered why they left us out there. I guess maybe that we were just [expendable] or something. Later on, my father and mother got a letter stating that I was out on outpost [assignment] and there was a firefight, and that they came out the next morning and found I wasn't there. So I got captured, and that was the end of my combat experience in World War II. It was the German First Army that we were against, and these were a couple of SS troopers who were good soldiers. We weren't too far from the German frontline because they had the chance to regroup. So they marched me past a bunch of the German Wehrmacht soldiers, who started hooting and hollering and calling me different names; I didn't know what they meant, but I don't think they were very kind. The guys that picked me up—captured me, I guess—checked me over for cigarettes and for D-Bars. That's what they wanted, I guess. So they took those away from me.

We walked quite a ways. They took me to a brick house and brought me in there. It must have been a central place or something because there were all kinds of telegraph lines, almost like movie stuff, people marching in and out with information. They took me in there and then they took me to another room and started asking me some questions, and of course, I was still a PFC at that time, and Eisenhower hadn't told me anything. [*Laughs*] I didn't have much information to give them except name, rank, and serial number. They knew what division I came from because I had the red diamond on my helmet. Periodically they'd get upset with me and give me a little jab with a bayonet, but otherwise it wasn't too bad.

They locked me in a room and the next morning two guys with skulls and crossbones on their uniforms put me in the back of what could be the German version of a jeep—in the back seat. One guy sat next to me and the other guy was driving. They tied my hands behind me, and we took off. And we came to a small stream and this German vehicle—the driver shifted gears of some sort and it became a floating jeep, a little boat—went across this stream. We drove maybe four or five hours and we stopped at a place where they locked me in a barn, and they brought me some meat and a piece of potato. They brought in this young fellow from Yugoslavia. In 1944, I had just turned twenty, and this guy was probably about sixteen or seventeen. They put him in the barn with me and he said something in his language, and I couldn't understand him, and we went through a couple of different things, and the next thing I knew he could speak French. He asked me an awful lot of questions. I started wondering what the heck he was doing there and why. Couldn't answer any of them. So I fell asleep in the pile of straw and woke up the next morning and he was gone. He was locked in. I often wondered why—I think he might have been quite interested in what was going on. I was picked up on Saturday night, the fourth of November. The following Tuesday was the seventh, Election Day back in the United States. Roosevelt was running for his fourth term against Tom Dewey.

Among the questions they kept asking me was, 'Are you getting ready to attack us?' We had been sitting still for a few weeks. I guess they were afraid that Roosevelt might pull an attack to maybe help solidify his possibility of becoming President again. It was his fourth term. I often wondered if that was the main point of the questions.

*

My two fellas with the skulls and crossbones picked me up again that morning and took me to a town called Forbush, as I found out later. I was put in the town jail in a cell by myself, and after I was there for a while, I heard some knocking on the wall. And a fella said, 'Are you American?'

I said, 'Yes, are you?'

He said, 'Yes.'

He was a fighter pilot that got shot down and parachuted and he had been there for a couple of days in that jail. They eventually took him out, and I heard some screaming and hollering. He never came back. I don't know whatever happened to him and I often wondered if some of the civilians maybe got to him because they were notorious that way if they caught anybody.

From Forbush, I was there for maybe four or five days by myself in the jail. One guy then took me out on a train. We went to Limburg, which was Stalag XII-A. At that place they took my picture and I felt kind of secure at that point in time that I was a POW. There had been rumors—and it happened on our side too—that periodically POWs never made it, never heard from them again; they became an MIA forever. But now I had my picture taken, I got my dog tag with my number on it, 078069, and Limburg was Stalag XII-A and there were British, Canadians, and Americans—all POWs there. I was there for maybe three weeks or so. Very boring. I felt very sorry for myself, what had happened. I felt sorry for the guys who were with me when I got hit. By the way, the shrapnel—a German medic got the shrapnel out. The biggest piece was in my elbow, and he sewed me up. They didn't have cloth bandages, they used crepe paper—they wrapped me up with crepe paper. I had a couple of other small pieces. But anyhow I was there—at Limburg—for a while.

They took a bunch of us out and put us on a train—a boxcar—there were forty-some of us. There was all straw on the floor and a big garbage can in the corner. There wasn't much room in it for forty-some guys and there was one fellow—I think he was from Chicago—all he kept talking about all the time we were on that boxcar was his mother's banana cream pie, and after about four days in the boxcar with him talking about banana cream pie, we were ready to shut him up. After a day, we took off in the train. I think there were a couple of other boxcars with GIs because when we did stop eventually, we met them. And we stopped periodically, and they'd put another boxcar on. Now, whether these were Jewish people that they were taking to someplace else, I don't know. Every once in a while—there was a little cubicle above the boxcar—the guard up there would drop some water and some bread down to us. We found out what the garbage can was there for after the second day. And then we really had problems. Some of the guys drilled holes with the dog tags to get the seepage out. It was horrible. About every third day they'd give us some bread. We had to stand up. Everybody couldn't lie down at the same time. These boxcars were too small, so we had to stand up.

We stopped someplace and we were there for a while and the Americans—it was daylight—they came over and bombed this railroad and we were screaming in the boxcar. We were targets of our own men. Fortunately, they didn't hit us. The boxcar ride took us seven days—an absolute horror—and one time they said we were going to Danzig; the German guard above said we were going to Danzig. We turned around apparently and came back, and we ended up at Neubrandenburg, which is Mecklenburg, thirty-some miles probably north of Berlin. They opened the doors to us, and they let us out and we were then herded into Stalag II-A, which was Neubrandenburg, which had Russian prisoners, beside British, and we were the first American prisoners to get in there. It was a big camp—a big prison camp. The first thing they gave us was cabbage soup, which was cabbage and water, and two slices of black bread. Most of us hadn't eaten much more than a slice of bread in over a week, so we devoured everything we got. Boy, did we pay for it in the next day or two. To have not eaten and to just get cabbage and everything else didn't do us any good. We were taken into the camp. I was there for probably three or four weeks. We got to the camp on November 29, Thursday, which was Thanksgiving Day in the United States. We had two Thanksgiving Days in 1944 in the United States, the original one, which was the last Thursday, and then they decided for some reason that they would have the third Thursday. So we got there on Thanksgiving Day, the 29th. After a time in II-A, it got very boring and I felt very sorry for myself. I didn't know what my mother and father knew, where I was, what happened.

The Work Detail

They came around and said, 'We're going to have work groups.' So they said, 'Anybody volunteer?' so I volunteered. They picked up twenty of us and they sent us to a place called Dunenwald, which was just outside of Neubrandenburg a few miles—they put us on trains to get there. We had two guards, two elderly men, and twenty of us, and among those that were with me was a fellow by the name of Jack Yole from Hudson Falls who I met. But anyhow, we went to Dunenwald and were told then—we were put into a barracks, just a small, one room, it had a stove in it—we were put there and we were going to be stump routers. They were building a new road. The two elderly men who I had met on the train, the two guards, they were the guys in charge. They took us out and they showed us where they had felled, knocked down, and cut down trees. The stumps were left, so we had to dig around the stump and get the roots. They had a tripod and we put the tripod down and put chains underneath the roots and everything, and then with the pump handle you would pump them up, for use as barricades against the advancing Red Army]. That was our job and we worked from dawn until dusk and we got our usual breakfast of ersatz tea. At noontime we had either potato soup or cabbage soup or turnip soup, and at night we had two slices of bread and that was our food.

The Prisoner Who Lost His Mind

At the time we were there we had an interpreter with us—one of the twenty. His name was Hank. He was from Brooklyn, a Jewish boy. They came around one day, and they checked our dog tags and they took Hank away from us and we never saw him again. We found out later that they did take out the Jewish-American boys, so we had to play games with our dog tags. The Jewish boys always hid theirs or got rid of them somehow and the rest of the guys would periodically hide their own too—the Gentile ones. So we lost Hank. A fellow by the name of Nixon who was from Colorado—I don't know if he was related to the future President—he and I were pretty good friends. Then, all of a sudden, he flipped. I woke up one night—we had to sleep on, there were two layers, not separate beds, but straw and then we had half a blanket to share—I woke up one night and Nixon's staring over at me and he's hollering, 'You know who I am?' I said, 'I know who you are.' He said, 'I am Jesus of Nazareth, King of the Jews.' Oh boy, he had really flipped. The next day I was walking out of the hole and Nixon was standing there and he clocked me on the jaw. The guys grabbed him and took him away. The next night he was standing over me again and said, 'Tonight I am a spot on the wall and I am watching everything you do.' They let him work the next day, and in my hole he took a shovel and he beat me on my back with the shovel, three shots, until the guys got him. They took him away on the back of a truck and I still can see him screaming; whatever happened to him I don't know. I had to work but the guys covered for me because I couldn't do anything.

Interpreting for the Germans

After quite a while, that job was finished, and we were taken back to the main camp. After a short period of time, I volunteered for another spot. While we were at Dunenwald with the guards and the civilians, I heard them speaking in German and I traded some cigarettes that I got from the Red Cross. I got a dictionary from German to French; when I heard different words, I could understand by hand signals and so on what the topic was, and I asked them to tell me what the German word was and then I got the French out of it. Having enough French in high school and so on, I was able to pick up enough so I knew what was going on.

With my dictionary I volunteered to go on another work group, and this was a big one. They picked 160 guys. They asked me to be an interpreter and I was an interpreter with a fellow from South Carolina who had been captured in North Africa. He was a medic. So we marched with this pretty good-sized work group. There was an under-officer and six guards and the usual wire around us and a small sleepaway tent. They brought us there and they said our job was going to be building a roadblock. Some of us were going to be building the scaffolding used to put the cement in, some of the guys were going to be mixing the cement, and the rest of the guys were going to lug it down and so on. So there we had two large barracks, eight rooms in each barrack with about twenty guys in it. We went to work building the roadblock. The under-officer thought he was a pretty good opera singer and he kept singing to me all the time and I had to listen to him.

While we there working on the roadblock, a couple of things happened. We had some information—a fellow by the name of Jack DeHuff from New Jersey was in charge of [camp] communications, and his job was mixing the cement for the roadblock. But he had a friend who was a French priest and he used to clue him in on what was going on. So one day, early April, Jack said the priest said that Roosevelt died. So, that was the evening. The next morning when we lined up for the count, they counted us out and took different groups to work. I called everybody to attention. I said, 'Face right,' and they all faced right. Some guy had traded cigarettes to get a bugle. He blew the bugle—taps. The German under-officer could hardly understand what was going on. He said, 'What happened?' I told him. He was shocked—he didn't understand how we knew. That was one of my first wins that had taken place.

I was pretty much upset. Roosevelt—he became quite a man once Pearl Harbor took place. He was on our side. He was a leader. He said, 'They are not going to get away with it.' He was good—he was right for the times. At that time there are people who are really specially made for various times—it was Roosevelt, Churchill of course, de Gaulle, yes, maybe—but they were all pretty strong people at that point in time. Although, I couldn't vote for Roosevelt because you had to be twenty-one. You could drink when you were eighteen, but you had to be twenty-one to vote. It has changed quite a bit.

*

After that, we had the Red Cross parcels come in. We used to be able to split them, maybe two boxes among twenty guys, and they had various stuff, the usual—cigarettes, soap, D-Bars, et cetera. We got some softballs and bats from the YMCA and we also got a record player with two records. One was, 'Into Each Life Some Rain Must Fall,' and the other one was, 'I'm Dreaming of a White Christmas.' Well, to have a bunch of American guys over there—we used to pass the Victrola around. It was a hand cranking thing; we used to pass that around with the two records. We had the balls and bats, but we couldn't do anything with them; we were working seven days a week.

We had one guard—we called him Peanut Head—and he was shell-shocked. One time he pointed his rifle at some of the guys who were working building the roadblock. He pointed his gun at them, and they were afraid he was going to shoot them, so they clocked him and carried him in. One of our guys was carrying his rifle; he was caught with Peanut Head, cleaning Peanut Head's rifle and Peanut Head was darning his socks. The under-officer, he came in and he couldn't understand why Peanut Head's rifle was being cleaned by an American POW and Peanut Head was darning the prisoner's socks. That was one bit of trouble. [*Laughs*]

The Work Strike

Soon we could hear the artillery. We were not far from Szczecin, which was Poland. The Russians were not that far away, they were almost to the Oder River, and we were not far from there. So we could hear the rumbling and so on. And finally, in true American style, we had elected a leader in each one of these eight rooms, and me as the interpreter. We met and the eight fellas said, 'We decided we're not going to work anymore on Sundays.' I said, 'Okay.'

They said, 'Okay, you tell them. Sunday morning, we are just going to go back in our rooms, and we are not going to work. And you tell them.' So that Sunday the guys did what they said they were going to do. Everybody went back in their rooms. I'm standing there with the under-officer trying to tell him that this is a strike; we are striking. But I didn't know the word for 'strike.' So he took me down to the guardhouse. He called in the bürgermeister, who is the mayor, and he called in a couple of majors, and they came up in a truck with twelve German guys, all military guys. So I tried to explain to them.

They said, 'No, you are going to work Sundays.' It became an argument.

He said, 'I'll give you two hours off this afternoon.' So I went back to the leaders of our 'union.'

I said, 'They are going to give us two hours.'

They said, 'No, all day or forget it!' So I went back down again, and this went on until about 2:00 in the afternoon.

I went outside and one of these groups was having a drill or something. Anyhow, a shot was fired, [maybe accidentally]; somebody had a hair trigger or something. The next thing I knew, there were two guards and a fellow prisoner, Earl Cross, who was from Oklahoma; he was half Native American as they call it, half Indian. He had taken over as interpreter when we lost Hank on the previous job. Earl came down and he said, 'What are you doing? We thought we got you killed.' Thanks a lot, fellas. [*Laughs*] Anyway, the upshot was—negotiating—I kept going back and forth.

My big ploy was that we could hear the Russians, everyone could hear the artillery, the Germans were not in good shape. This was April. Finally, they said, 'Okay, no more Sundays.'

They put me in solitary for the week. The following Sunday, the guys are out there playing softball in the eastern part of Germany and we were probably about two miles from a women's stalag with Russian and Polish girls—they used to walk by us in their blue and white uniforms. Well, these guys were out playing softball and showing off for these girls as they walked by. We never worked another Sunday after that.

It was time to unveil the roadblocks that would 'stop' the Red Army.

The only other [notable] thing that happened, [before we were evacuated], was the ['unveiling'] of the roadblock [we had been working on, to the townspeople]. They had the bürgermeister there and they had two guys with drums, and we had the morning off and some of the townspeople were out there. They had some speeches and they started to take the scaffolding off. Then something that DeHuff had told me, that nobody else knew, [became apparent]. Up at the top of one side, you could see a crack start and a little bit of sand would come down. DeHuff had reversed the [concrete formulation, with the ratio of] sand and cement, so that soon, this whole thing was going to fall down. He had been putting in four or five times the amount of sand into the cement mixture [than was called for]. Well, everybody was pretty upset about that, and that was the end of our work there.

The Captives Become the Lords

On the 27th of April, which was just after this occurred, the under-officer came to me and said, 'I have been told I have to take all 160 of your guys up to Denmark to continue the war.'

I said, 'When?'

He said, 'Tomorrow morning.'

So I told the fellas that we were leaving the next morning, and we were going to head towards Denmark, walking. So the first thing we did was throw away the Victrola, and the two records—they went flying out. The next morning we took off. We had the six guards and we walked all that day going west and we got to a barn, and we stopped there for the night. I went to sleep. The next morning, I got up at daybreak. A couple of fellas came over to me and said, 'We are ready to go.'

I said, 'Where are the guards?'

They said, 'They're not with us anymore!' They gave me the under-officer's pistol, which I had always recognized, so I kept the pistol and they left one guard, Kurt Papke was his name—he was the only guard left. Kurt and I used to talk about beer and girls, because we were both twenty years old, and I don't care where you come from, single guys talk about girls and beer. So, we'd talk about that. He was always with us; I don't know what happened to the other six guards—we never saw them again, but Kurt stayed with us. One night, I was asleep. We didn't get to bed until midnight. He came and he patted me on the back. He said, 'Come on—we're having a party.' And we went out and walked back along the road and up a little hill and there was a little fire going with rocks and things. There were four young German girls and they were cooking [wieners] and we had a party, we had a little beer. So we met these four girls out there and I woke up the next morning in a wagon with straw. Kurt leaned over—he was sleeping with me. I said, 'You smell bad.'

He said, 'I had a few beers.' Our relationship was fantastic. We needed him and he needed us.

We started going west and we kept going through woods and everything. Finally the road was clogged with people; everybody was going west because the Russians were right behind us. It was time to get out of there. There were men, women, and baby carriages, so we went on the road. Some of our guys were pretty weak—had some bad legs, and so on. So we kept looking until we finally found a horse alone; we took the horse and we got a wagon. Eventually we got a couple more horses and another wagon. We picked up a Latvian woman, who said she was a barber from Riga, Latvia, and we picked up a 12-year-old girl who was walking alone. They came with us.

We kept going west. Periodically the British and the Russians would strafe us, and the British, if you are going down the road, the British would go right down the road after you—they were strafing us—but really looking for any military people, vehicles or such. The Russians would go crossways; they didn't pick out a target, they'd just go crosswise. We got strafed a couple of times; some of the men and some of the civilians got killed. It was a real mess. I hid one time under a culvert—I was just small enough to do that—but we finally got to a town called Teterow. At the end of that long war, most of these people were hanging out white sheets, because the Russians were right behind us.

We kept walking. We always had a couple of scouts going out—true military style. A couple of them came back and said, 'There's a train leaving and there's room on it. We're going—does anybody else want to go?' I think there were a dozen of them who took off and got on the train and it was just ready to depart. And the Russians came by and strafed again and bombed the train, and we lost these twelve guys.

[Incidentally, back at the camp], the Russian POWs had their own compound. And the [other] Americans stayed in that camp and they were finally liberated by the Russians. But [normally], the Americans had their own compound and the

Russians had their own compound, and the Russians had been treated terribly. Almost every day, we saw them march by us with a body covered in brown paper. The Germans didn't feed them well, and they just kept working them.

Free

Anyhow, we [finally reached the lines of] the American 8th Division; it took us a little over a week, I think we covered pretty close to 150 miles. We reached the 8th Division, and we saw the MPs. I said, 'What do we do?'

They said, 'Go find some place to stay.'

So we took over an opera house. We still had Kurt Papke with us. We asked what to do with him.

They said, 'Keep him and we'll pick him up later.'

So after five or six days they came and said, 'We are ready to take you out of here.'

They put us on trucks and took us to a German airfield in Hildesheim, Germany. A C-47 took us to Namur, Belgium. I weighed eighty-eight pounds. From there, they took us to Camp Lucky Strike.

One day, they called us out. A guy was on a C-47 standing on the wing, and said, 'Does anybody want to go home?' Of course, we all hollered, 'Yeah!'

Home

A couple of days later I was on the SS *Explorer*, sleeping on the fantail, a Liberty ship. It took us twelve days to get to Norfolk, Virginia. From there I called my mother. The phone rang, and I said, 'Mom, it's Jack.'

She couldn't answer; I just heard her sob when I said, 'I'll be home soon.' She didn't say a word. I cried, too.

I get upset about this. I have the telegram that [my family received] when I got hit, early November 1944. Then they got a letter in March, and I was still missing in action. So it was a long time before they knew anything and of course in the meantime, I got captured. The Germans let me write from the prison—the war camp—and [my parents] heard from me in February. Before that, they just knew I was missing. The other three guys [who were with me] were killed. The Germans took their uniforms, and they used them [when they infiltrated American ranks during] the Battle of the Bulge. When I first got to Limburg, as a POW, the Germans took us in for delousing. We piled our clothes up and they took us in the shower; they poured all kinds of white dust on us [DDT]. Most of our clothes were gone; they took the American uniforms; we couldn't understand why. One of the pictures I have of Kurt and I leaving this group much later—you wouldn't know who the POWs were, because we had all kinds of outfits on, just [regular] clothes, some had wooden shoes. Again, we found out later that they used the uniforms for the Battle of the Bulge.

They shipped us to Dix and then sent us home for seventy days, so I was home all that summer of '45. Then they sent me up to Lake Placid for R&R. At that point, I had lost a bunch of teeth, so I was up there at Lake Placid with linen tablecloths, waiters and waitresses. Then they sent me from there to Camp J.T. Robinson down in Little Rock, Arkansas. I knew how to type, so they made me in charge of the typing pool. I had fourteen beautiful southern gals working for me. [*Chuckles*] I was discharged from there after I had enough points in December of 1945 and went back to Niagara and finished up; I got my degree in October of 1946. In February of 1947, I met a beautiful young girl on a blind date and on June 19, 1949, we were married.

*

The importance of World War II [should not be forgotten]. We had a real reason for World War II, and the whole country [was invested]. We had women working in factories, we had to get ration [cards] to get butter, to get shoes, to get tires. It was a war that everybody was involved with, either personally or through their families. My family was so involved and now we are faced with other wars and I wonder at times, why? I don't have that much to say. Everybody was involved in World War II and if we hadn't done what we did—I lost five friends [who were on that corner when we heard about Pearl Harbor], killed in WWII. So many—Bill Hoppe, Andy Hopkinson, Johnny English, Tommy Krone, and Bill Hill—I could go on, they were all killed in different places. I came back.

My Enemy is My Friend

Until he died two years ago, Kurt Papke and I had been in touch with each other for over sixty years—writing, talking about our kids, grandkids, wives. He was really a nice guy. [I feel like there were] two sets of Germans. There were Nazis and then there were the German people. And the German people were wonderful people. As it turned out later in life I became in charge of personnel and public relations for Nationwide Insurance. A young lady was working for us—she was German, and she had married a Hungarian fellow who had been drafted by the German Army. She came from Munich, and she came home one night from school and Munich had been bombed. She was about twelve or thirteen years old and her mother had hung herself. She couldn't take any more bombing.

I think that the German people were wonderful people. We traded cigarettes with them to get food. When we were finally liberated by the 8th Division, I weighed 88 pounds, [but I found that some of the Germans] were concerned about us. They would slip some food to us once in a while.

If they were strict Nazis, then we had a problem, because they came around at times, the German guards, and they checked dog tags. If they found that you were Jewish, which was on the dog tag, we never saw those guys again, they were put on trucks and they took them away. We had to play games with our dog tags. Whatever the German people thought [of Hitler], there was a lot of talk that the Germans after World War I did not get a really good shot at the Treaty of Versailles—that the treaty did not give them [a fair turn]. That's when Hitler began to rise, and he did a lot for Germany, building roads, et cetera, from what I understand of history. That's how he got involved, and he went off on a tangent to become what he did become.

[One of the important lessons of the war for me was about] relationships with people. Kurt Papke would steal food for us; he wasn't a Nazi. He was just a gentleman who had been wounded at Stalingrad on the Russian front, put in a hospital to recuperate, and after that they gave him an easy job taking care of field wounds. I think I learned so much more about humanity, about giving people a chance to show who they really are. That relationship is the basis for maybe sixty years of written conversation with Kurt and his family. Besides the horrors that I saw, that I had to be part of, to really sit back and take a look at that relationship is something that means an awful lot to me, to meet a man who was my enemy and become great friends for sixty years has meant a lot. I hope our kids and grandkids and great-grandkids know.

Jack Blanchfield died on November 3, 2012, at the age of 88.

Francis S. Currey, MOH. 1945.
Source: National Archives, public domain.

EPILOGUE

"Youth"

I rode the elevator up to the second or third floor. I don't remember what city it was in, nor exactly the year. Nashville? Savannah? Charleston? Probably not Fayetteville, because that was the very first time I met Frank Currey and Frank Towers, the vice president and president of the 30th Infantry Division Veterans of World War II, respectively, in 2008. I was the teacher who they had heard about, the one who taught history in the region of New York State just north of Currey's hometown. For the next ten years I had been helping Frank Towers track down survivors of the Holocaust all over the world, and for ten years we had been organizing presentations for the annual reunions of these World War II veterans, three times at my own high school. Four times I was with them at the reunions in Nashville, including the last gathering in 2015 to mark the 70th anniversary of the end of World War II and the liberation of a death train that these soldiers had encountered two weeks before Hitler blew his brains out in a bunker in Berlin, just a hundred miles east of where these guys wound up when the war in Europe ended. Spared being shipped out to the Pacific by the end of the war with Japan, for the next seven decades the former soldiers of the 30th Infantry Division held these reunions across many cities of the South, up to 15,000 veterans and wives strong, sometimes taking over more than one downtown hotel. On this evening, maybe there were a dozen veterans who were able to make the trip with their families.

The elevator door opened, and I made my way down the hall to the hospitality room, where one of the younger reenactor fellows was tending the makeshift bar. The 'farewell until next year' dinner was over, where Frank Towers always made sure I was seated at the head table. Me, a school teacher—not even a former soldier, sailor, airman, or Marine—but a veteran, I suppose, of the trenches of the American history classroom, where I made sure to introduce our nation's young people to the stories of their grandparents' generation and others, where I bonded these old soldiers with the kids who are now making their marks on our world today. And always seated next to me at that table was Francis Sherman Currey, MOH—the last surviving World War II Medal of Honor recipient from New York State—the man of whom Eisenhower himself speculated had single-handedly shortened the war in Europe by six weeks.

The two Franks were now relaxing at a small table to themselves, still in suitcoats, Currey with his Medal of Honor around his neck, Towers adorned with his beautiful French Legion of Honor, awarded to soldiers like him who liberated France. They motioned me to the table where I sat down and we sipped our mixed drinks; we talked, we caught up. War stories not traded, just conversation among friends, so casual it's difficult to summon exactly what we said. Yet it strikes me now again how lucky I was to be afforded a window—

and at the time, I had a subtle awareness, a prescient vision of sorts of the position I was in—another opportunity to absorb as much as I could from being in their presence, but this was a time to just sit and "be" with them.

What stands out from that last night we were together was what happened shortly before we broke up around 11:00 PM or midnight. A young couple, maybe in their early twenties, stumbled into the room. I can't remember if they were on the reunion manifest, or if it happened accidentally, but the young man appeared interested and looked around at the displays, some featuring nineteen-year-old Frank posing next to the arsenal of weapons he used on December 23, 1944, during the Battle of the Bulge, to hold off an entire German armored column.

"It was just one day in nine months of steady combat."
Source: National Archives, public domain.

The kid spied us and recognized the Medal of Honor around Frank's neck, and leading his girlfriend by the hand, came up to our table and introduced himself and his girl, and what an honor it is to meet you and shake your hand, and oh, can I have your autograph? Frank graciously obliged, and asked a little bit about them, no doubt having done this many, many times before. As the kids turned and left the room, he nodded and looked at me and smiled, perhaps with a trace of envy, uttered one word.

"Youth."

Frank Towers, Frank Currey, Matthew Rozell. September 2009. Credit: Twilight Studios.

Both Franks are gone now. When I get discouraged at the current state of affairs, when I wonder about the point of sitting so many hours trying to bring these World War II veterans back to life, I think back to Youth. I think about my former students hanging on to every word these veterans spoke in their presence, ten, and twenty, and thirty years ago. I think about this kid who actually knew what the Medal of Honor represented, and who sought out an old man for his autograph and served up his gratitude. He will carry that torch forever and may he himself pass it on. Because that is what our World War II veterans were fighting for in the end. For the future. For the young.

We will follow these 'Youth of Yesterday' in the next volume, *Across the Rhine*. In the meantime, join me in raising a cup to the Franks, to your own fathers, mothers, uncles and aunts, grandparents, all; to the youth who saved this country. Because dying for freedom isn't the worst that could happen.

Being forgotten is.

✱✱✱

THE THINGS OUR FATHERS SAW ® SERIES:

VOICES OF THE PACIFIC THEATER

WAR IN THE AIR: GREAT DEPRESSION TO COMBAT

WAR IN THE AIR: COMBAT, CAPTIVITY, REUNION

UP THE BLOODY BOOT-THE WAR IN ITALY

D-DAY AND BEYOND

THE BULGE AND BEYOND

ACROSS THE RHINE

ON TO TOKYO

HOMEFRONT/WOMEN AT WAR

CHINA, BURMA, INDIA

*

IF YOU LIKED THIS BOOK, you'll love hearing more from the World War II generation in my other books. On the following pages you can see some samples, and I can let you know as soon as the new books are out and offer you exclusive discounts on some material. Just sign up at <u>matthewrozellbooks.com</u>

Some of my readers may like to know that all of my books are **<u>directly available from the author, with collector's sets which can be autographed</u>** in paperback and hardcover. They are popular gifts for that 'hard-to-buy-for' guy or gal on your list. Visit my shop at <u>matthewrozellbooks.com</u> for details.

Thank you for reading!

I hope you found this book interesting and informative; I sure learned a lot researching and writing it. What follows are some descriptions of my other books.

Find them all at matthewrozellbooks.com.

The Things Our Fathers Saw: The Untold Stories of the World War II Generation from Hometown, USA-Voices of the Pacific Theater

Volume 1 of The Things Our Fathers Saw® series started with my first book on the oral history of the men and women who served in the Pacific Theater of the war.

"The telephone rings on the hospital floor, and they tell you it is your mother, the phone call you have been dreading. You've lost part of your face to a Japanese sniper on Okinawa, and after many surgeries, the doctor has finally told you that at 19, you will never see again. The pain and shock is one thing. But now you have to tell her, from 5000 miles away."

— *"So I had a hard two months, I guess. I kept mostly to myself. I wouldn't talk to people. I tried to figure out what the hell I was going to do when I got home. How was I going to tell my mother this? You know what I mean?"* — **WWII Marine veteran**

But you don't have to start with this book—I constructed them so that you can pick up any of the series books and start anywhere—but it's up to you.

The Things Our Fathers Saw—The Untold Stories of the World War II Generation-Volume II: War in the Air—From the Great Depression to Combat

Volume 2 in the series deal with the Air War in the European Theater of the war. I had a lot of friends in the heavy bombers; they tell you all about what it was like to grow up during the Great Depression as the clouds of war gathered, going off to the service, and into the skies over Europe, sharing stories of both funny and heartbreaking, and all riveting and intense. An audio version is also available.

— "I spent a lot of time in hospitals. I had a lot of trouble reconciling how my mother died [of a cerebral hemorrhage] from the telegram she opened, announcing I was [shot down and] 'missing in action.' I didn't explain to her the fact that 'missing in action' is not necessarily 'killed in action.' You know? I didn't even think about that. How do you think you feel when you find out you killed your mother?"

—B-24 bombardier

— "I was in the hospital with a flak wound. The next mission, the entire crew was killed. The thing that haunts me is that I can't put a face to the guy who was a replacement. He was an eighteen-year-old Jewish kid named Henry Vogelstein from Brooklyn. It was his first and last mission. He made his only mission with a crew of strangers."

—B-24 navigator

— "The German fighters picked us. I told the guys, 'Keep your eyes open, we are about to be hit!' I saw about six or eight feet go off my left wing. I rang the 'bail-out' signal, and I reached out and grabbed the co-pilot out of his seat. I felt the airplane climbing, and I thought to myself, 'If this thing stalls out, and starts falling down backwards, no one is going to get out...'"

—B-17 pilot

The Things Our Fathers Saw—The Untold Stories of the World War II Generation-Volume III: War in the Air—Combat, Captivity, and Reunion

Volume 3 is about the Air War again, and this time I have some of my friends who were fighter pilots, including a Tuskegee Airman who had to deal with racism back home, on top of defeating fascism in Europe. There is also the story of my B-17 crew friends, sitting around a table and telling about the day they were all shot down over Germany, and how they survived the prisoner-of-war experience in the last year of the war. An audio version is also available.

—"After the first mission Colonel Davis told us, 'From now on you are going to go with the bombers all the way through the mission to the target.' It didn't always work, but that was our mission—we kept the Germans off the bombers. At first they didn't want us, but toward the end, they started asking for us as an escort, because we protected them to

*and from the missions." —**Tuskegee Airman, WWII***

— *"[Someone in the POW camp] said, 'Look down there at the main gate!', and the American flag was flying! We went berserk, we just went berserk! We were looking at the goon tower and there's no goons there, there are Americans up there! And we saw the American flag, I mean—to this day I start to well up when I see the flag."*

*—**Former prisoner of war, WWII***

— *"I got back into my turret. Fellas, the turret wasn't there anymore. That German fighter who had been eyeing me came in and he hit his 20mm gun, took the top of that Plexiglas and tore it right off!*

*Now we're defenseless. The planes ahead of us have been shot down, we're lumbering along at 180 miles an hour, and these fighters were just [warming up] for target practice." —**B-17 Turret Gunner***

The Things Our Fathers Saw—The Untold Stories of the World War II Generation-Volume IV: 'Up the Bloody Boot'—The War in Italy

Volume 4 in this series will take you from the deserts of North Africa to the mountains of Italy with the men and women veterans of the Italian campaign who open up about a war that was so brutal, news of it was downplayed at home. The war in the Mediterranean, and particularly the Italian Campaign, is one that for many Americans is shrouded in mystery and murkiness. Yet it was here that the United States launched its first offensive in the west on enemy soil, and it was here that Allied forces would be slogging it out with a tenacious enemy fighting for its life in the longest single American Campaign of World War II.

—*"There was an old French fort there, and we could look down on it during the day. We gauged the way we would hit that place so that the moon would set right between two mountain peaks; we timed it so* when we got there, that moon would silhouette them, but not us... We carried out the first and only bayonet charge [of the war] by our Rangers; we didn't fire; very few people knew that we carried out an overnight bayonet attack. I'll tell you, that's something. You see that, it'll shake you up real good." — **U.S. Army Ranger, WWII**

— "We attacked another hill, and I shot a German soldier. And then the Germans counterattacked on the hill, and I could not escape, so I decided to just lay down on top of that soldier and make believe I'm dead. They passed me by, I got up and [this German I shot] starts talking to me in English, he says he's from Coney Island, in Brooklyn; he went to visit his mother in Germany and they put him in the army. And he was dying, and he says to me, 'You can take my cigarettes; you can take my schnapps.' Then he died right underneath me. And I imagine he knew I had shot him...."

—U.S. Army scout, WWII

— "So there was a terrific fight going on in a place called Santa Ma-ria, south of Rome. While we were going through, in transit, we stopped at a big Italian barn; they had a kitchen set up, and we had our own mess kits. As we were going through the line, *we saw this huge rack of shelves with American Army duffel bags packed on there. And Hendrickson said to me, 'Hey, Tony, you know what? My brother must be in the area someplace. There's his duffel bag.' The name was stenciled on. So I said, 'That's nice.' [But] I was thinking, why is his duffel bag there? Well, there was a military policeman guarding these bags. I went back to the MP. I said to him, 'What are these bags doing here?' And I told him about Hendrickson. 'Well,' he said, 'I don't know if you want to tell him, but these guys are all dead. They were all killed at Santa Maria.'" —**U.S. Army map maker, WWII**

The Things Our Fathers Saw—The Untold Stories of the World War II Generation-Volume V: 'D-Day and Beyond'—The War in France

Volume 5 in this series will take you from the bloody beach at Omaha through the hedgerow country of Normandy and beyond, American veterans of World War II--Army engineers and infantrymen, Coast Guardsmen and Navy sailors, tank gunners and glider pilots--sit down with you across the kitchen table and talk about what they saw and experienced, tales they may have never told anyone before.

— "I had a vision, if you want to call it that. At my home, the mailman would walk up towards the front porch, and I saw it just as clear as if he's standing beside me—I see his blue jacket and the blue cap and the leather mailbag. Here he goes up to the house, but he doesn't turn. He goes right up the front steps.

This happened so fast, probably a matter of seconds, but the first thing that came to mind, that's the way my folks would find out what happened to me.

The next thing I know, I kind of come to, and I'm in the push-up mode. I'm half up out of the underwater depression, and I'm trying to figure out what the hell happened to those prone figures on the beach, and all of a sudden, I realized I'm in amongst those bodies!" —Army demolition engineer, Omaha Beach, D-Day

— *"My last mission was the Bastogne mission. We were being towed, we're approaching Bastogne, and I see a cloud of flak, anti-aircraft fire. I said to myself, 'I'm not going to make it.' There were a couple of groups ahead of us, so now the anti-aircraft batteries are zeroing in. Every time a new group came over, they kept zeroing in. My outfit had, I think, 95% casualties." —Glider pilot, D-Day and Beyond*

— *"I was fighting in the hedgerows for five days; it was murder. But psychologically, we were the best troops in the world. There was nobody like us; I had all the training that they could give us, but nothing prepares you for some things.*

You know, in my platoon, the assistant platoon leader got shot right through the head, right through the helmet, dead, right there in front of me. That affects you, doesn't it?" —Paratrooper, D-Day and Beyond

...And if you would like to learn more about our GIs and the Holocaust...

~SOON TO BE A MAJOR FILM~

"What healing this has given to the survivors and military men!"-Reviewer

FROM THE ABC WORLD NEWS 'PERSON OF THE WEEK'

A TRAIN NEAR MAGDEBURG

THE HOLOCAUST, AND THE REUNITING OF THE SURVIVORS AND SOLDIERS, 70 YEARS ON

–Featuring testimony from 15 American liberators and over 30 Holocaust survivors
–500 pages-extensive notes and bibliographical references

BOOK ONE—THE HOLOCAUST
BOOK TWO—THE AMERICANS
BOOK THREE—LIBERATION
BOOK FOUR—REUNION

THE HOLOCAUST was a watershed event in history. In this book, Matthew Rozell reconstructs a lost chapter—the liberation of a 'death train' deep in the heart of Nazi Germany in the closing days of World War II. Drawing on never-before published eye-witness accounts, survivor testimony, and wartime reports and letters, Rozell brings to life the incredible true stories behind the iconic 1945 liberation photographs taken by the soldiers who were there. He weaves together a chronology of the Holocaust as it unfolds across Europe, and goes back to literally retrace the steps of the survivors and the American soldiers who freed them. Rozell's work results in joyful reunions on three continents, seven decades later. He offers his unique perspective on the lessons of the Holocaust for future generations, and the impact that one person can make.

A selection of comments left by reviewers:

"**Extraordinary research** into an event which needed to be told. I have read many books about the Holocaust and visited various museums but had not heard reference to this train previously. The fact that people involved were able to connect, support and help heal each other emotionally was amazing."

"**The story of the end of the Holocaust and the Nazi regime** told from a very different and precise angle. First-hand accounts from Jewish survivors and the US soldiers that secured their freedom. Gripping."

"**Mr. Rozell travels 'back to the future'** of people who were not promised a tomorrow; neither the prisoners nor the troops knew what horrors the next moment would bring. He captures the parallel experience of soldiers fighting ruthless Nazism and the ruthless treatment of Jewish prisoners."

"**If you have any trepidation** about reading a book on the Holocaust, this review is for you. [Matthew Rozell] masterfully conveys the individual stories of those featured in the book in a manner that does not leave the reader with a sense of despair, but rather a sense of purpose."

"**Could not put this book down**--I just finished reading *A Train Near Magdeburg*. Tears fell as I read pages and I smiled through others. I wish I could articulate the emotions that accompanied me through the stories of these beautiful people."

"**Everyone should read this book**, detailing the amazing bond that formed between Holocaust survivors likely on their way to death in one last concentration camp as WWII was about to end, and a small number of American soldiers that happened upon the stopped train and liberated the victims. The lifelong friendships that resulted between the survivors and their liberators is a testament to compassion and goodness. It is amazing that the author is not Jewish but a "reluctant" history teacher who ultimately becomes a Holocaust scholar. This is a great book."

ABOUT THE AUTHOR

Photo Credit: Joan K. Lentini; May 2017.

Matthew Rozell is an award-winning history teacher, author, speaker, and blogger on the topic of the most cataclysmic events in the history of mankind—World War II and the Holocaust. Rozell has been featured as the 'ABC World News Person of the Week' and has had his work as a teacher filmed for the CBS Evening News, NBC Learn, the Israeli Broadcast Authority, the United States Holocaust Memorial Museum, and the New York State United Teachers. He writes on the power of teaching and the importance of the study of history at TeachingHistoryMatters.com, and you can 'Like' his Facebook author page at <u>MatthewRozellBooks</u> for updates.

Mr. Rozell is a sought-after speaker on World War II, the Holocaust, and history education, motivating and inspiring his audiences with the lessons of the past. Visit <u>MatthewRozell.com</u> for availability/details.

About this Book/

Acknowledgements

*

A note on historiographical style and convention: to enhance accuracy, consistency, and readability, I corrected punctuation and spelling and sometimes even place names, but only after extensive research. I did take the liberty of occasionally condensing the speaker's voice, eliminating side tangents or incidental information not relevant to the matter at hand. Sometimes two or more interviews with the same person were combined for readability and narrative flow. All of the words of the subjects, however, are essentially their own.

Additionally, I chose to utilize footnotes and endnotes where I deemed them appropriate, directing readers who wish to learn more to my sources, notes, and side commentary. I hope that they do not detract from the flow of the narrative.

First, I wish to acknowledge the hundreds of students who passed through my classes and who forged the bonds with the World War II generation. I promised you these books someday, and now that many of you are yourselves parents, you can tell your children this book is for them. Who says young people are indifferent to the past? Here is evidence to the contrary.

The Hudson Falls Central School District and my former colleagues have my deep appreciation for supporting this endeavor and recognizing its significance throughout the years.

Cara Quinlan's sharp proofing and suggestions helped to clean up the original manuscript.

Naturally this work would not have been possible had it not been for the willingness of the veterans to share their stories for posterity. All of the veterans who were interviewed for this book had the foresight to complete release forms granting access to their stories, and for us to share the information with the New York State Military Museum's Veterans Oral History Project, where copies of the original interviews reside. Wayne Clarke and Mike Russert of the NYSMMVOP were instrumental in cultivating this relationship with my classes over the years and are responsible for some of the interviews in this book as well; Lt. Col. Robert von Hasseln and Michael Aikey also conducted some of these NYSMM interviews. Please see the 'Source Notes.'

I would be remiss if I did not recall the profound influence of my late mother and father, Mary and Tony Rozell, both cutting-edge educators and proud early supporters of my career. To my younger siblings Mary, Ned, Nora, and Drew, all accomplished writers and authors, thank you for your encouragement as well. Final and deepest appreciations go to my wife Laura and our children, Emma, Ned, and Mary. Thank you for indulging the old man as he attempted to bring to life the stories he collected as a young one.

ACKNOWLEDGEMENTS

NOTES

—THE INTERVIEWS—

Source Notes: **Alfred H. Meyer.** Interviewed by Michael Aikey and Wayne Clarke, October 3, 2001, Latham, NY. Deposited at NYS Military Museum.

Source Notes: **Angelo B. DeMicco.** Interviewed by Michael Russert and Wayne Clarke, May 21, 2003. Mechanicville, NY. Deposited at NYS Military Museum.

Source Notes: **Robert F. Kirk.** Interviewed by Robert von Hasseln and Wayne Clarke, January 23, 2001, Syracuse, NY. Deposited at NYS Military Museum.

Source Notes: **Harold Leonard Bloom, Jr.** Interviewed by Wayne Clarke, April 19, 2012, Greenfield, NY. Deposited at NYS Military Museum.

494 | NOTES

Source Notes: **William E. Bramswig.** Interviewed by Michael Aikey, 14 February 14, 2001, Peekskill, NY. Deposited at NYS Military Museum.

Source Notes: **Sydney Cole.** Interviewed by Toby Ticktin Back, August 7, 1989, Buffalo, NY. Interviewed by Wayne Clarke and Kathleen Mathews, April 9, 2009, Buffalo, NY. Deposited at NYS Military Museum.

Source Notes: **Rosario Catalano**. Interviewed by Michael Russert and Wayne Clarke, March 21, 2003, Brooklyn, NY. Deposited at NYS Military Museum.

Source Notes: **Frederick S. Dennin**. Interviewed by Michael Russert, September 20, 2002, Saratoga Springs, NY. Deposited at NYS Military Museum.

Source Notes: **Martin Sylvester.** Interviewed by Robert von Hasseln and Michael Aikey, January 9, 2001, New York, NY. Deposited at NYS Military Museum.

Source Notes: **Gerald M. Daub.** Interviewed by Michael Russert and Wayne Clarke, February 6, 2003, Tarrytown, NY. Deposited at NYS Military Museum.

Source Notes: **John J. Blanchfield.** Interviewed by Michael Russert and Wayne Clarke, September 22, 2005, Lake George, NY. Deposited at NYS Military Museum. Interviewed by Dylan Keyser, December 22, 2009, for the Hudson Falls HS World War II Living History Project, Lake George, NY. Deposited at NYS Military Museum.

---

[1] Fact Tank-News in the Numbers. *On 75th anniversary of V-E Day, about 300,000 American WWII veterans are alive.* Pew Research Center. May 8, 2020. www.pewresearch.org/fact-tank/2020/05/08/on-75th-anniversary-of-v-e-day-about-300000-american-wwii-veterans-are-alive

[2] Lennon, Thomas and Mark Zwonitzer. *The Battle of the Bulge.* American Experience, PBS, 1994.

[3] Weiss, Robert. *Fire Mission!: The Siege at Mortain, Normandy, August 1944.* Shippensburg, Pa.: Burd Street Press, 2002.

[4] Atkinson, Rick. *The Guns at Last Light: The War in Western Europe, 1944-1945.* New York: Henry Holt & Co., 2013. 157.

[5] The 30th Infantry Division Veterans of WWII. *Mortain.*

[6] *Surviving was all you thought about-* Quoted at Bard, Mitchell G., *Berga am Elster: American PWs at Berga.* Jewish Virtual Library. www.jewishvirtuallibrary.org/american-pows-at-berga-concentration-camp.

[7] Anthony Acevedo. *Americans and the Holocaust.* United States Holocaust Memorial Museum. https://exhibitions.ushmm.org/americans-and-the-holocaust/personal-story/anthony-acevedo.

[8] Shapiro, William J., *Berga am Elster: A Medic Recalls the Horrors at Berga.* Jewish Virtual Library. jewishvirtuallibrary.org/a medic-recalls-the-horrors-of-berga

www.ingramcontent.com/pod-product-compliance
Lightning Source LLC
Chambersburg PA
CBHW070042080526
44586CB00013B/879